This history of the Strategic Defense Initiative ranges across politics, economics, strategic studies and international relations. It provides the results of research into the SDI interest groups, the distribution of contracts and the politics of influence. It also examines the wider contexts of 'Star Wars', such as alliance management, marketing and domestic politics, and its military spin-offs, especially for anti-satellite (ASAT) and 'space control' programmes.

The author tests the theoretical literature on the dynamics of the arms race by using SDI as a case study, and draws evidence from sources such as congressional hearings, interviews, the trade Press, restricted briefing papers and documents obtained under the US Freedom of Information Act. The book follows the fortunes of strategic defence into the changed global conditions of the 1990s, following the collapse of the Soviet bloc, the Gulf War and President Bush's announcement of a refocussed SDI, the Global Protection Against Limited Strikes (GPALS).

# THE STRATEGIC DEFENSE INITIATIVE

# CAMBRIDGE STUDIES IN INTERNATIONAL RELATIONS

# THE STRATEGIC DEFENSE INITIATIVE

**EDWARD REISS**

*University of Bradford*

CAMBRIDGE
UNIVERSITY PRESS

Published by the Press Syndicate of the University of Cambridge
The Pitt Building, Trumpington Street, Cambridge CB2 1RP
40 West 20th Street, New York, NY 10011–4211, USA
10 Stamford Road, Oakleigh, Victoria 3166, Australia

First published 1992

Printed in Great Britain by Redwood Press Limited, Wiltshire

*A cataloguing in publication record for this book is available
from the British Library*

*Library of Congress cataloguing in publication data*
Reiss, Edward.
The Strategic Defense Initiative / Edward Reiss.
     p.     cm. – (Cambridge studies in international relations: 23)
Includes bibliographical references and index.
ISBN 0 521 41097 5
1. Strategic Defense Initiative – History. 2. United States –
Military policy. 3. Arms race – United States. I. Title.
II. Series.
UG743.R44 1992    91–29650 CIP
358.1'74'09–dc20

ISBN 0 521 41097 5 hardback

WD

# CONTENTS

PART 5 CONCLUSIONS

# TABLES

# ACKNOWLEDGEMENTS

I would like to thank Owen Greene for his many constructive comments. I am indebted to the generosity of Gwyn Prins, Jack Mendelsohn, Professor Hilary Rose and her colleagues in Ashgrove. My research in Washington, D.C. was helped by John Pike, Thomas Longstreth, John Tower and Tori Holt. I am grateful to R.W.R. and Maureen and David Snook for checking proofs.

The work was made possible by a grant from the Joseph Rowntree Charitable Trust. Without the support of my family and friends I would have written nothing.

# ABBREVIATIONS

| | |
|---|---|
| ABM | Anti-Ballistic Missile |
| ADI | Air Defense Initiative |
| AEW | Airborne Early Warning |
| AFB | Air Force Base |
| AFSC | Air Force Systems Command |
| AFSTC | Air Force Space Technology Center |
| AI | Artificial Intelligence |
| AIAA | American Institute for Aeronautics and Astronautics |
| ALPS | Accidental Launch Protection Scheme |
| AOA | Airborne Optical Adjunct |
| ASAT | Anti-SATellite Weapon |
| ASW | Anti-Submarine Warfare |
| ATBM | Anti-Tactical Ballistic Missile |
| ATM | Anti-Tactical Missile |
| BAMBI | BAllistic Missile Boost Interceptor |
| BMD | Ballistic Missile Defense |
| BMDATC | Ballistic Missile Defense Advanced Technology Center |
| BMDO | Ballistic Missile Defense Organization |
| BMDSCOM | Ballistic Missile Defense Systems COMmand |
| BP | Brilliant Pebbles |
| BSTS | Boost Surveillance Tracking System |
| C$^3$I | Command Control Communication Intelligence |
| CONUS | CONtinental United States |
| DARPA | Defense Advanced Research Projects Agency |
| D&S | Defense and Space |
| DAB | Defense Acquisition Board |
| DEW | Defense Energy Weapons |
| DMS | Defense Marketing Services |
| DNA | Defense Nuclear Agency |
| DoD | Department of Defense |
| DoE | Department of Energy |
| EAD | Extended Air Defense |

| | |
|---|---|
| EDI | European Defense Initiative |
| EEC | European Economic Community |
| E$^2$I | Endoatmospheric/Exoatmospheric Interceptors |
| ERINT | Extended Range INTerceptor |
| ERIS | Exoatmospheric Re-entry vehicle Interceptor System |
| ESD | Electronic Systems Division |
| EXCOM | Executive COMmittee |
| FAADS | Forward Area Air Defense System |
| FACA | Federal Advisory Committee Act |
| FFRDC | Federally Funded Research and Development Center |
| FMS | Foreign Military Sales |
| FOC | Full Operating Capability |
| FO/FA | Follow-On Forces Attack |
| FOIA | Freedom Of Information Act |
| FY | Fiscal Year |
| FYDP | Five Year Defense Plan |
| GAO | General Accounting Office |
| GAO/NSIAD | GAO National Security International Affairs Division |
| GBI | Ground-Based Interceptor |
| GPALS | Global Protection Against Limited Strikes |
| HASC | House Armed Services Committee |
| HEDI | High Endoatmospheric Defense Interceptor |
| HIBEX | HIgh acceleration Booster EXperiment |
| HOE | Homing Overlay Experiment |
| HR | House Resolution |
| ICBM | Inter-Continental Ballistic Missile |
| IDA | Institute for Defense Analysis |
| IEPG | Independent European Programme Group |
| INF | Intermediate-range Nuclear Forces |
| IOC | Initial Operating Capability |
| ITP | Industrial Technology Policy |
| JCS | Joint Chiefs of Staff |
| KEW | Kinetic Energy Weapons |
| LoADS | Low Altitude Defense System |
| LPS | Limited Protection Scheme |
| LRTNF | Long-Range Theater Nuclear Forces |
| MAD | Mutual Assured Destruction |
| MBFR | Mutual and Balanced Force Reduction |
| MCTL | Military Critical Technologies List |
| MHV | Miniature Homing Vehicle |
| MIC | Military Industrial Complex |
| MIRACL | Mid-Infra-Red Advanced Chemical Laser |

| | |
|---|---|
| MIRV | Multiple Independently targetable Re-entry Vehicle |
| MIT | Massachusetts Institute of Technology |
| MITI | Ministry of International Trade and Industry (Japan) |
| MoU | Memorandum of Understanding |
| MRBM | Medium-Range Ballistic Missile |
| MRV | Multiple Re-entry Vehicle |
| MX | Missile Experimental. 'Peacekeeper' |
| NASA | National Aeronautics and Space Agency |
| NORAD | NORth American Air Defense |
| NRL | Naval Research Laboratory |
| NSDD | National Security Decision Directive |
| NST | Nuclear and Space Talks |
| NY | New York |
| OASD | Office of the Assistant Secretary of Defense |
| OSD | Office of the Secretary of Defense |
| OTA | Office of Technology Assessment |
| OTH-B | Over The Horizon Backscatter |
| PAC | Political Action Committee |
| PD | Presidential Directive |
| PE | Program Element |
| R&D | Research and Development |
| RDT&E | Research Development Test and Evaluation |
| RORSAT | Radar Ocean Reconnaissance SATellite |
| RV | Re-entry Vehicle |
| SALT | Strategic Arms Limitation Talks |
| SAM | Surface to Air Missile |
| SASC | Senate Armed Services Committee |
| SATKA | Surveillance Acquisition Tracking Kill Assessment |
| SBKKV | Space-Based Kinetic Kill Vehicle |
| SBR | Space-Based Radar |
| SDI | Strategic Defense Initiative |
| SDIAC | Strategic Defense Initiative Advisory Committee |
| SDII | Strategic Defense Initiative Institute |
| SDIO | Strategic Defense Initiative Office (or Organization) |
| SDIP | Strategic Defense Initiative Program |
| SDS | Strategic Defense System |
| SE&I | Systems Engineering and Integration |
| SLBM | Submarine Launched Ballistic Missile |
| SLKT | Survivability Lethality Key Technologies |
| SRBM | Short-Range Ballistic Missile |
| SRHIT | Small Rocket Homing Interceptor Technology |
| SSA-2000 | Space Systems Architecture 2000 |

| | |
|---|---|
| SSTS | Space Surveillance Tracking System |
| START | STrategic Arms Reduction Talks |
| THAAD | Theater High Altitude Area Defense |
| TIR | Terminal Imaging Radar |
| USAFB | United States Air Force Base |
| USASDC | United States Army Strategic Defense Command |

# INTRODUCTION

SDI was probably the most important new military programme of the 1980s. When it was announced, it was certainly one of the most controversial and unexpected. Eight years and $22 billion later, after the disintegration of the Warsaw Pact and the Gulf War, SDI was refocussed into a new scheme which attracted renewed, bipartisan support: a Global Protection Against Limited Strikes (GPALS). The Pentagon is still pushing for increases in its SDI/GPALS budget and preparing advanced experiments which would contravene the ABM Treaty. It hopes to start full-scale development of interceptors and command and control elements in 1993 or 1994.[1] The debate about strategic defence is sure to rage on long after. This book analyses the history of SDI, combining multiple perspectives to show how and why it has developed.

SDI was exceptional from the day it was announced. Never before had an American president offered a 'vision' of using advanced technology to make nuclear weapons 'impotent and obsolete'. Welcomed by the 'New Right' and decried by the arms control community, the plan to develop space weapons took centre stage in the superpower summits of the 1980s. The research promised, or threatened, to generate qualitative advances in other, offensive weapons: notably battlefield lasers, anti-satellite weapons (ASATs), space weapons and Command Control Communication ($C^3$). And so SDI became a key growth market.

Works on SDI could fill a library.[2] In general, the literature focusses on three main issues: (1) SDI's technological feasibility, (2) its strategic advisability, and (3) its geostrategic consequences (arms control, international repercussions).[3] Whilst drawing on these perspectives, this book offers something different: a history of SDI, exploring the *interaction* of factors strategic, political, economic, technological, institutional and cultural. It analyses the interest groups behind SDI and the extent and effectiveness of lobbying. It is based on interviews, congressional hearings, market analysis, business newsletters, the SDI

1

Office's own data base of contracts, internal Pentagon documents and data obtained under the US Freedom of Information Act.

The following three deceptively simple questions are crucial to an understanding of SDI:

(1) What is SDI?
(2) Why did SDI happen?
(3) Why did SDI develop in the way it did?

Ninety-eight per cent of the US Academy of Scientists expressed disbelief in Reagan's vision.[4] Elder statesmen joined senior scientists in outspoken criticism of SDI. Their indictments might be summarised in former President Carter's charge that it was 'infeasible, extremely costly, misleading and an obstacle to nuclear arms control'.[5] Yet the budget for SDI continued to grow: and that demands some explanation.

In the following chapters SDI will be analysed in terms of the politics of influence; as an aspect of industrial technology policy; and as a symptom of the weaponisation of space, inextricably linked to controversies about anti-satellite weapons (ASATs). These issues are all related to vital questions of policy. In particular, understanding of the dynamics of the military programmes becomes ever more important at a time of 'new détente'. Why is it that, notwithstanding the collapse of the Soviet Union, the process of weapons development judders on, with 'modernisation' of short-range attack missiles, further military research and continuing funds for space weapons? With bright prospects for arms control and a lasting détente, study of the weapons procurement process and the barriers to disarmament is all the more timely.

## THE STRUCTURE OF THE BOOK

Part 1 summarises theories about the dynamics of the arms race. It outlines the main strategic, political, bureaucratic, economic and psycho-political perspectives; and identifies those with most promise as explanations of SDI. Strategic defence is later examined by applying theories of the arms race; and they in turn will be tested against strategic defence as a case study. Chapter 2 gives the prehistory of SDI: the 'ABM debate' of the 1960s and the history of Ballistic Missile Defense (BMD) from 1945 to 1983. It shows how the BMD infrastructure was established well before Reagan's announcement of SDI; and it considers the causes of the President's speech.

Part 2 studies the first two years of the SDI programme. It describes how a constituency gathered around and then shaped SDI. It sketches the international context of SDI, arms control controversies and the inconsistent strategic rationales offered for the programme. It then analyses non-strategic factors, with a close look at the institutions which stood to gain and contracts awarded. Part 3 describes SDI from 1985 to 1988. It gives a detailed account of the constituencies of interest which advocated the programme or won funds from it; and shows how the SDI Office tried to rush the programme into early deployment.

Part 4 describes the European response to Reagan's plan and the extent of participation by the Allies. It then considers the broader contexts and conditions surrounding SDI. After describing the programme's other military spin-offs, it shows how SDI fits into broader plans for 'space control', especially through its contribution to ASAT technologies. A separate chapter reassesses the subject in terms of culture and emotion. SDI texts and congressional hearings indicate that fear, fantasy and anxiety feed into 'professional' discussion. An anaesthetic 'technostrategic' discourse – used alike by SDI's supporters and opponents – has shaped the 'experts' debate' in favour of the programme. SDI, with deep resonance in US popular culture, was effectively marketed, affecting domestic and electoral politics.

Part 5 is about the radical changes to SDI since the accession of President Bush. It describes the new plan for Global Protection Against Limited Strikes: GPALS. It then considers the future of strategic defence, under Bush and beyond. It highlights recurrent themes in the history of BMD and draws conclusions.

'Theories about the causes of the arms race illuminate the dynamics of BMD and SDI.' Some elementary definitions are in order. 'Causes' should be understood throughout in the sense used by the humanities, not in the narrower usage of the natural sciences. The 'arms race' is the generic term for hundreds of military programmes, produced in the context of antagonism between the superpowers, manifested since 1945 in ways quantitative, qualitative and doctrinal, at varying levels of intensity. Since the term 'superpower' was in the 1980s almost universally applied to the USSR, I have retained that usage. The relationship of SDI to the dissolution of the Soviet Union is addressed directly in the final chapter and, more obliquely, in Chapter 11. In the rest of the book, the main framework for analysing SDI is the arms race and the theoretical literature about its dynamics.

'Strategy' usually refers to military strategy, as opposed to political, economic or corporate strategies. A 'strategic defence' is one against long-range, strategic missiles, as opposed to tactical, 'theatre', short- or intermediate-range missiles. Strategic defence is also called Ballistic Missile Defense (BMD), or, especially in the 1960s, Anti-Ballistic Missiles (ABM). The 'BMD Infrastructure' consists of the institutions involved in BMD, those with a financial or material stake in

BMD: laboratories, research establishments, military agencies, government departments, defence corporations, colleges and universities. These comprise the overall 'constituency of interest' in the programme.

'SDI' means the set of Program Elements (PEs) included in the SDI Program (SDIP). On occasion it refers to the idea announced by Reagan and later modified. 'Star Wars' refers to both the SDI Program and other programmes, closely related to SDI, yet officially excluded from it, notably ASATs. 'SDI' is therefore a subset of 'Star Wars'.

Theories of the arms race can be categorised as 'supply' or 'demand' models.[6] Demand models see weapons as responses to policy needs, or instruments to pursue military strategies or foreign policy objectives, stated or covert. In the case of BMD, they would focus on the strategic case, from the 1940s to the 1960s, for supplementing air defence with BMD; the arguments at stake in the ABM debate of the 1960s; the case made in 1967 for deploying the 'Sentinel' ABM against the Chinese: and the changing strategic and international climate, which caused Nixon to modify 'Sentinel' into 'Safeguard', a defence of missile silos from the Soviets. Demand models would study the strategic implications of the ABM Treaty of 1972; the strategic furore over SDI; and how new regimes of strategic defence might be constructed.

Supply models, by contrast, link weapons production to decisions about the allocation of resources between institutions and industrial sectors. Aware of the role of interest groups, they concentrate on the allocative at the expense of the strategic, emphasising factors other than the official rationales of strategy and foreign policy. They would focus on the sizeable constituency which sustained BMD even before Reagan's SDI speech; the opportunities for corporations and bureaucracies resulting from the speech; and the interest groups promoting the programme, in Congress, in the media and in public. Since they are less familiar and thus perhaps more in need of introduction, 'supply' perspectives will be prioritised in the following chapter.

# PART 1
# CONCEPTION

# 1 THEORY

## THE POLICY PROCESS

If, as many assume, the government as a whole, or its leaders, arrive at decisions through impartial analysis of logical problems, SDI might then be the result of a more or less rational decision taken by President Reagan.

In reality, the making of a military budget is not so simple. The government is seldom a unitary actor coherently synthesising issues to transcend sectional interest. The arms race is the sum of innumerable micro-decisions, each of which seems the almost inevitable response to a situation which is highly predetermined. It is often hard to pinpoint these decisions, or to distinguish between the formulation of a decision, the 'decision' itself and its implementation, which often alters the initial decision.

The process of weapons innovation passes through many stages, lasting 15–20 years. There is, for example, the discovery of new technological possibilities (the 'technocratic initiative'); the process of consensus-building which engages the military-technical community in the new possibility; the promotion of the idea to military leaders, Congress and the Executive; the formulation of a strategic case for a new weapon and the discovery of new threats (the 'open window'); and high-level endorsement.[1] Implementation of the high-level decision starts another round of decision-making. The decisions involved in this lengthy process are themselves diffused across different organisations, with divergent priorities and perspectives. Decisions are taken or avoided through a complex organisational process, or through governmental politics, often lacking in control and accountability.[2]

Individual decisions may affect many different values or objectives, and the government may not analyse and order the trade-off between them. As decisions are demanded in a state of uncertainty, imperfect information and limited feed-back, decision-makers may respond with narrowly focussed attention and a highly programmed response. They

7

may approach parts of problems sequentially, by established procedures, rather than seeing the problem as a whole, considering all the policy options and imagining a wide range of alternatives.[3] A web of institutions and committees may spread the decisions so thin as to lose them. A laissez-faire, wait-and-see attitude connives with an absence of decision or even an absence of policy. Each decision-maker in the arms race can plausibly deny responsibility. Politicians, civil servants, scientists, the enemy country, the strategists: each can blame the others. The buck stops nowhere: it cannot even be found.

This view of decisions as outputs from a complicated, ill-defined process challenges the more 'classical' view of policy as simply handed down from above. It also highlights the opportunities for interest groups vying to influence policy at its various stages.

## INTEREST GROUPS

Budgetary success depends on support from the agencies concerned. Different factions, with diverse motivations and priorities, gather around the same bandwagon; and may wrestle for control of the steering wheel, to direct the programme where they want. The main interest groups – bureaucracies, corporations and research laboratories – will now be identified.

The theme of 'bureaucratic policies' is central to many studies, notably Sapolsky's research into the Polaris programme and Holland and Hoover's work on the MX.[4] Levine argues that in the case of the Cruise missile, bureaucratic organisations embraced, assimilated and altered the plans thrust on them by politicians, to make the externally imposed mission compatible with self-chosen priorities.[5] 'Bureaucratic politics' has obvious applications to SDI. The SDI Office has been a principal advocate of SDI, and the Army Strategic Defense Command, the Air Force Electronic Systems Division, the Naval Research Laboratory, DARPA and the Defense Nuclear Agency (DNA) have all benefited.[6]

The arms bazaar also profits some of the most powerful corporations in the world. The market is characterised by imperfect competition (often sole source procurement) between large corporations which, if they do not diversify, come to rely on the defence budget.[7] Their attendant bureaucratic and profit-driven momentum may amount to an 'industrial imperative' for weapons production.

The power of a corporation can be gauged by a study of its board of directors, personnel transfers from and to the Pentagon, contracting history, location, size and value, the number of its employees, its relationship with members of Congress, membership of defence trade associations, entertainment funds, questionable payments, representation on advisory committees, the size of its offices in Washington, D.C., public relations budget, consulting agencies used, its bank and its lenders, and its budget for congressional liaison, education and grass-roots lobbying.[8]

Kurth, who charted the correlation between military aerospace systems and the major production lines, postulated a 'follow-on' or 'bail-out' imperative: 'about the time a production line phases out production of one government contract, it phases in production of a new one, usually within a year'. He offers this explanation:

> a large and established aerospace production line is a national resource – or so it seems to many high officers in the armed services. The corporations, managers, shareholders, bankers, engineers and workers, of course will enthusiastically agree, as will the area's congressmen and senators. The Defense Department would find it risky and even reckless to allow a large production line to wither and die for lack of a large production contract . . . Thus there is at least latent pressure upon the Defense Department from many sources to award a new major contract to a production line when an old major contract is phasing out.[9]

SDI was not a follow-on contract in the sense of a new contract structurally similar to the old and in the same functional category or production sector. But it did provide 'follow-on' contracts for pre-existing BMD work, as well as opportunities in a new high-tech area and a slightly different production sector for other military contractors. This prompts the accusation that SDI has been driven by the US arms industry; and that firms dependent on SDI will fight hard for its survival.

> Once they get a couple of hundred million dollars under their belt, that is what turns an operation with 10 people into one with 500, it turns division chiefs into vice presidents . . . The ultimate question is whether this [SDI] develops such a constituency that it leaves the realm of sensible discourse so that by the time we have a new president it's too late.[10]

Contractors have a stake in SDI which may be measured in terms of funds won, SDI-dependent employment and profit. It is harder to quantify the benefits accruing to others, especially shareholders in SDI corporations, for several reasons, including the following. First, it is not possible to aggregate the proportion of a dividend which correlates to SDI activities. Second, many of the shareholders are large entities:

9

pension funds, banks, insurance companies. Whilst there is a benefit to this large constituency from SDI, it is too dispersed and indirect to be quantified. Since they have no immediate dependence on SDI, the shareholders could invest elsewhere at equal profit.

In his farewell address to the nation, President Eisenhower warned that 'public policy could itself become the captive of a scientific-technological elite'.[11] The theme has since been developed, notably by Lord Zuckerman, former chief scientific adviser to, successively, the Ministry of Defence and the British government.

> It is he, the technician, not the commander in the field, who is at the heart of the arms race, who starts the process of formulating a so-called military nuclear need . . . The men in the nuclear weapons laboratories of both sides have succeeded in creating a world with an irrational foundation, on which a new set of political realities has in turn to be built. They have become the alchemists of our time, casting spells which embrace us all.[12]

The military chiefs 'usually serve only as the channel through which the men in the laboratories transmit their views'. The inherent secrecy in developing weapons creates an elite, which may use its privileged knowledge to propagate a myth of expertise, to delegitimise opposing points of view, to dictate which debates are significant or which assumptions correct. Unsure of technical and strategic details, officials readily defer to the 'experts' in charge of a weapons programme. Far from being the servant of security policy, military science becomes a relatively autonomous process, which generates its own powerful pressures for funding and for incorporating new research into procurement programmes. The politicians' nominal oversight creates a façade of democratic control.

The 'Zuckerman hypothesis' refers both to the inertia and creeping incrementalism of weapons laboratories as institutions and also to the role of key *individuals* from the labs, whose restricted knowledge wins them undue influence. It singles out day-to-day processes which have no political challenge to their legitimacy and so germinate within established guidelines beyond publicity. Decisions do not reach the desk of the 'high policy-makers', or they arrive there too late, or already shaped by unelected scientists or R&D institutions. BMD was in this position of closed secrecy until Reagan's speech, which cast the spotlight on to a hitherto shady area.

Since the 'Zuckerman hypothesis' applies best to the R&D phase of a weapon's development, we might expect it to illuminate SDI – an R&D programme. The chairman of the Joint Chiefs of Staff later attributed

SDI to a sort of sociolinguistic misunderstanding, wilful or not, on the lines of Zuckerman's postulate:

> I think generally when scientists say we're making a tremendous amount of progress what they mean is they're understanding the problem better. They don't normally mean we're real close to [a solution]. That was part of the problem all along [because] when they said we're making tremendous progress, many leaders said, 'hot dog, we're getting ready to go into hardware production'.[13]

Federal research laboratories are at the heart of the BMD infrastructure. Though scientists from these labs had ample chance to influence policy-makers, including Reagan, they alone could not have created SDI, and most did not apparently believe in a 'perfect defence'.[14] The wider scientific community has provided many of SDI's most informed critics.

### THE POLITICS OF INFLUENCE

On the need to sustain SDI, the interest groups outlined above were unanimous. Attention to them can therefore explain the dynamics of the programme and how it established institutional momentum. On more specific issues about the shaping of SDI, coalitions tended to be looser and more fragmentary. One must then focus on the priorities of different factions and on in-fighting. How can the various interest groups influence the policy process?

'Coincidence of interest' theories study the relationships between the institutions involved in the supply of weapons.[15] Some focus on the 'Iron Triangle' of the Pentagon, Congress and the manufacturers. Others look to a wider Military Industrial Bureaucratic Technological (MIBT) complex,[16] or a 'steel heptagon' of the 'Military Industrial Technological Labour Academic Managerial Political (MITLAMP) complex'.[17]

> The interest of the defense industry in sustaining a constant (or expanding) level of procurement coincides with the interest of military officers in developing new weapons systems for which they have been assigned programme responsibility. It coincides also with the interests of labour union leaders in keeping their members on the job; with the interest of individual congressmen in maintaining full employment and prosperity in their congressional districts; and with the interests of lawyers, bankers, public relations men, trade association executives and journalists and a host of others whose professional and personal fortunes depend on this major sector of the US economy.[18]

11

Interest groups may be clustered in particular areas or broadly distributed. The B-1 bomber, with over 5,000 subcontractors and suppliers, was notorious for the geographical spread of interest groups, which contributed to the extraordinary resilience of the programme.[19]

As people move jobs between the different interest groups, especially between the Pentagon and the arms industry, the spread of expertise and information may coincide with what Eisenhower called the 'acquisition of unwarranted influence'.[20] The 'revolving door' produces a closed community of insiders, with (potential) conflicts of interest; recently retired Pentagon officials can exploit insider contacts, or confidential knowledge, for their new company. In March 1969, the top 100 defence contractors employed 2,072 retired military officers of the rank of Colonel or Navy Captain or above.[21] In 1985 the General Accounting Office discovered that only 30 per cent of DoD personnel legally required to report post-government employment with defence contractors were doing so.[22] It found the same in following years.[23] Enforcement of the reporting requirement remained lax, and some submissions failed to say which major systems the individual worked on at DoD or at the defence contractor. Legislative loop-holes remain in the 1990s.[24] Whilst 'revolving door' employment is not in itself evidence of malpractice, it is a symptom of a closed community and a sign of potential conflict of interest.

The classified nature of much military information debars outside observers without security clearance. In the executive branch, far from the prying eyes of Congress, free from independent audit and control, questionable practices can thrive. Each year, the DoD is involved in roughly 15 million different purchases, costing more than the combined purchases of General Motors, Exxon and IBM. The ten largest defence contractors employ some 6,000 buyers. In the two and a half years up to April 1986, only nineteen buyers from large defence firms were convicted for receiving bribes.[25] Other evidence suggests that the practice of 'kickbacks' is more widespread. US Attorney Robert Bonner said that bribes were 'something that has come very close to being a way of life': 'there's even, I'm sad to say, a going rate that we've seen based upon the prosecutions that we've brought here in southern California, and the going rate is about five to ten per cent of the amount of the subcontract'.[26] From 1986, renewed probes into fraud, which uncovered $600 hammers and $2,000 airborne coffee pots, prompted the Pentagon to reconsider its procurement policies.[27] Though SDI, *qua* concept, received exceptional publicity, the programme's secretive character ruled out independent oversight and management.

Nominally impartial advisory panels, supposed to serve decision-makers, are usually dominated by members from military agencies, laboratories and corporations. This may promote efficiency by fostering 'informal communications loops' and trusted contacts, so that red tape is cut and business expedited. But it also creates a special potential for corruption and 'back-scratching'.[28] The closeness and closedness of the community encourage common presuppositions and mutual favours; and reproduce a self-perpetuating congregation of the like-minded. The formal restraints on this 'buddy system' are mostly ignored. The Federal Advisory Committee Act requires that no committee be 'inappropriately influenced by any special interest', that records be kept and salaries limited to about $250 a day. But, as will be seen later, SDI committees have failed to provide financial disclosure forms and reasons for individuals' membership.[29]

Military expenditures have to be authorised by Congress, the legislative branch. Congress is in a sense an interest group itself, since congressmen have substantial interests in the process they monitor, and seek to win investment and jobs for their district.[30] According to one congressman, SDI supporters include 'Republicans and Democrats who simply see economic benefit to their congressional district or state and don't care too much about the issues one way or another'.[31] Congress is also the arena in which different interest groups confront each other and have their disputes resolved.

'Congressional oversight' is an appropriately ambiguous term, since much is indeed overlooked during congressional examination. The 1980s saw a sharp rise in classified, 'black' programmes, not monitored by Congress. Hearings leave much unquestioned, sources unattributed, presuppositions unchallenged. The size of the committee often stops a member from pursuing a sustained line of enquiry. Thanks to its plentiful resources, the Pentagon can usually produce testimony superior to that of its critics. It can dominate a session with insider exegesis, viewgraphs, videos and the repetition of background information. Since it is privy to 'the latest classified intelligence', its statements on threats, feasibility and cost carry much credibility.

In extraordinary circumstances, corporations can mount public campaigns. As a matter of routine, they sponsor (and thus buy access to) congressmen through Political Action Committees (PACs).[32] The effect of such lobbying is unquantifiable. The best advocacy may be a discreet telephone call, passing unrecorded. Lobbyists may diplomatically understate their influence, or their opponents exaggerate it. All this may amount to what one senator called 'a devastatingly effective lobby working on both the executive and legislative branches. In every state and almost every congressional district, labor, public

13

officials and management combine to convert many a congressman into a fighting advocate of more military contracts.'[33] If, one should add, the congressman was not already disposed by background to favour Pentagon requests.

In sum, diverse interest groups have a crucial role in the policy process for SDI. The politics of influence are examined in parts 2 and 3 below.

## ARMS ECONOMY THEORIES

'Arms economy' theories argue that the arms industry sustains the economy *as a whole*. They point to long-term, structural causes, which cannot explain the details of SDI, but may contribute to an understanding of its underlying determinants. The classic 'army economy' theory, associated with Ernest Mandel and Michael Kidron, holds that, by absorbing surplus value, armaments maintain demand and prevent a realisation crisis. Another theory links SDI to 'long waves' in the economy of the kind originally proposed by Nikolai Kondratiev.

SDI has been interpreted as a way of securing federal funding for generic industries such as electronics and computing: and as a subsidy for the commercial development of space. Noam Chomsky has argued that the 'Pentagon system' is a device for the public subsidy of 'private' enterprise; and that Star Wars expenditures 'correspond closely to those of Japan's state-coordinated industrial system, which the US is unable to duplicate directly for a variety of social and historical reasons'.[34] Emergent technologies are therefore militarised in the USA, whereas in Japan their commercial potential is prioritised.

Chomsky and others have also maintained that the US economy depends on the repatriation of profit from abroad. This necessitates access to overseas markets and to foreign factors of production: natural resources, strategic minerals, oil and cheap labour. Sealanes must be protected and investments safeguarded. Socialist states must be contained and radical nationalist movements intimidated. From this perspective, the arms race stems from imperialist or neocolonial policies towards the socialist bloc and the Third World. Security Assistance programmes and Foreign Military Sales (FMS) bolster shaky allies and regional gendarmes and ensure access to overseas bases. They foster increased dependence of the host country on the USA and facilitate market penetration by US firms.

These could be considered 'strategic theories', since they focus on a 'demand' for weapons, stemming from an alleged need to dominate the

14

Third World. However, these theories concentrate on political economy and the (exploitative) relations between metropolitan countries and the periphery. In this respect they differ radically from orthodox strategic studies. If, as argued in Chapter 11 below, SDI has many conventional military applications, then it might be explained as a military/political force which underwrites US power.

Baran and Sweezy combine the various 'arms economy' theories. They place 'militarism and imperialism' under the rubric 'the absorption of surplus'.[35] They conceptualise the arms budget as a way to create demand and 'prime the pump of' the economy. The military sustains the economy by playing 'the role of an ideal customer for private business, spending billions of dollars annually on terms that are most favourable to the sellers'. The Pentagon also satisfies 'the giant multinational corporations which dominate American policy' by ensuring 'monopolistic control over foreign sources of supply and foreign markets', enabling 'American Big Business' to operate on its own terms, wherever it chooses. Moreover, militarism furthers 'the class interests of the oligarchy' by fostering 'all the reactionary and irrational forces in society'. This latter claim verges on another set of non-strategic dynamics which could be categorised as psycho-political.

### PSYCHO-POLITICAL OR CULTURAL THEORIES

In that different ethnic groups are united by a fear of a common enemy, 'defence' can foster national consensus.[36] In the USSR, severe ethnic tensions were once resolved by invoking the great Satan, 'imperialism'. The abandonment of Cold War rhetoric in the USSR is concurrent with a rise in ethnic strife. To this day, fear of 'Communism' binds diverse groups in the USA. Some have suggested that without the one to scare the other, the two great superpowers could fall apart. President Reagan introduced SDI as an appeal to American ingenuity and swathed it in the values of the Stars and Stripes. Such nationalism fosters people's sense of belonging, their group identity, perhaps at the expense of their awareness of others' perceptions or the need for change.

Prominent among cultural approaches are feminist critiques, which see militarism as an extension of masculine aggression, a result of the cultural construction of gender roles and masculinity, ultimately connected with the unequal sexual division of labour.[37] Others speculate about how people come to terms with, or avoid, the fear of holocaust;[38] and how the military gains cultural support or acquiescence.[39] It has been claimed that the sheer quantity of nuclear weapons and their

15

destructive power are hard to conceive and comprehend: and in order to 'accept' and make sense of the terror of nuclear weapons, many people come to believe that there must be an enemy as terrible and lethal as the Bomb itself. The Absolute Bomb requires an Absolute Enemy. It may be too that in some way the (subconscious) mind, yearning for security, imagines that the Absolute Bomb must be matched by an Absolute Defence. In this case, Reagan's offer of a shield to eliminate the threat of nuclear weapons was playing to the American, or even human, Dream.

It could be objected that theories about culture, psychology or 'arms economy' are too conjectural and explain nothing specific about SDI. It is indeed hard to find empirical data by which to verify or falsify direct causal links in the area. As with much social science (and indeed natural science), this difficulty may be taken as a measure of the complexity and importance of the issues. The end of enquiry is to 'extend the historical questionnaire'. The theories refer to a deeper (structural) level, the undercurrents beneath the surface flotsam, the foundation beneath the finery. In Braudel's terms, they illuminate the 'longue durée' and 'conjoncture', rather than merely 'l'histoire événementielle'. Whether these 'supply-side' approaches be far reaching or far-fetched, we must return to the more trodden paths of strategic theory.

## STRATEGIC THEORY

President Reagan introduced SDI as a new strategy, formed 'after careful consultation with my advisers, including the joint chiefs of staff',[40] and it has been widely discussed in terms of strategic theory ever since.[41] Such theory interprets new weapons in a fairly 'commonsense' way as contributions to military strength or national security. It may then continue, in a more remote fashion, to define and refine strategic criteria, such as 'assured deterrence' or 'strategic stability'; or model the changing 'threat scenario', to improve military posture and war-fighting capability.

For the last four decades funds for BMD have been justified as a 'hedge' against technological breakthrough by the Soviets. BMD might thus be understood as an instance of 'action/reaction', whereby each side rationalises its own activities as a response to the other's. The long lead times needed to engineer modern weapons require that developments be anticipated perhaps ten years in advance. The range of possible reactions is wide and contingent on many factors. R&D by one side on a new bomber may serve to legitimise the other side's new bomber, or interceptor, or, in the case of action/overreaction, both.

16

Since accurate information is scarce because of mistrust and secrecy, each side tends towards 'worst case assumptions' about the other, which creates exaggerated threat assessments. This pessimism may be matched by the optimistic ('best case') assumption that research by one superpower will *deter* the other side. Instead it usually helps to justify the opponent's own work, leading to a self-fulfilling prophecy and an upward spiral of weapons developments.

Reagan's presentation of SDI as a full defence to *replace* deterrence conflicted with the strategic case that it was a partial defence to *fortify* deterrence. This inconsistency and the lack of a strategic consensus for SDI indicate that the programme was not driven by strategy alone and that further reasons for its development may be found elsewhere.

### POLITICS

Political theory, in the sense understood in international relations, serves to explain the general context of the arms race. Without the underlying antagonism between the USA and the USSR, SDI would not have emerged in the way it did, as the last great outgrowth of the US arms build-up of the early 1980s, reinforcing the drive to 'get tough' with the Soviets and 'negotiate from strength'. As superpower relations have thawed since 1985, planned requests for SDI have also been partially reduced.

Weapons developments may be a response to the demands of allied states, an attempt at alliance management. The 'dual track decision' to deploy Cruise and Pershing II in Europe was, for example, widely understood as a signal that the USA would not be 'decoupled' from Europe. SDI may, likewise, be seen as an attempt to manage relations between the USA and its European allies; or, conversely, as an industrial technology policy aimed at reasserting US hegemony.[42]

Arms programmes may equally be understood in terms of domestic politics, as a signal to the public. Nuclear weapons are commonly depicted as symbols of 'strength', 'the resolute approach' and 'firm commitment to the national defence'. The 'modernisation' of US nuclear forces in the 1980s was portrayed as a sign of a reinvigorated America 'riding high in the saddle'. Chapter 13 below considers SDI in terms of marketing, mass politics and the popular political debate.

### TECHNOLOGY

Technology straddles the division between supply and demand. Mainly strategic theories, especially about SDI, also focus on

17

issues of technical feasibility, for practical reasons, rather than in search of causative dynamics. Matters of technological feasibility are inevitably linked to stated or covert policy prescriptions. The most credible advice masquerades as the most impartial. 'Behind many, if not most, more or less optimistic technical arguments concerning the feasibility of space weaponry, lurks a strategic policy proponent of one or another persuasion.'[43]

More on the 'supply side', a theory sometimes called the 'technological imperative' sees the arms race as being driven by the onward march of technology, the constant innovation which results from human ingenuity and scientific research.[44] Since 1945, each superpower has striven to gain a technological edge over the other. New capabilities look too scientifically 'sweet' to forgo, even though their development might in the longer run damage national security. Chapter 4 below considers how far SDI was dictated by the forward march of technology.

The theory of 'overdeveloped technology' links the 'technological imperative' with study of the institutional conditions in which military innovation is produced.[45] It proposes that the implementation of official policy by military, industrial and academic institutions (the 'Steel Triangle') creates weapons whose capabilities far exceed the requirements of the initial strategy. The excess is rationalised ex post facto. Superfluous applications are pursued because of 'worst case planning' and accommodated by strategists and politicians into a more sophisticated and demanding policy. As this new policy is implemented, the cycle continues. The president of LTV, an SDI contractor, puts the idea slightly differently. 'All too often before the ink is dry, "requirements" become "desirements" or industry starts pushing the "better biscuit". Everyone contributes to this problem.'[46]

Thus, an official policy of nuclear deterrence led to overdeveloped weapons, free-fall atom and hydrogen bombs, which were incorporated and used to justify a new policy (early 1950s to mid 1960s) of MAD, supplemented by limited nuclear war-fighting capability. Implemented by the Steel Triangle, this developed ICBMs and tactical nuclear weapons. These in turn were rationalised into the modern doctrines of 'flexible response' and 'counterforce'. These policies fed back into the Steel Triangle, which responded with MIRVs, cruise missiles, fast and accurate missiles suitable for a first strike, improved $C^3I$ and Anti-Submarine Warfare (ASW).[47]

BMD could be seen in this light, as an 'overdeveloped technology', which evolved out of a demand for air defence. SDI itself could in turn produce 'overdeveloped' technologies, which will improve $C^3I$ and offensive weapons. It is sure to improve capabilities for anti-satellite weapons (ASATs) and could spawn new battlefield laser weapons. These offensive military spin-offs, described in Chapter 11 below, conflict with the *defensive* rationale for SDI and could lead to declaratory policy being changed ex post facto into one for space warfighting.

When not proffering surplus capabilities, institutions may *degrade* strategic and technical plans. For example, promising new technologies for the M-16 rifle were neglected by the Army Ordnance Corps, which, wary of outside designs, clung to inappropriate performance criteria. A similar fate befell the F-16 fighter aircraft.[48] According to the theory of the 'baroque arsenal', discussed in Chapter 11 below, the armed forces are conservative in character and tend to defend their established roles.[49] They therefore seek to assimilate new technologies so as to minimise disruption to established organisational structures and strategies. New technologies are incorporated into existing weapons systems, perhaps beyond a point of saturation, in which case the weapon becomes overly sophisticated, unreliable, 'baroque'.

### CONCLUSION

The theories of the arms race outlined above are not mutually exclusive. They all contribute to a syncretic account of strategic defence. None will be discounted for sins of omission. Take three at random: the 'Zuckerman hypothesis', the action/reaction model and corporate momentum. Each focusses on one group: the weapons scientists, strategists and corporate contractors. The interaction of these groups is synergistic. They work together (not always in the same direction) to produce a whole greater than the sum of its parts. Much writing unites strategic debate with technical detail. Some mix supply theories, more or less consciously. Marek Thee, for instance, sees military R&D as 'the forge and engine of the arms race', supported by the staying-power of a military-industrial-bureaucratic-technological complex, energised exogenously by rivalry between the great powers and internally by the 'competitive process of procurement'.[50]

The binary opposition of supply and demand is, doubtless, intrinsically flawed, wide open to deconstruction. Technology is the obvious aporia, tugging at the threads of the dichotomy. Perhaps all 'supply' theories narrate the construction of 'demand'. But I keep the distinction because it is useful.

Of the approaches described, strategic theory, the only one to have been accepted as a major academic discipline in its own right, is accorded primary importance by many writers. Although 'supply' theories have produced outstanding studies, they violate traditional academic boundaries, and have been pursued more by mavericks than mainstream academics. The following chapters will pillage every available resource to illuminate the course and causes of SDI.

# 2 THE HISTORY OF STRATEGIC DEFENCE IN THE USA

The chequered story of SDI is but one chapter in the saga of Ballistic Missile Defence (BMD) or Anti-Ballistic Missile (ABM), as strategic defences have variously been known. In the USA, waves of hope and disillusionment about the prospects for intercepting nuclear missiles have only partially affected the relatively steady expansion in the infrastructure of laboratories, corporations and field agencies developing BMD. The history of strategic defence illuminates the causes of SDI and offers important clues as to the course SDI may now take.

## EARLY BMD

With Nazi Germany defeated, the two new superpowers strove to develop their own rocketry, using the German V-2 as a prototype. The US Army mounted 'operation paperclip' to recruit the inventors of the V-2, including Wernher von Braun. By 1945, 120 German rocket engineers were working for the Americans at Fort Bliss, Texas.[1] They helped to develop Medium-Range Ballistic Missiles (MRBMs) and, later, Inter Continental Ballistic Missiles (ICBMs), which both superpowers had successfully tested by the end of the 1950s.

During the Cold War, the superpowers invested heavily in air defences. This research laid the foundations for the first ABM programmes. It seemed that BMD could be allocated an increasingly important share of the defence budget and, in the United States, the army and the air force competed for the job of running the programme.

In claiming a right to the ABM role, the army could point out that it was already developing an air defence of the Continental United States (CONUS).[2] Straight after the war, it started Project Nike to build defences against manned aircraft.[3] These systems, which became known as Nike-Ajax and Nike-Hercules, were the beginning of the US ABM programme, the prehistory of SDI. The US Air Force (USAF) also had a stake in air defence. Its interceptor aircraft were designed to provide a general 'area' defence against enemy fighters. The air force

21

started researching ABM in 1946, but it terminated the projects, called Thumper and Wizard, because of inadequate technologies for radar, data processing and rocket guidance. The air force continued to work on ABM in the 1950s with research into BAMBI (Ballistic Missile Boost Interceptor), a space-based ABM system, and SAINT, a 'satellite interceptor'.

In 1956, Secretary of Defense McElroy announced that the army would run the ABM programme. This decision served to maintain the balance of bureaucratic power. The army had had no stake in the expanding budget for strategic nuclear missiles and was falling behind in its budget allocation. The air force, by contrast, had a large budget for strategic nuclear missiles, such as Minuteman, as well as nuclear bombers. So too did the navy, with Polaris and Poseidon. The ABM programme was the army's opportunity to win a role in strategic nuclear matters.

ABM was given a new urgency after the Soviets launched Sputnik-1 in October 1957. In reaction, the United States established NASA and the Advanced Research Projects Agency (ARPA), which later became the Defense Advanced Research Projects Agency (DARPA). ARPA conducted long-term research for ABM, under its Project Defender, which in the early 1960s accounted for half of its budget.[4]

The Nike programme continued in the form of Nike-Zeus. The army and other members of the ABM constituency repeatedly proposed that a system should be deployed, and they won firm support in Congress. The advocates of ABM were fired with a potent mixture of strategic concerns and economic or bureaucratic self-interest. The combination is well expressed in the call of the House Majority leader to 'muzzle the mad dog missile threat of the Soviet Union, loose the Zeus through America's magnificent production line'.[5]

Wary of the blandishments of the military industrial complex, in 1958 President Eisenhower vetoed funds for the production of Nike-Zeus, even though Congress had voted $137 million for that purpose. Eisenhower believed that the defence was not technically feasible and could easily be defeated by an attacker. The resulting campaigns in favour of Nike-Zeus were, according to one observer, 'particularly vigorous and included very large and effective advertising campaigns in the national periodicals peddling a mixture of military security and economic benefit'.[6] Western Electric and eight subcontractors bought full-page advertisements to show where the funds for ABM would be spent. In the face of congressional pressure, Eisenhower relented and allowed the money to be spent on Nike-Zeus, but only for research.

The Nike programme had some success in making intercepts of

single missiles in laboratory and test range conditions. Thirteen intercepts were judged to be 'successful'. In 1963, there was a successful satellite intercept demonstration codenamed 'Mudflap', and for the next year Mudflap missiles were maintained in a 'ready' state on their base at Kwajalein Atoll in the Pacific.

The Nike programme grew through creeping incrementalism. Budgets and bureaucracies sustained themselves and expanded. Nike-Zeus was up-dated and in 1964 became known as Nike-X, which had improved data processing and phased array radars, with a perimeter acquisition radar for long-range detection and a missile site radar for discrimination and interceptor guidance. It also incorporated faster interceptors: the Spring missile and, later, the Spartan missile.[7] Work on BMD was well established by the mid 1960s. The infrastructure was in place and a solid constituency of interest had developed. This constituency was fostered by the monies invested in BMD research, which amounted to about $4 billion between 1955, the start of the Nike-Zeus project, and 1967.[8]

One barrier to deployment of BMD was the Secretary of Defense, Robert McNamara. His opposition to ABM was shared by the Office of International Security Affairs (ISA) in the Office of the Secretary of Defense (OSD).[9] This office had no links with defence contractors and was intended to give independent advice, untainted by special pleading. Secretary Dean Rusk of the State Department also opposed ABM because of its political repercussions, and the Budget Bureau opposed it because of the expense. The President's Science Advisory Committee was sceptical, as members doubted that a secure defence was feasible.

The Service chiefs had long argued for ABM in their testimony to Congress. Leaders of the Senate were keen supporters of the concept. The idea of building defences against nuclear weapons is inherently attractive, and ABM was an obvious response to the new US vulnerability against Soviet missiles. In the post-Sputnik period, ABM could symbolise America's commitment to keep a technological edge over the Soviets and a military role in space. More generally, it was a token of US ingenuity, power and prestige. Senators and congressmen saw ABM as a vote-winner, and the time seemed propitious to expand the programme.

The main advocate of BMD was the army, since BMD was its best opportunity to win a role in strategic nuclear forces. The army had failed to become involved in other aspects of strategic nuclear forces, which were swallowing an ever larger share of the defence budget. The other Services backed, or at least did not oppose, the army's bid for BMD for their own reasons. The navy hoped that army BMD might lead

23

to an eventual Sea-based Anti-Ballistic Missile System (SABMIS). The air force, which had its own Air-borne Ballistic Missile Intercept System (ABMIS), was prepared to support the army, in return for army support for the air force's strategic programmes. To some extent the navy and the air force may also have been making the best of a fait accompli by the army. Some in Strategic Air Command did not want the army to be defending Minuteman silos, which were the province of the air force.[10] They feared that the army might appropriate funds to defend Minuteman at the expense of the air force budget. But, as long as the army cast ABM as an area defence, the air force as a whole would endorse it. The Director of Defense Research and Engineering (DDR&E) favoured an ABM deployment, since it seemed technically 'sweet'. To forgo deployment might cause demoralisation amongst the research teams. The Systems Analysis Office saw an ABM programme as preferable to yet another expansion of strategic nuclear forces.[11]

Research laboratories and private contractors also stood to gain from deployment of an ABM system. 'Thin Nike, fat orders' ran the headline in one trade magazine.[12] A brokerage house described the announcement of Nike-X as 'the day they will shake the money tree for electronics companies. All will stand to benefit. The demands will be too high not to be felt by all in the industry.'[13]

Western Electric Company, as prime contractor, had won over $1.5 billion for ABM between 1963 and 1967, and it could expect a large share from full-scale procurement. *Business Week* remarked that Western Electric 'has succeeded in spreading out the design and development work among close to 3,000 different companies'.[14] Hersh (1968) wrote that 15,000 companies, including 12,000 small businesses, were expected to profit from deployment. Raytheon, Martin and McDonnell Douglas could each expect some $600 million over five years, and General Electric could look forward to some $400 million.[15]

Throughout the early stage, the BMD infrastructure and its constituents showed remarkable continuity, whatever the shifts of strategic rationale. For example, the army's main contractors for Nike, established in 1945, were Bell Telephone Laboratories (BTL) and Western Electric. These companies were subsidiaries of the American Telephone and Telegraph Company (AT&T). AT&T effectively took over the programme for defensive guided missiles. It won $2.25 billion for the Nike-Ajax anti-aircraft missile and went on to run the Nike-Hercules programme.

As the superpowers expanded their arsenals of Inter-Continental Ballistic Missiles (ICBMs), Submarine Launched Ballistic Missiles (SLMBs) and Intermediate Range Ballistic Missiles (IRBMs), the army

Table 2.1. *Contractors for Nike-X*

| | |
|---|---|
| Western Electric Company[ab] | Prime contractor |
| Bell Telephone Laboratories[ab] | Systems integrator |

*Major subcontractors*

| | |
|---|---|
| Burndy Corp.[a] | Connectors for data processing |
| Burroughs Corp. | Operator displays |
| General Electric Co.[ab] | Perimeter acquisition radar |
| Martin Co.[ab] | Sprint missile |
| McDonnell Douglas Corp.[ab] | Spartan missile |
| Raytheon Co.[ab] | Missile site radar |
| Sperry Rand Corp.[ab] | Data processing |

*Second-tier subcontractors*

| | |
|---|---|
| Avco Corp.[ab] | Radar and optics |
| Block Engineering | Optics |
| Control Data Corp. | Recording equipment |
| Cornell Aeronautical Laboratory | Radar |
| Hughes Aircraft Co.[ab] | Recorders |
| RCA[ab] | Data reduction |
| Sperry Gyroscope | Engineering |
| TRW[ab] | Re-entry measurement vehicles |
| Wheeler Laboratories Inc. | Radar |
| World Airways | Flight services |

*Large lower-tier subcontractors*

| | |
|---|---|
| Hercules[ab] | Spring propellant |
| Honeywell[b] | Gyros |
| Ling-Temco-Vought[b] | Freon injection valves |
| Microwave Associates | Phase shifters |
| Motorola[a] | Semiconductors |
| Thiokol Chemical Corp. | Spartan propellant |
| Varian Associates | Klystron tubes |
| Westinghouse Electric Corp.[b] | Transporter-loader |

*Notes:* [a]Contractors for the subsequent Safeguard programme; [b]SDI contractors.
*Source:* Data on Nike systems from *Business Week* (23 September 1967), p. 37.

paid Bell Telephone Laboratory to study possible responses. Bell Telephones advised in 1956 that Nike-Hercules could indeed be modified into an effective ABM, and the company benefited handsomely from the advice it was paid to give.[16] Bell Telephones and Western Electric became prime contractors for the system they had advocated. When the Nike system was upgraded into 'Sentinel' in 1967, the main contractors for it were still Bell Telephones and Western Electric.

The centre of the army's ABM work was at Huntsville, Alabama. The

Nike-Zeus programme had been based there under the Army Ballistic Missile Agency in 1957. Nike-X and Sentinel were also based at Huntsville, which is a centre of SDI research to this day.

A formidable constituency therefore supported ABM. It could point to the potential military spin-offs from advanced BMD research. Hovering over ABM, and later SDI, was the enticing prospect of a major technical breakthrough which might usher in a new era of 'futuristic' laser and beam weapons. In 1958, the USA started highly classified research on particle beam weapons (Project Seesaw).[17] The first working laser appeared in 1960; by 1965, scientists in the USA had developed chemical lasers and carbon dioxide lasers. This had a clear military potential. Tactical laser systems were already used for range-finding in Vietnam. Analyses of rocket plumes made it possible, by 1967, to detect the launch of ballistic missiles. This opened the *prospect* of destroying missiles in their boost phase, although the ABM systems discussed in the 1960s did not have that capability.

The pressures to announce a deployment of ABM came to a head in 1967. The Soviets had been working hard on ABM and were planning to deploy the rudimentary 'Galosh' ABM around Moscow. They refused to negotiate a joint ban on ABM development, stating that as a purely defensive weapon, ABM was harmless. Both superpowers thought that they might gain unilateral advantage from BMD research.

President Johnson, who had no great ideological affinity to ABM, feared that the issue might be exploited as a symbol of negligence in defence. Kennedy had won votes on account of a mythical 'missile gap' two elections previously, and one Republican contender for the presidential election of 1968 had already spoken of an 'ABM gap'.[18]

*Business Week* ran a special report on the '$30 million Nike-X debate'. Prospects for an ABM bonanza had never looked brighter. The Secretary of Defense, Robert McNamara, was increasingly isolated in his opposition to ABM, even in his own office, where Paul Nitze, a supporter of ABM, had replaced Cyrus Vance as Deputy Secretary.[19]

### SENTINEL

The announcement of a new ABM system came in an unexpected way. Speaking to United Press International in September 1967, McNamara announced a 'light' defence, estimated by him to cost about $5 billion, against missiles which might be launched by the Chinese Red Army.[20] It was to be called Sentinel and would use the components of Nike-X.

McNamara opposed an ABM defence against Soviet missiles. He had long been telling Congress that the technologies were immature and that the Soviets could easily defeat a system by using decoys or Multiple Re-entry Vehicles (MRVs). Announcing Sentinel, McNamara reiterated this judgement: 'none of the systems at the present or foreseeable state of the art would provide an impenetrable shield over the United States'. He repeated that an ABM defence against Soviet missiles would be both infeasible and counter-productive:

> The so-called heavy ABM shield – at the present state of technology – would in effect be no adequate shield at all against a Soviet attack, but rather a strong inducement for the Soviets to vastly increase their own offensive forces. That, as I have pointed out, would make it necessary for us to respond in turn – and so the arms race would rush hopelessly on to no sensible purpose on either side.[21]

The Secretary of Defense had the same message for Congress: 'in all probability, all we would accomplish [by deploying Nike-X] would be to increase greatly both their defense expenditures and ours without any gain in real security to either side'.[22] McNamara also told Congress that 'there will be such a huge amount of fall-out generated by our own anti-ICBM system and the incoming warheads of the strike that it would be foolhardy to spend funds of this magnitude without accompanying it with a civil defense program'.[23] As McNamara well knew, a major civil defence programme was not politically viable.

Nonetheless McNamara was under pressure to endorse ABM. He compromised with a defence against China. The items which he had ordered would take some years to produce, and arms control talks might intervene to prevent full-scale deployment of ABM. McNamara did not himself believe that the Chinese would attack the United States. Such an attack would be tantamount to suicide. Like Reagan, sixteen years later, he used a rhetorical question to suggest a remote eventuality:

> Is there any possibility then that by the mid-1970s China might become so incautious as to attempt a nuclear attack on the United States or our Allies? It would be insane and suicidal of her to do so, but one can conceive conditions under which China might miscalculate. We wish to reduce such possibilities to a minimum.[24]

At the time, the Chinese did not have any ballistic missiles able to reach the United States. McNamara had pointed out that 'the lead-time required for China to develop a significant ICBM force is greater than that required for deployment of our defense – therefore the Chinese threat in itself would not dictate the production of an ABM system at this time'.[25] Even if the Chinese *were* mad enough to attack the US, with

27

missiles as yet not invented, they would probably use bombers launched from a ship or terrorist means, against which Sentinel was powerless. It seems that McNamara was not convinced by his public reasoning, even after announcing the change to his own staff. According to one account:

> When Warnke saw McNamara later that day, he asked 'China bomb, Bob?'
> McNamara looked down, shuffled some papers around on his desk and muttered, 'What else am I going to blame it on?'[26]

The danger of the compromise, as McNamara implicitly acknowledged in his speech, was that Sentinel might generate unstoppable momentum.

> There is a kind of mad momentum intrinsic to the deployment of all new nuclear weaponry. If a weapon system works – and works well – there is a strong pressure from many directions to procure and deploy the weapon out of all proportion to the prudent level required.

The truth of this was soon apparent, for no sooner had McNamara announced a 'thin' defence than congressmen were calling for it to be 'thickened'.[27]

McNamara had wanted an ABM deployment which was unambiguously aimed at China and which could not be construed as a defence against Soviet attack. But he was increasingly preoccupied with Vietnam and had little time to supervise the implementation of his ABM announcement. This being so, the Services began to deploy the system in the way they wanted, so that it could be used against Soviet missiles just as much as Chinese ones.[28]

The Sentinel programme gave a big boost to existing work on BMD. McDonnell Douglas would provide the Spartan rocket, and Martin the shorter-range Sprint interceptor. These would be guided by a Raytheon missile site radar and Sperry Rand computer complex. General Electric would provide the perimeter acquisition radar. The US Army established a Sentinel System Command (SENSCOM) at Huntsville, which had been the base for the army's ABM work since the 1950s. It also appointed the first official BMD programme manager, Lieutenant-General Starbird, who continued to enjoy direct access to the army chief of staff.[29] SENSCOM concentrated on engineering development. The Advanced Ballistic Missile Defense Agency (ABMDA) took over advanced work from Nike-X, and also ARPA's Project Defender.

Those who assumed that citizens would welcome a defence, even an unreliable one, against nuclear weapons, were proved wrong. There were protests in the cities involved – Seattle, Boston, Detroit and Chicago – and also in New York, San Francisco and Salt Lake City.[30] Mass meetings, demonstrations, picketing and letter-writing campaigns forced the Pentagon to reconsider its policy. The Church, liberal and anti-war groups opposed to Sentinel found powerful allies, including the former Vice-President, Hubert Humphrey, who said that Sentinel would encourage the Soviets to build more nuclear missiles and would hinder arms control. This view was probably shared by others within the Administration. Trade unions also opposed Sentinel. The United Automobile Workers (UAW) executive board said that it would be 'hypocritical' to ask other countries to sign the pending nuclear non-proliferation treaty, 'while flaunting our own lack of restraint' on a 'useless and unnecessary' ABM system. The United Mine Workers (UMW) said that ABM would only inflame the arms race and drain funds from welfare programmes.

Following reports in the press, the army admitted that it had undertaken a large-scale public relations campaign to win support for the ABM programme.[31] In February 1969, the Secretary of Defense released details of the plan for the campaign. Its objectives were 'gaining public understanding of the necessity' for ABM and establishing 'a favorable public attitude'. The campaign was planned by the Secretary of the Army and included congressional lobbying, co-ordination with contractors and efforts to influence editors and reporters. It would encourage articles 'supporting the technical feasibility and operational effectiveness' of ABM. Public relations tactics included orientation tours for the media, congressmen and scientific and civic groups.

Overall, the coalitions for and against Sentinel were powerful and evenly matched, and they both campaigned vigorously. The balance was probably tipped by factors outside the immediate control of either coalition.

### SAFEGUARD

The rationale of a defence against Chinese missiles, which had always been tenuous, was to become even less plausible in the light of Nixon's rapprochement with China. Sentinel had been met with unforeseen opposition, and there was no political capital in continuing it. The new Nixon Administration therefore announced that construction would be delayed whilst the Pentagon reconsidered the programme. Opposition to Sentinel was strong enough to force a revision of policy, but not able to halt the ABM programme altogether.

On 14 March 1969, President Nixon announced that Sentinel was to be changed into a new system, intended as a limited 'point' defence, called Safeguard. He said that Sentinel 'could not prevent a catastrophic level of US fatalities', adding that 'it might look to an opponent like the prelude to an offensive strategy threatening the Soviet deterrent'.[32] Safeguard was to use components similar to Sentinel's: a perimeter acquisition radar, a missile site radar and two missiles, Spartan and Sprint. The Administration justified Safeguard as a response to the Soviet SS-9 and to the development of MRVs (Multiple Re-entry Vehicles). The Administration said that a BMD system would be placed around twelve sites, to defend Minuteman missiles. ABM thus reverted to the role envisaged by the Nike-X Threat Analysis Group, which McNamara had established in 1964.

Contractors for Safeguard were much the same as those for Sentinel. Some, such as Martin Marietta, McDonnell Douglas, Raytheon and General Electric, kept working on BMD in the 1970s and became major contractors for SDI in the 1980s. Some discontinuities are also apparent. Western Electric, a subsidiary of AT&T, has lost its leading role in BMD and has very few SDI contracts. The federal laboratories (Los Alamos and Lawrence Livermore) and the four leading contractors for SDI – Lockheed, Boeing, TRW and Rockwell – all emerged after the 1960s as leading BMD contractors.

Whereas the Nike systems of the early 1960s had enjoyed firm support in Congress, Safeguard encountered deep scepticism. The initial funds for it were approved only by the narrowest of margins, with the Vice-President breaking a 50–50 tie vote in the Senate.

The senator from Kansas reported that an army General had threatened that a plane built in that state would be stopped if ABM was thwarted by Congress.[33] Apart from such anecdotal evidence, there is no systematic record of telephone calls and other techniques of the lobbyist. It is certain, however, that the major contractors had both the motive and the means to influence Congress. Three large ABM contractors – Lockheed, General Electric and Motorola – funded the 'American Security Council', which supported ABM through radio and direct mail campaigns.[34] The council's 'national strategy committee' also published a pro-ABM booklet which was mailed to twenty thousand opinion-formers in Congress, the Pentagon and the media. The committee responsible for the report was chaired, and the report signed, by the chairman and chief executive officer of Motorola, a firm which won $9.495 million from Safeguard. Furthermore, 8 of the top 12 Safeguard contractors belonged to the Aerospace Industries Association, a large coalition of arms manufacturers, which furthers the interests of its members in Congress.

Table 2.2. *Contractors for Safeguard and SDI: continuity and discontinuity*

| Prime contractors | FY 1968–9 ($ million) | FY 1985–8 ($ million) |
|---|---|---|
| Western Electric (Bell Telephone Lab.) | 1,028.294 | 5.906 |
| Stanford Research Inst. | 2.455 | 11.818 |
| Brown Engineering | 1.564 | 0 |
| Boeing | 1.240 | 634.022 |
| *Subcontractors* | | |
| General Electric | 45.289 | 64.024 |
| IBM | 7.569 | 14.308 |
| Lockheed | 1.746 | 658.329 |
| McDonnell Douglas | 90.385 | 282.963 |
| Martin Marietta | 70.232 | 187.051 |
| RCA | 15.140 | 27.732 |
| Raytheon | 109.023 | 103.863 |
| Sperry Rand | 15.772 | 0.800 |
| Burndy Corp. | 4.157 | 0 |
| Air Research | 1.653 | 7.234 |
| Thiokol | 6.300 | 9.319 |
| Hercules Inc. | 8.040 | 3.087 |
| Motorola | 9.495 | 1.555 |
| Texas Instruments | 16.127 | 15.821 |
| American Machine & Foundry | 1.685 | 0 |
| Varian | 4.470 | 1.268 |
| Gardner Denver Corp. | 2.919 | 0 |
| Brunswick Inc. | 1.608 | 0 |

*Sources:* Figures for Safeguard contracts, at dollar value of that year, are from Safeguard Command Office, Department of Defense, *Congressional Quarterly* (30 May 1969), p. 848. Figures for SDI are from the SDI Office contract data base (5 August 1988). The figures are for *outlays*: funds obligated at the dollar value when the contract was signed. Some firms have been changed by takeovers and mergers between the 1960s and 1980s.

Policy-makers were concerned that the interceptor missiles for Safeguard would use nuclear warheads. In order to test them adequately, it would be necessary to renounce the Partial Test Ban Treaty, one of the few existing successes of arms control. There seemed no compelling need to defend twelve Minuteman bases at great political and financial expense. The technology was immature and members of the Administration had testified that the system would not be cost-effective at the margin. Indeed, the Director of Defense Research and Engineering (DDR&E) stated that the US would have to spend four times as much to limit damage as the Soviets would have to spend to create damage.[35] In other words, offensive forces would win in any arms race between offence and defence.

The things which stopped Sentinel finally stopped Safeguard as well. The budget increases needed to deploy Safeguard were swallowed up by the Vietnam War. The war increased public disillusionment with the Pentagon, whilst a rise of superpower détente undermined 'hawkish' arguments for ABM.

By 1969 the Soviets had also come to the conclusion that neither side could gain from an ABM race. Their own efforts at ABM around Moscow (the 'Galosh system') had merely served as a justification for the US to develop ABM and MRV. Whilst the Soviets continued to build and upgrade 'Galosh', they sought some kind of mutual restraint on ABM deployment. The prospects for a secure ABM defence were receding, as the Americans planned to develop Multiple *Independently-targetable* Re-entry Vehicles (MIRVs) and build Poseidon and Minuteman III.

### THE ABM TREATY AND AFTER

In a new spirit of détente, both superpowers realised that a competition for ABM defences would only produce a new spiral in the arms race and generate even more offensive weapons. Negotiations began to ban ABM deployment and to agree limits for the offensive nuclear arsenal. The ABM Treaty of 1972 forbade deployment of ABM systems and restricted their development. Each country would limit itself to two ABM sites. The ABM budget could therefore be reduced. In 1973, Congress restricted US deployment to one site, at Grand Forks Air Force Base, North Dakota. This unilateral initiative was reciprocated the following year when a protocol to the ABM Treaty formally limited both sides to one ABM site with no more than 100 missiles and launchers.

The treaty was a massive blow to the prospects of BMD deployment and to the fortunes of the BMD infrastructure. It led to reorganisation and cuts, although the core elements of the research infrastructure remained unscathed. The Sentinel System Command (SENSCOM) at Huntsville, Alabama, which had been renamed SAFSCOM under Safeguard, was now relabelled the Ballistic Missile Defense Systems Command (BMDSCOM).[36] In 1974, the Advanced Ballistic Missile Defense Agency (ABMDA) became the Ballistic Missile Defense Advanced Technology Center (BMDATC). Both BMDSCOM and BMDATC were under the same manager at the Ballistic Missile Defense Organization (BMDO) at Huntsville. This organisational structure remained until the creation of the US Army Strategic Defense Command (USASDC) in 1985.

On 1 October 1975 the Safeguard system moved to Full Operating Capability (FOC) at Grand Forks, North Dakota. Five months later, Congress closed the base, even though the Pentagon wanted to retain it for operational experience. The perimeter acquisition radar became part of the air force's early warning system. The closure of the site may be seen as a victory for the arms control community and those who sought to strengthen the ABM Treaty and to reduce the chance of ABM being once again proposed for deployment in the near future.

### CONCLUSION

The extensive BMD programmes which existed before SDI originally evolved out of air defences. Given the climate of the Cold War, the inherent appeal of 'defences' and the absence of an appropriate treaty, it was almost inevitable that the superpowers should research BMD. In the USA, the BMD programme gained some additional momentum from the rivalry between the army and the air force and from the corporate constituency, which had a vested interest in the BMD budget.

Whilst the army, backed by the Pentagon and many in Congress, was calling for a new ABM, many policy-makers were persuaded of the undesirable strategic and political implications of ABM deployments. The announcement of Sentinel in 1967, an ABM against the Chinese, was a compromise, announced by Robert McNamara against his better judgement.

In the early years, ABM could be seen as an instance of the 'technological imperative', in that new technological possibilities, which seemed too attractive to forgo, propelled the programme forward. The quiet influence of research laboratories could be adduced to support 'Zuckerman's hypothesis' that it is the technician 'who is at the heart of the arms race, who starts the process of formulating a so-called military nuclear need'.[37] Within the Executive, scientists were probably most influential in providing legitimisation for decisions based on primarily political considerations.[38] A band of independent scientists opposed to ABM campaigned hard in public and in Congress.

In the late 1960s, as a controversial public issue, ABM was also affected by larger political affairs. The transformation of Sentinel into Safeguard, intended as a 'point defence' of missile silos against the Soviets, was caused by public protest against Sentinel and by Nixon's new policies towards China. The demise of Safeguard can be ascribed

33

to the Vietnam War, which dominated the Pentagon budget, and to the Soviets' acceptance of the need for some restrictions on ABMs. The ABM Treaty of 1972 and the subsequent protocols are instances where the advantages of mutual restraint have triumphed over mutual distrust, institutional inertia and the self-interest of the BMD constituency.

From early debates about ABM to later controversies over SDI, old habits were followed with predictable and usually damaging results. In 1970, Herbert York wrote that ABM is destabilising because it is 'simply another step in the arms race':

> It presents a technical challenge (again, not a political provocation!) to the technologists who design the offense. In designing around the ABM, these latter will usually come up with a more complex, more expensive, more deadly and more volatile offense. Our ultimate response to the Soviet ABM was MIRV. If current plans continue, fewer than one hundred Soviet ABM missiles now deployed around Moscow, will have resulted before very long in an increase in the number of US warheads by more than five thousand. *Thus, as a matter of historical fact, the Soviet ABM program has been fantastically counter-productive and has had anything but a stabilizing effect.*[39]

York's prognosis was proved correct and, whether the 'Galosh' system was a cause or pretext, the US proceeded to MIRV its missiles. In 1967, Robert McNamara, then US Secretary of Defense, had emphasised a similar, fundamental fact about BMD:

> What is essential to understand here is that the Soviet Union and the United States mutually influence one another's strategic plans.
>
> Whatever be their intentions, whatever be our intentions, actions – or even realistically potential actions – on either side relating to the buildup of nuclear forces, be they either offensive or defensive weapons, necessarily trigger reactions on the other side.
>
> It is precisely this action–reaction phenomenon that fuels an arms race.[40]

McNamara also warned about the illusion of seeking a 'technological fix', or security through new weapons.

> As the arms race continues and the weapons multiply and become more swift and deadly, the possibility of a global catastrophe, either by miscalculation or design, becomes ever more real. More armaments, whether offensive or defensive, cannot solve this dilemma.[41]

Fifteen years later, the lessons drawn by McNamara and York were publicly spurned. The President asked his people to turn to 'the very strengths in technology' that made the country great. The SDI Office spoke of SDI as if it were the 'last move', which would never be used to justify further refinements in the offensive arsenal, such as penetration aids, stealth technology and other counter-measures. Any defence can look good against a static threat. Improved BMD technology means little in itself, as long as the Soviets track the improvement. Improved international relations are likely to mean much more.

The anxiety about a Soviet first strike which haunts strategic texts also drives BMD onward. The rationale for Safeguard in 1969 was that it would prevent a pre-emptive strike by the Soviets. This was a worst case justification, for there was little chance of a deliberate first strike against the United States. In the words of the director of defense research and engineering at the DoD, speaking six years after Safeguard had been announced, when the Soviets *had* increased their arsenal, there was still no prospect of a successful first strike.

> At the present time, to my knowledge, there is no way, when one thinks of the location of all our forces, the coordination and synchron- ization that would be required in such an attack, there is no way they can attack all our forces simultaneously as a pre-emptive counterforce capability and wipe them out.[42]

BMD was again proposed as a defence of land-based missiles in the late 1970s. Some US strategists were concerned about a 'window of vulnerability' through which the Soviets might launch a first strike and destroy America's land-based missiles. If the Soviets destroyed the accurate counter-force nuclear missiles, the US Administration would be left with only 'counter-value' nuclear weapons, ones which destroy cities. These might not be a credible deterrent: if the Soviets kept enough missiles in reserve, they could then threaten that if Washington responded, the remaining Soviet missiles would wipe out the United States. Subjected thus to nuclear blackmail, the USA could be defeated.

This widely feared scenario was extremely far-fetched. For geo- graphical reasons it is impossible for the Soviets to have simultaneous launch and also simultaneous detonation, should they contemplate a first strike. There was therefore no chance of the Soviets destroying the US nuclear triad in one fell swoop. Some US bombers carrying nuclear warheads could 'scramble' and so survive an attack. Just one US sub- marine could wreak a devastating revenge on the Soviet homeland. Moreover, it is unlikely that such a drastic plan could be kept secret from US intelligence. The 'window of vulnerability' was a strategic argument whose premise had more to do with psychopathology. It rested on a deep fear that the Soviets were ruthless and callous enough to invite massive radioactive fall-out, international opprobrium and the obliteration of tens of millions of their own citizens.

In the late 1980s, BMD was once again justified as a means to 'increase the uncertainty of an attacker'. By defending some missile silos, it would supposedly deter a Soviet first strike. The argument was as tenuous as ever in that any attacker always faced a great deal of 'uncertainty', not to mention the prospect of assured destruction from ICBMs, SLBMs and nuclear warheads carried on bombers. Although the 'window of vulnerability' and related arguments had no more substance than the 'missile gap' or the 'bomber gap' of a preceding generation, they still won support for BMD and other 'modernisation' programmes.

History, it is well known, teaches no lessons (and not even that one). But certain features do recur throughout the evolution of strategic defence, notably the counter-productive consequences of being fixated on weapons gaps, worst case scenarios, technological fixes and final steps. If the lesson of BMD was to beware of these illusions, it was to be honoured more in the breach than the observance.

# 3 THE 'SDI' SPEECH

On 23 March 1983, President Reagan startled nearly everyone with a speech which, if taken literally, signalled his intention to overturn the entire basis of official US nuclear strategy. The bulk (four-fifths) of the address was the familiar 'threat speech', given by many presidents. The sting was in the tail, when Reagan spoke of his 'vision of the future which offers hope'.[1] His actual formulation was quite careful: 'I am directing a comprehensive and intensive effort to define a long-term research and development program to begin to achieve our ultimate goal of eliminating the threat posed by strategic nuclear missiles.'[2] But what captured the public imagination and scandalised the arms controllers was the memorable style: the talk about 'changing the course of human history', 'the cause of mankind and world peace' and 'rendering these nuclear weapons impotent and obsolete'.[3] Who could not be moved by the President's resonant rhetorical questions? 'Would it not be better to save lives than to avenge them? Are we not capable of demonstrating our peaceful intentions by applying all our abilities and our ingenuity to achieving a truly lasting stability?' 'But what if free people could live secure in the knowledge that their security did not rest upon the threat of instant US retaliation to deter a Soviet attack; that we could intercept and destroy strategic ballistic missiles before they reached our own soil or that of our allies?' 'But is it not worth every investment necessary to free the world from the threat of nuclear war?'[4]

In terms of logic or strategic theory, Reagan's speech was extremely lightweight, neither defining the new policy nor examining its implications. But it still had great public impact. The media were primed to give a high profile to Reagan's pronouncements. Only two weeks previously, the President's 'evil empire' homily had identified the USSR as 'the focus of evil in the modern world'. As an effort to sell a new military programme, as a rhetorical and emotional construct, the SDI speech worked superbly. It was a triumph of suggestion over-statement, skilfully structured to appeal first to fear and then to hope, to the wish for protection and invulnerability and the American feeling that technology is the nation's forte and space its destiny.[5]

General Alexander Haig, the former Secretary of State, characterised the announcement as a public relations initiative, emanating from the White House:

> The White House guys said 'Hey, boss, come on. You're going to make a big splash. Big P.R. You're going to look like the greatest leader in America. Go out there and give that speech.' And he did . . . But the preparation had not been made. I know the aftermath, the next day in the Pentagon, where they were all running around saying 'What the hell *is* strategic defense?'[6]

Senior advisers had scant notice of the speech. The joint chiefs of staff, the Secretary of Defense and the Secretary of State had only two days' warning of its contents.[7] Richard DeLauer, Under-Secretary of Defense for Research and Engineering, and Fred Ikle, the Under-Secretary of Defense, had only nine hours.[8] The director of DARPA and the director of defensive systems first heard the news on television.[9] The head of directed energy weapons development had told a Senate subcommittee only that afternoon that, because of disappointing performance, such systems did not merit extra funds.[10] The communications director in the White House and the Pentagon officials who had drafted the rest of the speech were equally taken aback.[11]

Reagan's chief scientific adviser, George Keyworth, had five days' notice of the President's intention:

> Most people saw the speech very close to the time of delivery and most – myself included incidentally – had the same reaction: 'My God, let's think about this some more. Let's think about the implications for the allies. Let's think about what the Soviets are going to think. Let's think about what's technically feasible . . . Let's think about the command and control problems.'[12]

The difficulties with directed energy weapons had been highlighted in a report on BMD made two months previously for the White House Science Council, over which Keyworth presided.[13] Having assumed the matter closed, one member of that council recalled his subsequent consternation:

> I was terribly surprised; 'stunned' would be a better word for it. To see it all emerge in that form, to see a whole notion change from offense-dominated policy to a defense-dominated policy, it was all new. I don't think any of us understand it.[14]

38

## GENESIS

To understand the origins of Reagan's announcement, one must return to the ABM Treaty and its aftermath, when Congress was reluctant to invest indefinitely in a programme without clear objectives or visible returns. Things looked bleak for the BMD interest groups: the army's BMD Organization at Huntsville, Alabama; the air force Space Command and the laboratories at Lawrence Livermore, Sandia and Los Alamos. Nonetheless, these federal institutions, coupled with the private sector, provided the 'experts' who addressed congressional committees, who dominated the advisory panels, and who thus secured the BMD budget. Slowly the programme began to recover. In 1977 the head of the BMD Organization convinced the Senate Armed Services Committee to give the BMD budget an increase for inflation each year, which, he later observed, laid the foundation for the layered defence work of the 1980s.[15]

The requisite technologies were gradually improved. Advances in micro-electronics and artificial intelligence would help in producing software to track missiles and co-ordinate defence operations. Miniaturisation and improvements in materials and space technologies in general opened new possibilities for space-based weapons. That, combined with breakthroughs in high-intensity lasers, offered the promise of destroying enemy missiles in their boost phase, before they had deployed MIRVed warheads or decoys. Whilst all this increased the chances of intercepting a single missile, it did not significantly improve the prospects for a reliable overall defence, whose security requires that one side cannot emulate or counter-act the technologies of the other.

Wider political conditions began to favour a revival of BMD. In the dusk of the Carter Administration, draft registration was restored, the Olympic Games boycotted, grain sales embargoed and new nuclear war-fighting strategies enshrined in Presidential Directive 59, which ordered preparations for protracted nuclear war. By 1980, 'Middle America' was concerned about relative US economic decline; loss of US strategic superiority; the failure of détente; and perceived vacillation among NATO allies. Events in Iran, Afghanistan and Nicaragua coincided with a wave of militarist revanchism in the USA and the resurgence of a 'New Right', which sought a technical or military solution, unilaterally enforceable by the US, to the problem of super-power relations.[16] The Committee on the Present Danger pinned the blame on to liberalism, negligence and arms control. Reagan's 1980 campaign attacked Carter's weak spot: the anti-nuclear rhetoric of his early days, which by the late 1970s he had abandoned but not explicitly renounced. Reagan portrayed Carter's erstwhile idealism as a continuing and dangerous *naïveté*, even though Carter was actually presiding over a major rearmament. Presenting itself as the party of prudence, the Republican platform of 1980 called for a massive military build-up, 'more modern' ABM technologies and 'overall military and technological superiority over the Soviet Union'.

Members of the Committee on the Present Danger who took office in 1981 included Jeanne Kirkpatrick, George Schultz, Paul Nitze, Kenneth Adelman, William Casey and Ronald Reagan himself. The radical war-fighting views of the committee were articulated by one of its members, English by birth, Colin Gray: 'the United States should plan to defeat the Soviet Union and to do so at a cost that would not prohibit US recovery'.[17] The committee formed part of a powerful and disparate coalition which had never accepted the arms control accords of 1972. By the end of the 1970s disillusion with détente was widespread. The Senate had refused to ratify three of the four treaties signed with the USSR between 1974 and 1979. These included SALT II and the Threshold Test Ban. In 1982 the United States failed to renew the Outer Space Treaty. Right-wingers called for the sacred cows of arms control to be turned into hamburger. In 1981, *Fortune* magazine wrote that 'a few career bureaucrats in the State Department, including holdovers from the Kissinger era, still support the 1972 Treaty and intend to lobby for a five year renewal, but it has few friends in the White House or Pentagon'.[18]

The first Reagan Administration sought a more dynamic and aggressive space policy. BMD could symbolise restored American pride and strength, a point noted by *Fortune* magazine:

> The Administration's new commitment to BMD is bound to rain down hundreds of millions of dollars on such defense contractors as McDonnell Douglas, Martin Marietta, Boeing and Hughes Aircraft, which have already done much development work. And if the Pentagon ultimately does try for a full-scale system, the bill could run into the tens of billions over the next decade or so.[19]

On 4 July 1982, the President announced a new 'National Space Policy', which spoke of an 'aggressive, far-sighted program' and of an 'ASAT capability with operational deployment as a goal'.[20]

BMD was justified in Congress by some rather lacklustre rationales: as a 'hedge' against Soviet break-out from the ABM Treaty, a means of keeping the US lead in the field and maintaining options for deployment.[21] It might also 'support the US position in Strategic Arms Limitations negotiations – by maintaining and providing visible demonstration of BMD technological superiority over the Soviet Union.

Table 3.1. *Planned BMD funds, pre-SDI ($ million by fiscal year)*

| Agency | 1985 | 1986 | 1987 | 1988 | 1989 | TOTAL |
|--------|------|------|------|------|------|-------|
| DoD | 1,527 | 1,802 | 2,181 | 2,699 | 2,982 | 11,191 |
| DoE | 210 | 295 | 365 | 439 | 505 | 1,814 |
| TOTAL | 1,737 | 2,097 | 2,546 | 3,138 | 3,487 | 13,005 |

*Source:* SDI Office figures. Quoted in D. C. Morrison, 'Shooting down Star Wars', *National Journal* (25 October 1986), p. 2544.

[And] support offensive forces and intelligence assessments – by aiding in the design and evaluation of penetration aids and by providing the technological basis for understanding and interpreting Soviet BMD R&D activities and capabilities.'[22]

Preoccupied with winning funds for counter-force ICBMs, the Pentagon 'wanted to keep BMD low key and primarily invisible so as not to jeopardize MX'.[23] Once MX was underway, however, it offered BMD a much-needed new rationale. There was a prolonged, embarrassing debate about the best means for siting the new missile so as to minimise its vulnerability. The army proposed that its Low Altitude Defense System (LoADS) could protect MX sites, thereby helping to close the 'window of vulnerability'. History was repeating itself, for in the late 1960s Safeguard had been proposed as a defence of Minuteman sites. In both cases, 'hard site' defence of specific points was a sufficiently limited goal to seem realistic.

Even without the full backing of the Pentagon, BMD was flourishing in the years of plenty which accompanied Reagan's arms build-up. Table 3.1 shows retrospective SDI Office calculations for the planned level of BMD research before Reagan's SDI speech. The figures are rather large because they assume that plans for a ground-based BMD and missile and satellite tracking would have been funded if Reagan had not announced SDI. Under the opposite assumption, BMD funding would have remained between $1 billion and $2 billion per annum, giving a total of about $8 billion.

The difference between these plans made before Reagan's speech for BMD funding between 1985 and 1989 and SDI funds actually won over the same period is surprisingly low: under $4 billion.

### INFLUENCES ON RONALD REAGAN

In the early 1980s, therefore, the tide was running in favour of strategic defence. To show more precisely the origins of the dramatic speech on 23 March 1983, one must review the history of BMD with a more specific focus: in relation to the President himself.

Reagan's predilection for 'rescue scripts' might be traced back to his teenage years as a life-guard, credited with some seventy-seven life-savings.[24] One of his films featured an SDI-type super-weapon, and perhaps that fiction affected his interpretation of facts. In 1967, just after becoming Governor of California, he visited the Lawrence Livermore Lab, getting his 'first chance to hear about defensive weapons'.[25] Twelve years later, in the summer of 1979, Reagan toured North American Aerospace Defense Command at Cheyenne Mountain, Colorado. Here he was impressed by the possibility of tracking objects in space and the irony that there was still no defence against nuclear attacks.[26] After the NORAD visit, Reagan received a memo proposing an anti-missile shield from his domestic policy adviser, Martin Anderson.[27] This called for new strategic defences, along with 'a reasonable build-up in our conventional forces, and an acceleration in development of cruise missiles, laser beam technology, and conventional nuclear missiles like the MX'. A protective missile system would, Anderson observed, be 'probably fundamentally far more appealing to the American people' than MAD.

Anderson later stated that all the 'key people' in Reagan's campaign supported the idea of strategic defence.[28] It is not entirely clear *which* idea of it each favoured: or how pleased each might be with how SDI has since fared. They agreed on the goal of reinvigorating the BMD programme and that debates about the method or desirability of actual deployment should be deferred.

In the early days of the new Republican Administration, at least four groups in Washington, D.C. were advocating more funds for strategic defence. The first was the 'laser lobby" in Congress: Senator Malcolm Wallop; his aide, Angelo Codevilla; and Senator Harrison Schmitt. The second band was High Frontier, led by Lt-Gen. Daniel Graham. His manifesto proposed a three-tiered layered defence, coupled with civil defence. Graham claimed that the US could build orbiting battle stations with existing technology, at astonishing speed: a 'point defence' by the mid 1980s, an initial space defence by the turn of the decade and a 'second generation' space defence 'in the early 1990s'.[29]

The third group started to meet at offices provided by the right-wing Heritage Foundation in July 1981. It consisted of old affiliates of Reagan, members of his so-called 'kitchen cabinet': Karl Bendetsen, a conservative Democrat and retired chairman of Champion International; the brewer Joseph Coors; the oil magnate William Wilson; and Jaquelin Hume, a Californian businessman. Also present was Edward

Teller and, initially, General Graham. Teller and Bendetsen favoured compact, short-wavelength, nuclear-powered lasers. Whilst these had the disadvantage of requiring a nuclear explosion to generate their energy, they seemed less vulnerable to Soviet counter-measures than the larger, long-wavelength chemical lasers favoured by Wallop and Codevilla.[30]

The fourth group, ensconced in the White House, contained three of Reagan's senior advisers – Martin Anderson, Edwin Meese and Richard Allen – along with George A. Keyworth II, a former nuclear physicist from Los Alamos, privy to recent advances on lasers, who had become the President's science adviser in May 1981. Anderson recalled in his memoirs how 'we did something that, by the book, we should not have done. Without ever formally acknowledging it, even to ourselves, a small, informal group on strategic defense was formed within the White House.'[31]

These groups knew of Reagan's antipathy to MAD. Schmitt, for example, recalled discussing strategic defence with the President shortly after his inauguration. 'When I heard his speech, the phrases sounded very familiar. The words had the same ring.'[32] The concept was on or in Reagan's mind: it was a matter of hatching it into a definite commitment.

By Anderson's account, 'things started to roll in early September [1981] with a series of phone calls involving Karl Bendetsen, General Graham, Ed Meese and myself'. These culminated in a meeting on 14 September 1981, attended by Meese, his aide, Anderson, Keyworth, Bendetsen, General Graham and Edward Teller. Anderson felt a 'rising sense of excitement' as it became clear that they all 'deeply believed it could be done'. At a second meeting in the White House on 12 October 1981, Graham and Bendetsen produced a status report which was 'glowing and encouraging' about strategic defence.[33]

At about this time, the end of 1981, the Heritage group started to split and General Graham was edged out.[34] His emphasis on 'off the shelf' technology clashed with Teller's predilection for advanced research and the X-ray laser. Graham's eccentricity always posed a credibility problem, and his proposal was rejected by a Pentagon report of September 1981.[35] Henceforth he failed to win consistent access to Reagan in the White House.

The Teller/Bendetsen cluster and the caucus in the White House had more success. On 8 January 1982, Teller, Bendetsen, Hume, Wilson, Coors, Anderson, Meese, Keyworth and William Clark (the new national security adviser) had a quarter of an hour scheduled with Ronald Reagan. They overran by forty-five minutes. Bendetsen recalled that Reagan was briefed on technological advances and told 'that the public would definitely welcome this'.[36] This meeting, which Anderson considered 'a critical turning point', was followed by three more. Though the outside advisers probably exaggerated the promise of BMD, they did not apparently argue that BMD could make nuclear weapons obsolete. The hard questions were never asked. Bendetsen said it was 'too early to make a distinction between city protection and silo protection and we ought to get on with it. The president answered "You're right" . . .'[37]

Reagan raised the issue of strategic defence at a monthly discussion with the joint chiefs of staff in December 1982. His national security adviser, William Clark, subsequently instructed both the joint chiefs and his own deputy, Robert McFarlane, to research the matter.[38] Prior to their presidential audience in February 1983, the joint chiefs gathered to set an agenda. 'We decided we didn't just want to tell him readiness was up and so forth', recalled a participant. 'We wanted to bring the president something new, different and exciting.'[39] Admiral James Watkins mooted the idea of strategic defence, using a rhetorical question which later resonated in Reagan's speech: 'Would it not be better to save lives than to avenge them?'

When the joint chiefs met Reagan on 11 February 1983, Admiral Watkins gave his briefing on strategic defence. The President 'perked up', and no one put the case against. One of those present, Robert McFarlane, told three of his staff on the National Security Council to prepare an announcement of a new defence-orientated strategy. Their efforts were collated by McFarlane, 'using the ultimate means of secrecy, his own typewriter'.[40]

McFarlane and his superior, William Clark, met the President on 18 March. It was then apparently that they decided to add McFarlane's draft to the President's speech of 23 March. The so-called 'annex' would temper Reagan's call for a 10 per cent increase in the arms budget with some long-range hope, or 'uplift'.[41] During the following days, the insert was altered to fit its new context and to accommodate the anxieties of the few officials informed.[42] Reagan added some final flourishes in longhand. The stage was set and the script ready.

For Martin Anderson, insider and advocate, 'Star Wars was a carefully thought out proposal, developed over many years, with the advice and consultation of some of the best nuclear weapons experts in the world.'[43] He gives credit to the BMD enthusiasts on the White House staff, whilst also emphasising the proper participation of the joint chiefs. Thus, he states that on 11 February 1983, the joint chiefs 'recommended' Reagan to abandon MAD and 'move ahead with the research and development of a missile defense system'. By contrast, Greve writes that the subject of missile defence was originally low on the chiefs' agenda.[44] Herken claims that the joint chiefs proposed five options, including more conventional forces, a bigger navy or more submarine-based missiles: 'Reagan personally selected strategic defense'.[45] The outsiders, mostly critics, emphasise the role of a techni- cally ignorant president; the amount of lobbying; and the lack of wider consultation. They focus on the capricious, the impulsive and the bizarre.

Whilst most of the New Right backed strategic defence a bare hand- ful subscribed to notions of impenetrable area defences, population protection or rendering nuclear weapons obsolete. General Graham foreshadowed some of Reagan's rhetoric, calling MAD a 'dangerous doctrine', a 'brooding menace', a 'horrendous legacy' and an 'immoral and militarily bankrupt theory'.[46] He toyed with the idea of a 'stable world of Mutual Assured Survival'.[47] But he rejected 'perfectionist demands' for 'impermeable or invulnerable defenses', for he saw space weapons as a way of increasing uncertainty for an aggressor, thereby enhancing deterrence, rather than replacing it.[48] Likewise Edward Teller, never one to understate the promise of BMD, explicitly repudi- ated the idea of a 'complete 99.9 per cent defense'.[49] That 'Utopian' vision was confined to marginal groups, though ones of the kind with whom Reagan associated. It was also aired in publications which Reagan might have seen:

> The nuclear weapon may therefore be an anomaly in military history, and the end of its reign of terror may now be coming with the advent of the directed- energy weapon based in space . . . nuclear disarmament will come about because of continued weapon development, which makes nuclear warfare impossible and therefore obsolete.[50]

Policy-makers might pooh-pooh such notions, but Ronald Reagan did not: and the portion of his speech which undermined faith in deterrence into the indefinite future, the quixotic quest to eliminate the threat of nuclear weapons, was very much the brainchild of the President himself.[51]

## CONCLUSION

After 1972, BMD returned to the state of relative obscurity which it had enjoyed before the 'ABM debate' of the 1960s. It continued to win funds as a hedge against Soviet research, as a potential limited defence of land-based missiles and as a convenient way of funding research which might produce spin-offs for conventional and nuclear forces and 'space control'. The BMD infrastructure therefore survived to become the basis for SDI.

By the start of the 1980s, the cause of strategic defence was once again in the ascendant. Conditions favoured the partisans of BMD: 'hawkish' strategists, right-wingers, opponents of arms control, military space enthusiasts and advocates of a 'technological end-run' with the USSR. McFarlane, author of the 'annex', named his concerns as the 'window of vulnerability'; new Soviet, mobile ICBMs; the burgeoning Freeze movement; 'the east–west political dynamic, congressional politics, trends in domestic thinking and arms control strategy'. All these, he concluded, made strategic defence 'an initiative whose time had come'.[52]

Scientists from the weapons laboratories and their military associates had long been building interest in strategic defence among the military-technical community. Was SDI, as Herbert York, himself a former head of Lawrence Livermore Laboratory, suggested, 'an instance of exceedingly expensive technological exuberance sold privately to an uninformed leadership by a tiny in-group of especially privileged advisers'?[53] Progress on the X-ray laser encouraged a new 'technocratic initiative' by the group at Lawrence Livermore, who promoted the new laser as the defensive weapon of the future. To the ordinary self-promotion of the BMD infrastructure was added the extraordinary evangelism of key individuals. Edward Teller introduced Reagan to ABM technology in 1967; helped to convince Reagan's staff in the White House that 'a nuclear missile defense was technically possible';[54] recommended his protégé George Keyworth to be the President's science adviser; allied with Bendetsen and the 'kitchen cabinet'; brought Admiral James Watkins, chief of naval operations, the technical information 'that got him so interested in SDI';[55] urged Reagan to give more funds for Excalibur, Livermore's X-ray laser;[56] 'met repeatedly' with members of the joint chiefs of staff and officials in the DoD, including Robert McFarlane;[57] and dined with Reagan and Schultz on the night of the SDI speech.[58] Discussing the role of the X-ray laser in the genesis of SDI, Robert McFarlane later said that the crucial factor 'was Edward Teller – who could have been talking about anything – more than the technology he explained, which Reagan grasped only superficially'.[59] General Graham was equally zealous. He advised Reagan in the 1976 and 1980 presidential campaigns; lobbied the strategic defence caucus in the White House; spoke with General Vessey, the future chairman of the joint chiefs of staff, who gave him a 'pretty positive' response;[60] and 'went public' with his book *High Frontier*. These BMD evangelists combined ardour and persistence with access and power. Graham's book, for example, was made at a cost of $500,000 donated by private sources;[61] compiled by two dozen consultants; 'scrubbed' by a group from the Boeing company; and endorsed by the President.[62]

If Reagan made his own speech, he did not do so just as he pleased: he made it under circumstances directly encountered, given and transmitted from the past. Most of the script was written by Pentagon officials, and the 'BMD annex' penned by the deputy head of the National Security Council. The main preconditions were the resilience of the BMD infrastructure and the favourable political climate. The speech was precipitated or prompted by the determined lobbying of individuals with ideological, institutional and financial interests in BMD. Their backstage efforts set the scene for the President's *coup de théâtre*. Reagan's contribution was first to have 'bought' the idea of strategic defence and then to sell it, endowed with the promise, or burden, of rendering nuclear weapons obsolete.

# PART 2
# CONSTRUCTION: 1983–1985

# 4 CONTEXTS

Between 1983 and 1985, SDI was established and came to be the Pentagon's largest single research and development (R&D) programme. Part 2 examines the different rationales given for SDI; how the programme was established and shaped; and why it flourished, despite fierce criticism from senior scientists and statesmen. After summarising the development of SDI during this period, it analyses the role of interest groups, which, since funds were expanding rapidly, had little need to fight among themselves to shape the details of the programme. The emphasis is therefore more on how the interest groups worked together to establish the programme as a whole.

Following the President's speech, plans for a renewed BMD programme were formulated. Official advisory panels (the Fletcher, Hoffman and Miller panels), which completed their reports in October 1983, gave qualified support to Reagan's idea. It was christened the 'Strategic Defense Initiative' by National Security Decision Directive 119 (NSDD–119), signed on 6 January 1984. The SDI Office (SDIO) was established in April 1984, based in Washington, D.C. and headed by Lt-Gen. James A. Abrahamson.

The Administration's first SDI budget submission to Congress, made on 1 February 1984, requested $2.001 billion for SDI in FY 1985. On 12 October 1984, Congress authorised a total of $1.621 billion, of which the Department of Energy took $224 million. The new SDI programme comprised five main Program Elements (PEs), each defined according to its stated aim.[1] These PEs were created for military service and defence agency programmes. By way of example, the table below shows how the Surveillance Acquisition Tracking Kill Assessment (SATKA) PE was formed.[2] In the FY 1985 budget, work valued at $366.5 million from ten former PEs was amalgamated into a single new PE, 'Surveillance, Acquisition, Tracking and Kill Assessment'.

## THE DIFFERENT STRATEGIC RATIONALES FOR SDI

The orthodox explanation for SDI is couched in strategic terms and sees the programme as being what its name implies: a *strategic initiative*. The official rationales for SDI were summarised in the Hoffman Report, which, without directly denying the President's goal of an area defence to render nuclear weapons obsolete and replace deterrence, set out a 'preferred path': namely, a 'flexible R&D program designed to offer early options for the deployment of intermediate systems'.[3] This was the doctrinal opposite of Reagan's vision, since it involved defending nuclear weapons rather than eliminating them. Technologically, it was far more realistic:

> an approach explicitly addressing the utility of intermediate systems offers a hedge against the possibility that nearly leakproof defenses may take a very long time or may prove to be unattainable in a practical sense against a Soviet effort to counter the defense.[4]

The panel argued that a partial BMD system could 'reinforce or help maintain deterrence by denying the Soviets confidence in their ability to achieve the strategic objectives of their contemplated attacks as they assess a decision to go to war'.[5] It could help towards 'improving the deteriorating military balance'[6] and 'would also provide operational experience with some components of later, more comprehensive and more advanced defense systems, increasing the effectiveness of a development effort'.[7]

One intermediate option was for a defence of the Continental United States (CONUS), 'initially to defend critical installations such as C³I nodes'.[8] The Hoffman panel noted the need for a study of review air defence technology against other threats, notably attack by advanced bombers and cruise missiles.[9] It saw SDI as an addition to increases in offensive forces, not as an alternative to such increases, or as Reagan had suggested, as an alternative to offensive forces: 'while additions to our forces are needed to maintain the continued viability of our nuclear deterrent, such additions alone may not preserve confidence in our alliance guarantees'.[10]

The Hoffman Report's ambivalence towards Reagan's speech was mirrored in contradictory, public statements of US officials between 1983 and 1985. Some insisted that the main goal was still an area defence 'to replace deterrence'. Others steered towards a partial defence 'to enhance deterrence'. Some presented SDI as a grand initiative. Others said it was a mere response. SDI proponents did not settle on a unified, coherent case. Their differences indicate

52

Table 4.1. *Previous (1984) budget structure of the SATKA programme element (PE63220D)*

| Former PE name | SDI-associated $m. | Program Element |
|---|---|---|
| Army BMD Advanced Technology | 82.0 | 63304A |
| Army BMD Systems Technology | 172.4 | 63308A |
| Geophysics | 5.1 | 62101F |
| Missile Surveillance Technology | 7.7 | 63424F |
| Advanced Warning Systems | 20.8 | 63425F |
| Space Surveillance Technology | 22.5 | 63428F |
| Defense Research Sciences | 6.3 | 61101E |
| Strategic Technology | 31.2 | 62301E |
| Experimental Evaluation | 10.0 | 62711E |
| Defense Nuclear Agency | 8.5 | 62715H |
| TOTAL | 366.5 | |

*Sources:* United States Congress, Congressional Budget Office, 'Analysis of the Costs of the Administration's Strategic Defense Initiative', p. 12. Some details are modified in the light of the FY 1987 RDT&E Program Descriptive Summary.

that there was no single, compelling strategic underpinning to SDI.[11]

The President and some of his advisers insisted that the point of the programme was a perfect defence to replace deterrence:

> We seek to render obsolete the balance of terror – or Mutual Assured Destruction as it's called – and replace it with a system incapable of initiating armed conflict or causing mass destruction, yet effective in preventing war. Now this is not and should never be misconstrued as just another attempt at protecting silos.[12]

Caspar Weinberger seconded this aspiration:

> The defensive systems the president is talking about are not designed to be partial. What we want to try to get is a system . . . that is thoroughly reliable and total. I don't see any reason why that can't be done.[13]

The President's science advisor, George Keyworth, reiterated the policy:

> SDI is intended to protect populations, not weapons. And it's intended to protect not just the United States, but our Allies as well.[14]

And again:

> Protecting weapons represents no change in present policy. It simply strengthens, entrenches, a de facto doctrine of Mutual Assured

53

Destruction. Protecting people, on the other hand, holds out the promise of dramatic change. This clear purpose of the president has been repeated time and time again by Cap Weinberger, Bud McFarlane and myself.[15]

The quite different argument, that SDI was about limited defence to enhance deterrence, had also been repeated time and time again. On occasion, the President himself denied that he was seeking a perfect defence to replace deterrence:

> Oh, I've never asked for 100 per cent. That would be a fine goal: but you can have an effective defensive weapon, even if it isn't 100 per cent. Because what you have is that the other fellow would have the knowledge that if they launched a first strike, that it might be such that not enough of their missiles could get through, and in return we could launch a retaliatory strike [sic].[16]

The director of the SDIO stated that 'a perfect astrodome defence is not a realistic thing';[17] and that 'this argument that it's got to be perfect is, I think, badly founded'.[18]

The 'Utopian' idea of a perfect defence to replace deterrence is associated with Reagan and a number of 'ideologues' in the Administration. It held sway at the top and also, in the sense of public opinion, at the bottom. The intermediate professional layers who implemented the programme knew that the realistic option was partial defence to enhance deterrence. What Weinberger publicly said was not what his Department privately did.

A White House paper on the SDI, published in January 1985, sought to reconcile the dispute over the programme's rationale. The paper suggested that whilst the ultimate goal of SDI was indeed the abolition of nuclear weapons, another aim was 'finding ways to provide a better basis for deterring aggression'. SDI was also simply a research programme which would provide a future president and a future Congress with the technical knowledge required to support a decision on whether to develop and later deploy advanced defensive systems. This became the main official rationale for SDI, although the Administration never publicly withdrew the more popular idea of a 'space shield'.

It is possible to reduce the appearance of contradiction by refining the concept 'deterrence'. Some strategists spoke of SDI as 'defensive deterrence', or deterrence 'by denial', as opposed to a pre-existing regime of 'offensive deterrence'.[19] However, these elaborations do not resolve the uncertainty as to whether SDI was meant to 'eliminate nuclear weapons' or to defend them.

The promise of 'perfect defence' enabled the President to appeal for the SDI programme over the heads of Congress, direct to public opinion. Key Democrats were probably 'swung' this way, especially as the first SDI budget was debated in the shadow of elections for the House of Representatives, as well as for the presidency, in November 1984. Many Democrats were anxious not to appear 'soft on defence' by opposing yet another programme, especially one which held such psychological appeal.

The uncertainty surrounding SDI gave great scope for creative strategic thinking, conveyed at times as a heady feeling that the nuclear stalemate could be broken, that anything was possible. Reagan provoked much speculation with some of his musings on SDI:

> If we had the defensive weapon and no-one else had it, but we also had the missiles, wouldn't it be proof of our sincerity if we said: 'Look, we've got it made. We've got both now. And we tell you we will eliminate ours, along with everyone else.'[20]

Exactly what Reagan had in mind was never fully clarified. Nor was the larger debate about the strategic rationale for SDI resolved. The cardinal issues about whether and how SDI was intended to revolutionise, or reinforce, existing doctrines were left open, or avoided by emphasising the R&D nature of the SDI programme.

Reagan's initial speech made no mention of any Soviet BMD competition, but presented SDI as an imaginative initiative heralding a new strategic era. Whilst continuing to present SDI as an exciting innovation, at times the Administration resorted to an older argument: that BMD research was a prudent hedge against Soviet break-out from the ABM Treaty. Some called the 'Strategic Defense Initiative' a misnomer, and said that the 'Strategic Defense Response' was more accurate, because the Soviets instigated increased BMD research. Sometimes even Reagan argued that the USSR was well ahead: 'the Soviets are way ahead of us in that field. They've been at this for about ten years or more. And we are just at the field of beginning research.'[21] This assertion was contradicted by the director of the SDIO: 'in the key technologies needed for a broader defense – such as data processing and computer software – we are far, far ahead'.[22]

The divergence stems more from a difference about how best to justify BMD than from examination of the evidence. Whilst enthusiasts were won by rhetoric about a bold initiative, sceptics could be swung by references to Soviet research. One such, Richard DeLauer, argued for SDI as 'a necessary and vital hedge against the possibility of a one-sided deployment'. Thus Reagan's first report on 'Soviet Noncompliance with Arms Control Agreements', sent to Congress on 23 January 1984, pinpointed the Phased Array Radar (PAR) at Krasnoyarsk as a violation of the ABM Treaty, whilst ignoring the American PARs at Fylingdales and Thule. It suggested that the USSR could be preparing a BMD break-out, and these 'findings' were repeated in the reports of the following years.

Little public attention was paid to the apparent discrepancy in the 'double presentation' of SDI, as initiative and response. If the Soviets were ahead, as claimed, there was almost no chance of a secure area defence, since the Soviets would have the know-how to counteract a US system. Given the inconsistent strategic rationales for SDI, how far was the programme driven by other factors? Was it, for example, dictated by irresistible breakthroughs in BMD technologies?

## BMD TECHNOLOGIES

The confusion over the strategic response of SDI was matched by doubt about its technical feasibility. This became one of the most contested issues in the public debate about SDI. The most striking coup for SDI during this period was Lockheed's Homing Overlay Experiment (HOE) of 10 June 1984, which destroyed a mock ballistic missile in mid-flight. The video sequence, relayed around the globe, encouraged widespread belief in 'Star Wars' systems. The interception of one missile in a benign environment, with knowledge of the target's flight path, was, however, a far cry from dealing with the whole arsenal of an enemy who could use an array of counter-measures, including underflying, overwhelming or outfoxing defences, as well as fooling them through surprise or decoys.

Major problems were raised by each tier of proposed systems. In particular, it would be difficult to make the crucial space-based layer survivable, militarily effective and cost-effective at the margin. The Scowcroft Commission, which reported in April 1983, endorsed the Trident programmes, cruise missile and bomber programmes, Anti-Submarine Warfare (ASW) and, especially, modernisation of C³I and battle management, but registered a major proviso about BMD research:

> No ABM technologies appear to combine practicality, survivability, low cost and technical effectiveness sufficiently to justify proceeding beyond the stage of technology development.[23]

Scowcroft's report was written before the SDI programme had gathered momentum; perhaps even before Reagan's SDI speech. Its judgement is significant in that it shows a 'hawkish insider' saying in effect that an expanded BMD programme was not justified on technical merit. It explicitly ruled out one of the subsidiary rationales for SDI, as a partial defence of missile silos. Instead it called for passive defences (hardened silos) and a shift towards small ICBMS, the Midgetman. The technical feasibility of the SDI concept was also challenged by the reports produced in 1984 and 1985 for the Office of Technology Assessment, an independent arm of the US government.[24] Other independent scientists made further, trenchant criticisms.[25]

Although the technical debate was often arcane, some of the fundamental considerations were quite simple. One of these is human error. All agree that an operational strategic defence would be enormously complex and would rely on the near-perfect performance of all its systems in battle. It would require almost instant decision-making, with minimal time to check data, think or consult, in crisis. Urgency or panic might increase the risk of error, with possibly catastrophic consequences.[26]

Any defence is only as good as its weakest link. The enemy can concentrate forces to overwhelm the defence in one spot. A 'spasm attack' of some of the opponent's arsenal would be hard to counteract. If the Soviets received some of SDI's specifications, they could take appropriate counter-measures. Absolute security is almost impossible when the programme employs so many people. Any espionage team can choose where to concentrate efforts, where to break into the chain of information. Thefts did occur at the SDI Office,[27] along with security lapses at the State Department and at foreign embassies.[28] The SDI Office failed to investigate the background of foreigners who won SDI contracts.

The SDI Program is vulnerable in that it is computer-based. The National Test Bed, which simulates SDI scenarios, is a glorified computer network. If teenage hackers have accessed sensitive Pentagon data bases, it is safe to assume that KGB professionals can too. One 'computer virus' in the SDI software, placed by mistake, by malice or by an enemy, which could lie dormant until the system was operated 'for real', could ruin the performance of a Strategic Defense System.

Proponents of SDI suggested that it was a question of reaching a technological goal: simply of developing the means to destroy nuclear missiles.[29] However, building a successful Strategic Defense System, of the kind envisaged by Reagan, would involve *far more* than simply reaching a certain point of technological capability. It would require the establishing and then maintaining of an insuperable technological and military lead over an adversary. The trend towards freedom of information and the vulnerability of computer networks makes such confidence wholly unrealistic.

For these fundamental, almost a priori reasons, it was extremely unlikely that a strategic defence of the kind intended by Reagan could work reliably against an enemy determined to defeat it. However, there was a high chance that some kind of partial defence, with limited capability, could be built.

## INTERNATIONAL RELATIONS: A BARGAINING CHIP?

If the strategic desirability and technical feasibility of SDI were so dubious, one alternative explanation for the programme's success in winning support is the state of superpower relations, which remained fraught between 1983 and 1985. The Soviet shooting down of flight KAL 007 in September 1983 was denounced by the US as 'wanton, calculated, deliberate murder'[30] and produced a new flurry of belligerence. Many probably saw SDI in the most general sense as a tool of power politics, which evidently frightened the communists. This perception and fears of Soviet expansionism doubtless helped the establishment of SDI.

Although Reagan was adamant that his programme would not be negotiated away, his insistence could be seen as an initial bargaining position in itself, an opening gambit in the informal negotiations about negotiations. Arguably, SDI could extract concessions or aid in 'negotiating from strength' or 'forcing the Soviets back to the table'. Abrahamson extended the prospect of arms control to influence the waverers in Congress.

> It [SDI] opens up a whole new regime for leverage with negotiations. We may even do some trading. We might say, 'OK, we won't put something up for three years if you take out five hundred warheads.'[31]

Whilst hostility between East and West may be a necessary precondition for SDI, it is not itself a sufficient explanation. General hostility could have manifested itself in many other ways, as could desires for 'bargaining chips'.

## CONCLUSION

There was no compelling evidence, let alone proof, that the USA's security interests compelled it to maintain a lead (or even parity) in relation to Soviet BMD research. There was only sufficient uncertainty for inveterate worst-case analysers to believe that, in the absence of a major American effort, the USSR might take a lead in the field in the coming years.

The strategic case for SDI remained uncertain while the programme was established. The reasons for SDI given by the Administration were at best inconsistent, as worst contradictory. Senior officials, including the President, insisted that the goal of SDI was to eliminate nuclear weapons and end the era of 'Mutual Assured Destruction'. Officials also argued for SDI as a way of defending nuclear weapons and stabilising a regime of retaliatory 'deterrence' into the future. Sometimes the Administration presented SDI as a grandiose, historic initiative, a 'flagship' policy. On other occasions, officials maintained that it was mere research, a prudent 'hedge' in line with established US policy.

Independent scientists, the Office of Technology Assessment and the Scowcroft Commission reported severe doubts about the feasibility of achieving the President's goal and about the desirability of increasing BMD funds in the way envisaged under SDI. But strained relations between the superpowers encouraged support for SDI, which was sometimes presented as a bargaining chip for negotiations with the Soviets.

Neither the strategic case for SDI nor the state of technology nor even the state of superpower relations can singly or together explain adequately the success of SDI in establishing itself. The reasons proffered for SDI were at best uncertain. The following chapters examine why the uncertainty was resolved in favour of the programme, and why, in the face of informed criticism, the programme was none the less constructed.

# 5  INTEREST GROUPS

## GREAT EXPECTATIONS

In material terms, SDI was a rising star, a growth market. The keen expectations which it generated reinforced support for the programme. The budget was projected at $26 billion for the first five years, rising to $69 billion for the first ten years, 1985–94.[1] Much larger sums, – the 'gigabucks' – would come with a decision to deploy, which would initiate a costly full-scale RDT&E programme. A declassified DoD study on laser weapons in 1982 put the cost of a limited system for 'damage denial' at $500 billion.[2] A former Secretary of Defense estimated the cost of a full Strategic Defense System (SDS) at $1 trillion.[3] Richard DeLauer, Under-Secretary of Defense for Research and Engineering, said that each element of the programme was 'equivalent to or greater than the Manhattan project': 'When the time comes that you deploy any of these technologies, you'll be staggered at the cost that they will involve.'[4]

Whatever the exact figure, the long-term prospect could not fail to excite the military-industrial interest groups, including the groups in the Pentagon. It is hard to quantify the SDI constituency of interest – even if the term 'interest' is restricted to those with a direct monetary stake in the programme. Many researchers were employed in work of multiple applications, which could be defined as 'SDI work' or otherwise. One estimate was that there were about 5,000 scientists, engineers and technical workers employed on SDI work in 1984 and that the number would rise to 18,600 by 1987.[5]

## BUREAUCRATIC INTEREST GROUPS

Many accounts of SDI focus on the debates prevailing in Washington, D.C. and the strategic think-tanks. But the programme was more than a series of commands issuing from the centre. Those commands were often influenced and modified by the far-flung field agencies assigned to implement them. It is necessary to specify those groups outside Washington, D.C. which constituted the programme and, in so doing, to indicate the magnitude of the SDI infrastructure.

Many agencies in the Department of Defense were involved in BMD, long before the creation of SDI. These included the USAF Space Division, the army's BMD Organization, DARPA and the main DoE federal laboratories. These and other agencies retained their work, co-ordinated by and contracting to the SDIO, under the procedures of the Federal Acquisition Regulations (FAR), used by all government agents.

The air force, always keen to expand its interests in space, was a major beneficiary of SDI.[6] Nearly all the USAF SDI funds were channelled to the subsidiaries of Air Force Systems Command (AFSC), whose headquarters are at Andrews Air Force Base (AFB) in Maryland. A major subsidiary of the AFSC is its Space Division at Los Angeles.[7] As a lead agency and integrator for the SDI, Space Division is working in many areas: natural backgrounds, advanced cryocoolers (for super-cooling of sensors), infrared focal plane, radiation hardening, focal mirrors, space boosters, threat analysis, large optics, atmospheric composition and space logistics.[8] Space Division's technology arm is the Air Force Space Technology Centre (AFSTC), at Kirtland AFB, just south of Albuquerque, New Mexico. AFSTC was created in 1982 and has a budget of over $650 million a year; it employs nearly 2,300 people.[9]

Amongst the laboratories managed by the Air Force Space Technology Center is the Air Force Weapons Laboratory, which has an annual budget of nearly $350 million and employs over 1,100 people.[10] This laboratory, whose predecessor was the Air Force Special Weapons Center, has contributed to all USAF nuclear weapons, including the Minuteman ICBM, the B-52, the MX, the B-1B, ground launched cruise missiles, as well as developing superhardened silos and hard mobile launchers. It 'continues to be the premier USAF research center for laser devices and beam control innovations'.[11]

The Air Force Weapons Laboratory was divided into five technology offices. The Advanced Radiation Office develops military high-energy lasers, as well as the optics and beam control technologies needed to point and track the lasers' output in weapons applications. The Advanced Weapons Technology Office researches charged and neutral particle beams, X-rays, microwaves, high-velocity plasmas and pulsed power physics related to military applications. The Technology Assessment Office tests directed energy concepts. The Air Force Weapons Laboratory was working with TRW Corporation on the hydrogen fluoride chemical laser, called Alpha; on the High Energy Laser (HEL); and on neutral particle beams.

Air Force Systems Command also ran the Electronic Systems Division (ESD) at Hanscom AFB (Massachusetts). ESD researched artificial intelligence and the software problems associated with battle management. Its Rome Air Development Center (RADC) at Griffiss AFB, New York, researched computer architectures and expert systems to analyse sensor data.[12]

The Air Force Geophysics Laboratory at Hanscom AFB (Massachusetts), with its annual budget of over $100 million, employed some 600 people.[13] It hoped to devise space-based infra-red sensors to locate boosters and warheads. The Air Force Rocket Propulsion Laboratory at Edwards AFB, California (450 employees and an annual budget of $90 million) also participated in SDI research.

Amongst other air force units working on SDI were the Armament Division at Eglin AFB, Florida, and the Aeronautical Systems Division (ASD) and its Wright Aeronautical Laboratories, both at Wright–Patterson AFB, Ohio.[14] The Ballistic Missile Office at Norton AFB, California, which ran a penetration aids programme, is believed to have worked closely with the SDIO. There was similar co-operation with the long-range planning staff at AF Space Command, Colorado Springs, Colorado, who would have the task of integrating SDI weapons into the central co-ordinating computers of Space Command.[15]

Along with the air force, the other main Service in receipt of SDI funds is the army. Its main agency for BMD was the Ballistic Missile Defense Organization (BMDO), which will be examined in detail later in this chapter. Other army organisations to benefit from SDI were the Army Material Commands Armament Research and Development Center at Dover, New Jersey and the Army Materials and Mechanics Research Center at Watertown, Massachusetts.

Although the navy has a strong interest in military communications satellites, ASATs and space war-fighting, it won only about 5 per cent of SDI contracts. Individual navy agencies to benefit from SDI included the Naval Ocean Systems Center, San Diego, California; the Navy Space and Warfare Systems Command, Arlington, Virginia; and the Navy Center for Advanced Research in Artificial Intelligence, which is located at the Naval Research Laboratory (NRL), Washington, D.C. and run from the Office of Naval Research in Arlington.[16]

The Department of Energy's triad of major laboratories specialise in high-energy optical weapons, especially short-wavelength lasers, and also in 'third-generation' nuclear weapons, such as the nuclear-pumped X-ray laser. The Lawrence Livermore National Laboratory

(LLNL), Livermore, California, developed charged-particle beams.[17] Los Alamos National Laboratory, in New Mexico, investigated neutral particle beam devices.[18] The Sandia National Laboratory (also in New Mexico) built new laboratory space for research into kinetic energy weapons.[19] This affords one example of the expansive character of the SDI infrastructure. It was initially justified on the grounds that future strategic defence systems would require new laboratory space. Once that space has been provided, that is, of course, further argument for carrying out more research and development. The DoE laboratory at Brookhaven also won contracts in 1984 and 1985 for work on neutral particle beams.[20]

The Defense Advanced Research Projects Agency (DARPA), at Arlington, Virginia, conducted SDI research. The Defense Nuclear Agency (DNA) ran the SDI's target lethality and hardening programme.[21] The Defense Communications Agency researched into SDI Battle Management.

## BUREAUCRATIC POLITICS: RELATIONS BETWEEN THE SDI OFFICE AND OTHER BMD AGENCIES

SDI was both a challenge and an opportunity for all the bureaucratic interest groups outlined above. Although the rhetoric about eliminating nuclear weapons or sharing technology with the Russians was inimical to the Service chiefs, SDI did offer them several advantages. It could distract attention from controversial counter-force modernisation; in the event of budget cuts, it was a potential sacrificial lamb; and it offered a new rationale for a programme which had previously lacked clear purpose. The chairman of the joint chiefs later said that they 'felt if the system was promising and could be made reasonably inexpensive, we should probably build, but those were questions we could not answer for many years. The chiefs never felt we should go forward with SDI if it was going to emasculate the rest of the military.'[22]

The established BMD agencies had a stronger institutional base than the newly created SDI Office. Relations could have been strained. A major reason for a 'Special Projects Office', such as the SDIO, is to circumvent obstructions arising from any Service hostile to a new programme which encroaches on its turf.[23] One SDIO official described his organisation as 'an end-run around the bureaucracies'.[24]

Previous Special Projects Offices – for Polaris, Trident and the MX – had been under the Office of the Under-Secretary of Defense for Research and Engineering, subject to annual reviews and the Defense System Acquisition Review Council (DSARC). SDI was free from such constraints and exempt from DSARC.[25] Apart from its obvious benefits for the SDI Office, this relative independence presented opportunities to the other Armed Forces. For example, the Boost Surveillance Tracking System (BSTS), an air force project, failed to pass the first DSARC milestone. Instead of being cancelled, it was passed to the SDI programme, still to be managed by the air force. In this way the air force retained a project it might otherwise have lost.[26]

The SDIO was bound by its nature to be a major institutional supporter of SDI.[27] Its staff, who numbered about eighty in mid 1985, depended on the programme as their raison d'être. The director of the SDIO, Lt-Gen. James A. Abrahamson, came to be seen as a charismatic figure with a flair for steering a budget request through Congress.

Abrahamson seems to have minimised potential 'conflicts of turf' with his colleagues in different sectors of the Pentagon. In this he was helped by several factors. The SDI Office was nominally independent of the DoD in budgetary terms. It made its own budget request and did not compete directly with other military R&D budget requests. It was not immediately apparent that the expanded programme was taking funds from other military projects. Moreover, the SDI Office had no contracting capability itself until October 1985. Until then, it had to contract all work out to the other military agencies, who would either perform the work in-house or find an industrial contractor. Even when the SDIO had its own contracting authority, the bulk of work was still contracted out through the defence agencies.[28]

The SDI Office was careful to respect the interests of other agencies in its shaping of the programme. It successfully won and passed on large budget increases to BMD agencies in the Services. After Congress reduced the FT 1985 request by 21 per cent, the SDIO reported that it 'was reluctant to cut back' projects also 'required for other programs (such as improved missile attack detection and warning programs)'.[29] The SDIO was quick to use the multiple applications of SDI technologies to promote a larger coalition of interest in budgetary debates.

Abrahamson focussed on winning extra funds from Congress, instead of 'micro-managing' the programme. The SDI Office claimed to use 'centralized direction' and 'decentralized execution' for the programme. Stressing flexibility and improvisation, its officials spoke of an 'ad hocracy rather than bureaucracy'. Some executives thought 'ad hocracy' a euphemism for inefficiency. For example, General Abrahamson, busy promoting the programme to Congress, the media, defence corporations and US allies, was often absent from the SDI Office. This increased the importance of the SDIO Deputy Director. For two years, no one was appointed to occupy this crucial post full-time. It was covered by the chief scientist, Dr Gerold Yonas, who was also occupied with extensive other duties. The 'ad hocracy' allowed the established military agencies to expand their own BMD work free from interference or inconvenience, shaping the programme in their own way, to the perturbation of some in Congress:

> The 700 some odd contracts we have already gotten, that we have seen so many disappointments, so much wasted money, so-called Beltway Bandits. Everybody sets up a shop. They go and get a contract to study this, this feasibility study, that feasibility study. Now we have wasted a tremendous amount of money in the past in this regard, and we have 700-plus contractors already and more coming down the pike.[30]

Abrahamson seems to have fostered good morale among SDIO staff, aided by the plenitude of funds, the exciting aura of the programme and the low priority which he gave to federal regulations designed to limit conflict of interest.[31] It emerged that all personnel and conflict of interest matters at the SDI Office had been dealt with by just one part-time worker. When that worker left, the chief scientist kindly offered to oversee conflict of interest and to obtain financial disclosures and disqualification statements. But he lacked the time to do the job.[32] This created opportunities for the 'buddy system' to flourish.

In sum, the SDI Office was an extra organisational layer which did not gravely threaten other agencies interested in BMD. No US military agency was actively opposed to SDI. Funds were contracted out to them by the SDI Office, which interfered little and successfully won budget increases. Moreover, the programme came at a time of increased defence expenditure all round.

The case of the US Army Strategic Defense Command, to be examined below, shows how one component of the BMD infrastructure reacted to and benefited from SDI.

### A CASE STUDY OF THE ARMY STRATEGIC DEFENSE COMMAND (ASDC)

The Army Ballistic Missile Defense Organization offers a case study of how one of the 'field agencies' enacted and accommodated orders emanating from Washington, D.C. It flourished as a result of SDI, and in July 1985 was renamed the Army Strategic Defense Command (ASDC).

The US Army has worked on BMD at Huntsville, Alabama, since the 1950s under various different names. When SDI was announced, the

Table 5.1. *Companies participating in the 'defense in depth' study and SDI contracts later received by them*

| Company | Value ($m.) | Number of contracts |
|---|---|---|
| Teledyne Brown Engineering | 140.552 | 263 |
| Sparta Inc. | 35.027 | 46 |
| Science Applications Inc. | 60.247 | 150 |
| Kaman Science Corp. | 33.057 | 63 |
| Spectra Research Systems | 4.169 | 15 |
| TOTAL | 273.052 | 537 |

*Source:* Companies participating are named in United States, Department of Defense, Army Strategic Defense Command, Official History, p. 39. Data on SDI contracts are from SDIO Contract Management Information System (April 1988).

Army's BMD headquarters at Huntsville, the BMDO, ran the Ballistic Missile Defense Systems Command (BMDSCOM) and the Ballistic Missile Defense Advanced Technology Center (BMDATC). BMDSCOM projects included the Airborne Optical Adjunct (AOA), Terminal Imaging Radar (TIR), High Endoatmospheric Defense Interceptor (HEDI) and the Exoatmospheric Re-entry vehicle Interceptor System (ERIS). BMDSCOM also operated the Kwajalein Missile Range (KMR) in the Marshall Islands, some 4,000 km south-west of Hawaii. KMR is the main air force range for testing ICBMs and is used by the air force and NASA to monitor objects in space. It also supports research and technology validation programmes for SDI. BMDATC projects covered a wide range: radar, optics, missiles, discrimination, data processing and directed energy weapons.

In FY 1983, before the announcement of SDI, the budget for the BMDATC programme for the endoatmospheric non-nuclear kill programme had more than doubled. With these new funds the programme began to expand. The Scowcroft Report had ruled out ABM (such as SENTRY) for MX silos and the focus of research was shifted from low to high endoatmospheric. This became the High Endoatmospheric Defense Interceptor (HEDI). The new interceptor research invited a new strategy. In FY 1983 the army commissioned a study on 'defence in depth', published in three volumes during 1984 and written by some of the BMDO's principal contractors.

Whilst the political spotlight was on the presidential advisory panels, developments continued in the shades of the infrastructure. The army's BMDO conducted at least two internal management studies in

1983. They recommended the creation of two major new posts: a 'chief of staff' and a 'chief engineer' to help the deputy programme manager at Huntsville.[33] This is a small instance of creeping bureaucratic incrementalism, which usually occurs below the horizon of publicity.

The arrival of SDI demanded reorganisation and facilitated growth. Within BMDSCOM the SENTRY project office and the Systems Technology Project office closed. They were effectively replaced by two new offices. The Systems Development Directorate worked on problems of definition and engineering. Tests and evaluation of hardware were then carried out by a Systems Projects Directorate. The organisation's official history notes that the readjustment 'served to illustrate the resiliency of BMDO personnel and the soundness of previous initiatives. In addition to revolutionary thrusts that had spurted ahead of existing technology, the organization's approach had also been evolutionary and incremental. Thus, the new technologies pursued in the past became the foundations for the new efforts.'[34]

The corporate contractors for BMD continued to benefit from SDI. Thus, Lockheed's Homing Overlay Experiment led on to an ERIS contract, whilst the company's Talon Gold research grew into the Star Lab pointing and tracking equipment. For McDonnell Douglas, LoADS evolved into HEDI. As Manfred Hirt, manager of business development at Interstate Electronics Corporation, said, 'the formation of SDI gave the community the impetus to grow on what they had been doing already to make commitments to advance the state-of-the-art technologies in hopes of achieving additional business from SDIO'.[35]

The BMDO provides one example of the complex process of integration and accommodation. It assigned its Program and Analysis Evaluation Office to deal with the SDIO. Many of the work packages which formed contracts between the two agencies crossed directorate lines between the Systems Definition Directorate and the Systems Projects Directorate. The BMDO created an SDI task force to oversee this problem, and rejected the idea of immediately reorganising to come into line with the SDIO's Program Element structure:

> With SDIO volatile in its early stages, it seemed judicious to BMDO management to allow time for their permanent structure to appear.[36]

The BMDO decided instead 'to design a matrix concept that would serve the directives of SDIO with as little disruption as possible to BMDO. Close coordination between BMDO elements was necessary to accomplish this objective, for the task was complex.'[37]

Treated intelligently, the SDI was an opportunity for expansion. On

1 July 1985, the BMDO was renamed the US Army Strategic Defense Command (USASDC). Most of its funds came from the SDIO and were, therefore, theoretically at the mercy of an organisation based some 600 miles away, which had also become the final integrator for SDI R&D. But in practice the SDIO did not make any great attempt to integrate SDI technologies in this period or interfere with pre-existing work. Overall, the creation of the SDI programme strengthened the army's existing effort. For the first time since 1974, the army's BMD was to be headed by a Lieutenant-General, who reported, not to the SDIO, but to the Office of the Chief of Staff of the Army. His appointment put the leadership of the army's programme on a level with that of the SDIO. In a sense Lt-Gen. Wall was in a stronger position than Lt-Gen. Abrahamson, since he had a larger and more permanent staff. The SDIO had about eighty staff, whose career loyalty was to the Services from which they had been selected and to which they could ultimately return. The Army Strategic Defense Command, by contrast, was employing 772 civilian and 154 military personnel in April 1985.[38] For the established BMD agencies, far from Washington, D.C., SDI was something to be accommodated, an opportunity to increase the rate of programmatic incrementalism and expansion.

The military agencies and government 'in-house' facilities described above formed one sector which won funds from the SDIO and had high expectations of further work. The army industry, which manages contracts for the Services, had an equally compelling interest in the fortunes of SDI.

### THE ARMS INDUSTRY

The Nobel laureate Hans Bethe observed that 'when a trillion dollars is waved at the US aerospace industry, the project will rapidly acquire a life of its own – independent of its public justification; it will become an unstoppable juggernaut'.[39] Table 5.2 shows that most of the main SDI contractors were large defence corporations, already established customers of the Pentagon.

Apart from the 'household' names, many small firms – 'systems integrators' and 'beltway bandits' – won contracts for consultancy, 'architecture studies' and research.[40] Science Applications International Corporation is one such firm of 'paper warriors'. Established in California in 1969, its stock was privately traded at $1.11 per share. By 1985, it had 5,700 employees and revenues of $420 million, and the stock price had risen to $22 per share. All but 10 per cent of revenue came from federal government.[41] SAIC runs no assembly line. In the words

Table 5.2. *The top twenty SDI contractors by the end of FY 1985*

| Organisation | Value ($m.) |
| --- | --- |
| 1. Lockheed | 1,024 |
| 2. General Motors[a] | 734 |
| 3. TRW | 567 |
| 4. Lawrence Livermore Lab. | 552 |
| 5. McDonnell Douglas | 485 |
| 6. Boeing | 475 |
| 7. EG&G | 468 |
| 8. Los Alamos Lab. | 458 |
| 9. General Electric | 420 |
| 10. Rockwell International | 369 |
| 11. MIT | 353 |
| 12. Raytheon | 248 |
| 13. LTV | 227 |
| 14. Fluor | 198 |
| 15. Grumman | 193 |
| 16. Gencorp | 191 |
| 17. Honeywell | 151 |
| 18. Teledyne | 189 |
| 19. Martin Marietta | 134 |
| 20. Textron | 118 |

*Note:* [a]Through Hughes Aircraft Subsidiary.
*Source:* The *Washington Post* (20 October 1985), 'Major SDI contractors to October 1985'. Data provided by Federation of American Scientists. The figures show contracts awarded or appropriated, not outlays.

of its executive vice-president, its 'shipping platform is a Xerox machine'.[42]

SAIC was one of the most successful of the breed of small R&D firms to win SDI contracts. It contributed five of its members to the Fletcher panel, and the firm was also represented on the Hoffman panel. By April 1988, it had won $460.25 million in SDI contracts.[43] This placed it among the top thirty SDI contractors, ahead of much larger firms such as Westinghouse and General Dynamics.

Many defence corporations, small and large, showed a keen enthusiasm for SDI. 'Were we to proceed with deployment, it would be the biggest thing this industry has ever had happen to it, by far. It would be the greatest thing on earth.'[44] TRW was uninhibited about its pleasure. 'We're standing on the first rung of a defence development that will dominate the industry for the next 20 years.'[45] Others may have been equally excited, but expressed it more circumspectly, for they had no need at all to 'talk up' the programme at this stage.

Many companies which won SDI funds created special SDI divisions.

Boeing, for example, created a special division for SDI battle management/C³I. Some 600 Boeing employees were working on SDI by 1985. Marshall Gehring, manager of the SDI division, explained:

> There is an awful lot of money here and this is the type of activity Boeing is interested in. If we can do something for the government that is within our resources and make money, we will. We are not philanthropic.[46]

McDonnell Douglas, RCA and TRW were amongst those who appointed a vice-president to manage SDI subdivisions. Martin Marietta spent $9.2 million on a new facility for SDI research.[47] In that their very existence depends on the programme, new corporate sub-entities can become vigorous advocates of the SDIP.

The growth of specialist market research provides another index of corporate interest in SDI. John Bosma and Pasha Publications started a biweekly newspaper, *Military Space*, to provide executives with news on the SDI market. They also marketed a *Guide to the Strategic Defense Initiative* at $145.[48] A rival biweekly publication, the *Star Wars Intelligence Report*, retailed at $297 per annum.

Abrahamson outlined a 'horserace' approach 'to orchestrate a rollicking prelude of milestone-oriented development contracts'.[49] The ten $1 million awards for 'architecture studies' to shape an overall concept reportedly attracted more bidders than any other military contract of recent times.[50] Abrahamson and others suggested, probably correctly, that the contracts gave firms an 'inside track' in the race for contracts: 'if you didn't get one, you'll be a little bit behind the power curve'.[51]

However, even at this stage, there were limits to industry's enthusiasm. Irrespective of its future prospects, SDI remained a research programme, and profit margins at the R&D phase tend to be comparatively low. There was no guarantee of winning in the short run. Several companies reportedly invested $1 million of their own money in the SDI architecture studies and still failed to win a contract.[52] Some contracts were cancelled midway. For example, Boeing's Airborne Optical Adjunct (AOA) was scaled back in August 1985.[53] This resulted in the cancellation of work on long-wave infrared sensors by one of the main subcontractors, Aerojet Electro-Systems.[54] Whilst companies had a common interest in promoting SDI as a whole, they could be deeply divided about the shape of the programme.

Finally, there was a group whose interest in SDI was primarily 'ideological'. Many officials in the first Reagan Administration were 'ideologues': self-styled critics of the political establishment, driven by the agenda of the 'New Right', in defiance of consensus politics. These outsiders and 'Californian cowboys' were of course incorporated into a new consensus: by about 1985 Reagan's Administration was becoming more pragmatic in international affairs. Many of these 'ideological' adherents of SDI were also its most articulate spokesmen and helped to mobilise latent support for SDI among those in the political 'centre': moderate Republicans and conservative Democrats, concerned with 'hedges' and 'bargaining chips'.

## CONCLUSION

SDI seemed a key growth area, and the army and air force in particular could expect a major role. The director of the SDI Office, Lt-Gen. Abrahamson, proved adept at winning increased funds for the programme and minimised 'conflicts of turf' with colleagues in the Pentagon and the established BMD agencies. A wide range of 'field agencies' run by the army, air force, Department of Energy, navy and DARPA performed SDI research. Most of them had a long record of working on BMD, and SDI was an opportunity to expand existing facilities. The case of the US Army Strategic Defense Command shows how the army's main BMD agency adapted to and benefited from the SDI programme.

The main SDI contractors were large firms, like Lockheed, General Motors, TRW, McDonnell Douglas and Boeing. Many small firms won contracts for consultancy work. Some executives greeted SDI with unabashed enthusiasm. Corporations opened special divisions for SDI and there was new trade in SDI market analysis. Groups such as High Frontier supported SDI for their own reasons, which could be classed as political or ideological.

These political advocates, coupled with federal bureaucracies and arms corporations, constituted a formidable constituency of interest in SDI. They foster a community dedicated to the programme, which nourishes it in hard times and can ease its passage through Congress by the provision of 'expert opinion'. The SDI infrastructure and SDI interest groups grow together, reinforcing each other. Increases of the SDI facilities encourage budget growth, which leads to further expansion of the infrastructure. A virtuous circle develops. The next chapter examines the extent to which interest groups managed to support and influence the SDI programme.

# 6 THE POLITICS OF INFLUENCE

The previous chapter described a constituency with both motive and means to influence policy on SDI. Before assessing how much influence was in fact wielded, this chapter must describe the making of SDI policy. On 25 March 1983, Reagan issued National Security Decision Directive 85 (NSDD–85):

> I direct the development of an intensive effort to define a long term research and development program aimed at an ultimate goal of eliminating the threat posed by nuclear ballistic missiles.[1]

The programme was to be consistent with the ABM Treaty and 'recognizing the need for close consultations with our allies'.[2] On 18 April, NSDD 6–83 commissioned three panels to investigate BMD: the Fletcher, Hoffman and Miller panels. The Fletcher panel studied technological feasibility.[3] A declassified summary emphasised the need for strong, central management, multi-tiered defence and good survivability.[4] It pointed out that 'significant demonstrations' could be performed over the next ten years, giving visible evidence of progress. The panel reported that *'by taking an optimistic view . . . we concluded that a robust BMD system can be made to work eventually'*.[5] The notes of caution – 'by taking an optimistic view' and 'eventually' – were later overlooked.

Completed in October 1983, the studies were sent to the National Security Council, to be condensed for the President. Qualifications made in the original reports were, it seems, edited out in this summary; and totally ignored in the upbeat public presentation. Weinberger told a news conference that the experts had concluded for SDI after several months of intensive effort which began *'with a good deal of healthy scepticism'*.[6]

It appears that the abridged report recommended a vigorous programme which would initially respect the ABM Treaty. It set out four funding levels for the years FY 1985–9, ranging from $27 billion to $18 billion. It also seems to have edged further from the vision of a secure

72

population defence. It reportedly justified the programme as an aid to military and negotiating stances; and it argued that options for immediate deployment would play a significant role in deterrence.[7]

The name 'SDI' was announced by National Security Decision Directive 119 (NSDD–119) of 6 January 1984, ten months after Reagan's speech. This directive emphasised partial defence to enhance deterrence, without rebutting the original goal of an area defence to replace deterrence. It called for a focussed programme to demonstrate the technical feasibility of enhancing deterrence and thereby reducing the risk of nuclear war through greater reliance on defensive strategic capability. As author of NSDD–119, the National Security Council was in a sense the main agency responsible for SDI. But its decision was based on the advice of scientists and the speech of the President. And its proposals then had to be ratified by Congress.

Responsibility for SDI was dispersed institutionally – it was not attributable to any single agency or individual – and chronologically. The arguments for SDI stressed that it was simply a research programme with no hardware development. Later, someone else can recommend full-scale engineering and procurement, on the grounds that the foundations of this policy have already been laid.

### THE POLITICS OF INFLUENCE

In the year after Reagan's speech, SDI was moulded by the Pentagon, which dominated the executive committee in charge of implementing the idea. The Pentagon also influenced the decisions of the advisory panels by contributing members. The arms corporations were well represented on the panels, especially on the Fletcher panel, which recommended a structure and funding levels for SDI.

The initial shock of the President's speech was soon absorbed by the Pentagon. Within a week, it was agreed that Reagan's announcement would be implemented by an Executive Committee (EXCOM): the Defensive Technologies EXCOM. This was established by Caspar Weinberger and chaired by his deputy, Paul Thayer. It comprised the chairman of the JCS, the Under-Secretaries of Defense, the Director of Program Analysis and Evaluation and the Assistant Secretary of Defense (Comptroller).[8] It contained and was receptive to the significant interest groups in the Pentagon, which therefore gained the opportunity to shape Reagan's ideas in their own fashion.

In April 1984, the Defensive Technologies EXCOM was superseded by the SDIO EXCOM, which gave the DoD 'oversight and guidance for an internal management' of the programme.[9] It too was chaired by the

73

Table 6.1. *Composition of the Fletcher panel: private sector*

| Institution/panelists | Value (in $m.) | Number of contracts |
|---|---|---|
| *Lawrence Livermore Lab.*<br>Dr Walter R. Sooy<br>Dr Robert T. Andrews<br>Dr Richard J. Briggs<br>Dr Robert B. Barker<br>Dr Michael May | 224.422 | 55 |
| *SAIC*<br>Dr J. Richard Airey<br>Dr Clark DeJonge<br>Dr Julian Davidson<br>Robert Yost<br>Dr Edward Frieman | 60.247 | 150 |
| *Los Alamos*<br>Dr Delmar Bergen<br>Dr Gregory H. Canavan<br>Dr Robert W. Selden | 209.571 | 82 |
| *Sparta Inc.*<br>Dr Wayne R. Winton<br>Dr J. E. Lowder | 35.027 | 46 |
| *Sandia Lab.*<br>Dr Gerold Yonas<br>Dr Robert G. Clem | 77.842 | 66 |
| *MIT*<br>Dr Robert E. Nicholls<br>William Z. Lemnios | 302.341 | 87 |
| *McDonnell Douglas*<br>John L. Gardner | 191.095 | 109 |
| *General Motors* (Hughes Aircraft Co.)<br>Dr George F. Aroyan | 169.819 | 256 |
| *Gencorp (Aerojet)*<br>Robert G. Richards | 75.830 | 93 |
| *Flow General* (General Research Corp.)<br>Robert T. Poppe | 55.377 | 126 |
| *Raytheon Corp.*<br>Fritz Steudel | 68.459 | 53 |
| *Systems Planning Corp.*<br>Lt-Gen. Kenneth B. Cooper, USA (Ret.) | 3.091 | 12 |
| *W. J. Schafer Associates*<br>Dr Edward T. Gerry | 14.406 | 45 |
| *Logicon (R&D Associates Inc.)*<br>Dennis P. Murray | 14.634 | 86 |
| *General Atomic Technologies Inc.*<br>Dr Harold M. Agnew | 5.078 | 24 |

Table 6.1 (*cont.*)

| Institution/panelists | Value (in $m.) | Number of contracts |
|---|---|---|
| *Institute for Defense Analysis* Dr Alexander H. Flax | 5.899 | 4 |
| *Physical Dynamics Inc.* Charles R. Wieser | 0.750 | 5 |
| *Coleman Research Inc.* T. Jeff Coleman | 2.510 | 6 |
| *Mitre Corp.* Bert Fowler | 2.736 | 9 |
| *University of Pittsburgh* Dr James C. Fletcher (Chairman) | 0.368 | 3 |
| *Hewlett Packard Co.* David Packard | 0.083 | 5 |
| *Bell Laboratories* Dr Solomon Buchsbaum | 5.906 | 8 |

*Sources:* Data on panelists and their institutional affiliation come from United States Congress, Senate, Armed Services Committee, *DoD Authorization for Appropriations for FY 1985. Hearings, Part 6.* 98th Congress, 2nd session (Washington, D.C.: United States Government Printing Office, 1984), p. 3017. Data on contracts come from the SDIO Contract Management Information System (April 1988).

Deputy Secretary of Defense. It included the other members of the Defensive Technologies EXCOM and also brought in Service secretaries and chiefs, the chairman of the military liaison committee and the directors of DARPA and the DNA. The head of the SDI Office was to be executive secretary. In this way, the interests of established groups were heard and respected, which minimised potential conflict with the newcomer.

Reference to the 'expert' conclusions of the advisory panels bolstered SDI's case in Congress. Table 6.1 shows that members of the Fletcher panel held substantial financial stakes in the programme which they were examining.

Apart from these individuals drawn from institutions with a definite commercial interest in SDI, the Fletcher panel contained others from the Department of Defense.

The Fletcher panel also contained six who are listed simply as private consultants and another six from institutions which are not listed on the SDI's 1988 list of contractors.[10] Overall it was dominated by members of institutions with a direct financial interest in the subject under

Table 6.2. *Composition of the Fletcher panel: DoD members*

| | |
|---|---|
| Major-General John C. Toomay | (USAF Ret.) |
| Major Simon P. Worden | (Office of the Secretary of Defense) |
| J. Bachkosky | (Office of the Secretary of Defense) |
| Dr J. Mayersak | (USAF Armament Division) |
| Dr H. Fair | (DARPA) |
| Dr L. Marquet | (DARPA) |
| Dr Mangano | (DARPA) |
| Dr Sepucha | (DARPA) |
| Dr Katechis | (US Army BMD Systems Command) |
| Dr Fisher | (US Army BMD Systems Command) |
| Lt-Col. Gleszer | (Army HQ) |
| Lt-Col. Clements | (Army HQ) |
| Captain Joseph | (Defense Nuclear Agency) |
| Dr Somers | (Defense Nuclear Agency) |
| Dr Avizonis | (USAF Weapons Laboratory) |
| Captain Evans | (USAF Systems Command) |
| Lt-Col. Cooper | (US Army Ret.) |
| General Meyer | (US Army Ret.) |
| Lt O'Rourke | (Office of Chief of Naval Operations) |

*Source:* see Table 6.1.

discussion. Of its 65 members, over half (34) came from firms which have profited from the programme they recommended. Another 19 were drawn from institutions which have won SDI contracts. Fifty-three out of 65 have a direct, traceable financial interest in SDI.

A similar pattern emerges from a study of the Hoffman panel. Of its 24 members, the majority (17) were employees of firms listed as having won SDI contracts on the SDIO's data base of April 1988. Two other members of the Hoffman panel were military men: Gen. John Vogt (USAF Ret.) and Andrew Marshall from the Office of the Secretary of Defense. Nineteen out of 24 members of the panel therefore had good reason in purely institutional terms to support SDI. The other five members (see Table 6.4) did not come from companies listed in the SDIO's 1988 list of contractors. Some, however, had links to BMD work, and one, James Woolsey, had sat on the Scowcroft Commission.

Membership of an institution which later profited from SDI does not automatically imply 'bias' or pro-SDI views. Nor does membership of a firm which has won no SDI contracts necessarily imply impartiality about BMD. But overall, it is reasonable to expect a correlation between membership of an SDI contracting firm and pro-SDI views.

The panels were formulating judgements in an area of enormous uncertainty. The uncertainty was resolved in favour of the programme; and in favour of the demonstrable financial interest at both the personal

Table 6.3. *Composition of the Hoffman panel: private sector*

| Institution | Value ($m.) | Number of contracts |
|---|---|---|
| *Science Applications Inc.* Dr J. Martin | 60.247 | 150 |
| *Physical Dynamics* Craig Hartsell | 0.750 | 5 |
| *Martin Marietta* Dr Sauerwein | 80.431 | 114 |
| *Stanford Research Inc.* Frank Hoeber | 9.198 | 32 |
| *Northrop* Fritz Ermath | 3.733 | 14 |
| *R&D Associates (Logicon)* Lt-Gen. LeVan (Ret.) (Pan Heuristics)[a] Dr Fred Hoffman Dr Albert Wohlstetter[b] P. Kozemchak | 14.213 | 82 |
| *Riverside Research Institute* Dr Marvin King Dr L. O'Neill | 18.205 | 53 |
| *Lawrence Livermore Lab.* Dr May | 224.422 | 55 |
| *MIT* Prof. Deutch[c] | 302.341 | 87 |
| *Stanford Univ.* Prof. Rowen | 4.637 | 25 |
| *Rand Corp.* Dr Thomas Brown | 1.853 | 7 |
| *Boeing* Dr Thomas Rona | 475.386 | 127 |

*Notes:*
[a] Pan Heuristics is a division of R&D Associates, which is a subsidiary of Logicon.
[b] Albert Wohlstetter had been a prominent supporter of BMD since the 1960s. He had worked with Fred Hoffman, his colleague at Pan Heuristics and leader of the advisory panel, back in 1954 on a paper which predicted that by the end of the 1960s hardening of silos would no longer guarantee protection of offensive missiles. York, *Race to Oblivion*, p. 183.
[c] Deutch was to become a director of SAIC, a major SDI contractor.
*Source:* Members of the Hoffman panel are listed at the start of its report. Their institutional affiliation comes from miscellaneous sources. Figures on contracts from SDIO Contract Management Information System (April 1988).

Table 6.4. *Other members of the Hoffman panel*

| | |
|---|---|
| Leon Sloss | Leon Sloss Associates Inc. |
| M. D. Millot | Leon Sloss Associates Inc. |
| Dr Charles Herzfeld | ITT |
| Ambassador S. Weiss | SY Corporation |
| James Woolsey | Shea and Gardner |

and the institutional level of the panel members. The official history of the US Army Strategic Defense Command puts it this way:

> Key members of each committee were provided by the BMDO staff of competent and dedicated scientists and technicians. It was no accident that the conclusions of the DoD studies strongly resembled the programme the BMDO already had in place.[11]

Given that so many members of the advisory panels came from institutions with an evident financial interest in BMD, and that there was such potential for conflict of interest, it was all the more important that the panels should comply with the regulations of the Federal Advisory Committees Act (FACA), which is designed to maintain public confidence in the impartiality of advice given to government. The Fletcher and Hoffman panels signally failed to comply with the Act.[12] Later investigations by Senator Carl Levin revealed that those responsible for setting up the panels were told about FACA by DoD General Counsel's Office. But they did not wish to comply. General Lamberson proposed a way of obviating FACA by establishing the panels under an existing contract with a think tank. David Ream of the General Counsel's office specifically advised against this circumvention and wrote a memorandum about the incident to the General Counsel.[13] The panels were none the less set up under contract to the think tank and in circumvention of FACA.

Table 6.1 shows that the main federal weapons laboratories all sent members to the Fletcher panel. Lawrence Livermore, Los Alamos and Sandia provide ten members. The Institute for Defense Analysis and Massachusetts Institute of Technology are also represented. Gerold Yonas from Sandia later became the SDIO's chief scientist and acting deputy director, before departing through the revolving back door into the business of receiving rather than giving SDI contracts.

One incident which offers an unusual insight into an instance of powerful, unofficial advocacy by a weapons scientist is the 'Woodruff Affair'. A letter from Edward Teller, of 22 December 1983, to George Keyworth, the White House scientific adviser, was leaked to the head of the Livermore X-ray laser project, Roy Woodruff, who found its optimistic tone misleading.[14] The letter reportedly said that the laser was entering the engineering phase, a stage which in reality it had still not reached four years later. In December 1984, two more of Teller's letters found their way to Woodruff. Teller had advised Paul Nitze, Reagan's chief arms negotiator, not to compromise at Geneva, because the laser showed such promise:

> Some [of the schemes for Super Excalibur] were very innovative and deserved the highest praise. But to say that you had Super Excalibur just around the corner and that you ought to go to Geneva and base your policy on that being just around the corner – that was nonsense, utter nonsense. Yet that is what was said in the letter to McFarlane.[15]

In letters to Paul Nitze and Robert McFarlane, Teller made assessments which Woodruff, as head of the X-ray laser programme, considered unduly optimistic. Woodruff also learnt that, unknown to other scientists, Lowell Wood, head of the 'O' group at Lawrence Livermore and a protégé of Edward Teller, had been briefing policy-makers, including Abrahamson and William Casey (then director of the CIA).[16]

Woodruff filed a grievance, saying that Teller and Wood 'undercut my management responsibility for the X-ray laser program ... Dr Teller and Dr Wood conveyed both orally and in writing overly optimistic, technically incorrect statements regarding this research to the nation's highest policy-makers.'[17] On learning of another secret briefing by Lowell Wood to Abrahamson on the X-ray laser, Woodruff resigned as the programme's associate director.

The 'Woodruff Affair' demonstrates why such matters may never be disclosed. In the first instance, many career scientists accept defence orthodoxy. Woodruff states his belief in 'strong defence'. There are few channels to express criticism. In Woodruff's case, the director of the laboratory forbade him to send letters critical of Teller's exuberance. Pressure to conform mounts. Woodruff and some of his supporters risked gaol and broke 'top secret' strictures. Woodruff was warned that he could lose his salary, and he was eventually removed to a small windowless room far from his colleagues. Teller's advice to some senior policy-makers became public knowledge only because of unknown 'whistleblowers'. But for their leaks the story would remain untold.[18]

After the 'Woodruff Affair' had been made public, the screen of secrecy fell again. A letter from the DoE to the director of Livermore said that 'we do not believe the discussion of nuclear directed energy weapons concepts during media interviews is in the best interests of the Department of Energy or the national SDI programme'.[19]

Woodruff's stance was vindicated by the subsequent record. After peaking in 1987 at $349 million, funds for the X-ray laser declined. Although more than $1 billion had been spent on the project by 1990, it had produced no breakthroughs of the kind predicted by Teller. 'I don't know whether I would call lasers a disappointment', said the acting deputy director of SDI, 'but they have not come along as fast as I thought they would.'[20] In 1990 Congress eliminated the X-ray laser as a separate item in the federal budget. Henceforth it would survive as a minor effort, not developing hardware and dependent on general research funds. Its leader expected to lose half his workforce of 200.[21]

## CONGRESS

The announcement of SDI was greeted, predictably, with exultation on the Right, dismay in the arms control lobby and a good deal of scepticism and puzzlement in between. Even traditional 'hawks' such as Senator Barry Goldwater, were perturbed by the cost:

> We don't know how much it is going to cost. You don't even have an idea . . . If we wander off into something too exotic, then I have a strong feeling this is never going to be financed by the congress.[22]

The 'People Protection Act' was introduced in May 1983 by Representative Ken Kramer from Colorado. In an effort to win congressional support for BMD, it sought to establish a new agency dedicated to BMD, a unified space command and a review of the ABM Treaty. But, overall, Congress had comparatively little time for BMD in 1983.[23]

The first budget request for SDI, submitted in February 1984, sparked much closer congressional scrutiny.[24] Henceforth, Congress became a crucial actor in deciding the level of the SDI budget, questions of treaty compliance and other matters. It was in Congress that the army control lobby was pitted against the Pentagon and its supporters. SDI could count on some well-placed supporters to help establish it. A staff member on the House Armed Services Committee, which oversees SDI spending, told an industry conference in 1984 that prospects for SDI looked bright:

> Given a couple of billion dollars or more funding, there'll be a fairly good constituency built up and there'll be a lot of pressure placed on the various congressmen to vote for higher funding in this area.[25]

Even so, it was necessary to 'get letters in to your congressmen': 'hopefully Abrahamson will surround himself with some Madison Avenue type folks, because that's what it's going to take'.[26]

The corporations did not need a major public relations campaign for SDI: the President and political lobby groups were their advocate and the programme was growing well. A hard sell at this stage could have back-fired, for the papers were rife with stories of corruption, including the long-running scandal at General Dynamics. The corporations sensibly focussed on the corridors and backrooms of power, rather than the balconies. They could nurture SDI through membership of advisory panels and shape it at the same time, ensuring their own participation.

Some groups did make relatively minor efforts to mobilise public support for SDI. The American Defense Preparedness Association (ADPA), which had championed the arms build-up of the early 1980s, appointed a retired army colonel to manage a new Strategic Defense Division. Amongst its activities was a classified conference for some 350 industry executives at Huntsville, Alabama.[27] Aerospace consultant and former High Frontier member Jack Coakley tried to set up a more aggressive lobbying group to be known as the Strategic Defense Association. Coakley believed that 'SDI isn't going to go any place if it isn't pulled along by industry.'[28] The American Space Frontiers Committee, a Political Action Committee (PAC) formed in October 1983 to make the High Frontier strategy 'the prime defense issue in the 1984 elections', illustrates the informal collaboration of the SDI interest groups. Its chairman was the director of High Frontier, Daniel Graham. Its president was former talk-show host and Republican congressman Robert Dornan. Its host committee included Phyllis Schlafley, leader of the far Right Schlafley Institute, the Reverend Jerry Falwell of the Moral Majority, Admiral Thomas Moorer, Senator Jesse Helms, science fiction author Robert A. Heinlein and the Apollo astronaut Buzz Aldrin.[29]

The 'Coalition for the Strategic Defense Initiative' was launched on 5 August 1985. Of the eighty-six groups in the coalition, some were large and seemingly 'centrist'. These included the American Catholic Conference, the Association of American Physicians and Surgeons, the National Aeronautic Association, the National Jewish Coalition and Americans for a Safe Israel. But most of the groups were clearly conservative: the Moral Majority, Liberty Legion, Citizens' Committee for the Right to Keep and Bear Arms, etc. Moreover the coalition's chairman, Lt-Gen. Daniel O. Graham, was the head of High Frontier and was unlikely to attract broad support.

On 7–9 August 1984, the State Department hosted a secret symposium on SDI, organised by the American Institute of Aeronautics and

Astronautics (AIAA), officially supported by the SDIO and the Office of the Secretary of Defense and co-chaired by Lt-Gen. Abrahamson. Attendance was restricted to US citizens holding a security clearance. Speakers included the director, deputy director and assistant directors of the SDIO, senior army, air force and navy officials and James Fletcher, of the eponymous panel. According to the registration document, an objective of the conference was 'to foster development of a national commitment to the Strategic Defense Initiative'. This is one instance of the Pentagon and the arms industry working together, funded by the taxpayer, to influence policy, rather than simply to implement it.

Apart from PACs and congressional advocacy, the interest groups were well served by instances of the 'revolving door': individuals transferring between government and the private sector, making policy and then benefiting from it, or even awarding a contract and then being employed by the contractor. SAIC, a small company discussed in the previous chapter, was a firm believer in 'establishing and maintaining close liaison between key members of the company's professional staff and its customers',[30] its main customer being the Pentagon. SAIC's board of directors includes one former Secretary of Defense, Melvin R. Laird, and a former head of the National Security Agency, retired Admiral Bobby R. Inman. Inman was also a member of the Fletcher panel, which recommended SDI, as were four other SAIC representatives. Another director, John Deutch, also dean of science at MIT and former Under-Secretary of Energy, served on the Hoffman panel. Former Under-Secretary of State Lucy Benson was another director, along with ex-member of the National Security Council, retired General Welch. These directors exemplify the revolving door in that their contacts with former colleagues can facilitate acquisition of contracts from the Pentagon. Going the other way through the revolving door was SAIC director Donald Hicks, who became director of research at the Pentagon.

## CONCLUSION

Between 1983 and 1985, in the face of criticism from leading scientists and statesmen, the SDI programme established itself and won an initial budget of $1,621,000,000. The strategic case given for SDI was confused, even contradictory. The Scowcroft Commission, the Office of Technology Assessment and independent scientists all doubted the feasibility and usefulness of BMD. Many in the USA, including much of the political centre, favoured a policy of 'negotiating from strength' and, in the light of bad relations with the Soviets, they saw SDI as a bargaining chip.

The Pentagon, military agencies and federal laboratories all had a stake in SDI. Their representatives dominated the executive committee charged with implementing the President's ideas. Along with members of corporations which have since won SDI contracts, they also dominated the panels, which advised in favour of SDI. These panels contained almost no sceptics or critics of the programme. They circumvented the Federal Advisory Committee Act, despite potential or actual conflicts of interest. Some caveats about BMD, contained in the original reports, seem to have been omitted in the summary prepared by the National Security Council for the President.

It is hard to assess how far the panels were influenced by informal advice provided by weapons scientists. Edward Teller gave highly tendentious accounts, disputed by the head of the X-ray laser project, to policy-makers at the highest level. The informal and unrecorded influence of such scientists was probably very great.

In its first year, SDI was shaped by the Pentagon, which effectively controlled the SDI executive committee, and by the arms corporations, which, with the Pentagon, dominated the advisory panels. In a sense, it could not be otherwise, since these were the groups which were charged with fulfilling the President's idea. Reference to their opinions and judgements was necessary in order to assess the feasibility of SDI. But they dominated the advisory panels and executive committees to the virtual exclusion of critics and independent minds.

After the first SDI budget request, Congress had the potential to influence SDI significantly. The Pentagon and SDI contractors furnished expert evidence to Congress in favour of SDI. Despite opposition from individual members, Congress appropriated over 90 per cent of the Pentagon's greatly increased budget request for BMD.

The corporations did relatively little lobbying in public, although there were a few pro-SDI conferences and attempts to back SDI through Political Action Committees (PACs). A larger public relations campaign run by the contractors could have been counter-productive. The main public lobbying to win support for SDI was carried out by pressure groups, such as High Frontier, the Administration and the President himself. If one were looking at SDI purely through the lens of logic and strategic rationality, one might be surprised that the concept was ever developed into a programme. Consideration of the domestic politics of the programme and the formidable constituency of interest behind SDI provides a fuller explanation of the programme's initial success.

# PART 3
# CONSOLIDATION: 1985–1988

# 7 CONTEXTS AND CONSTITUENCIES

Part 2 showed how SDI was established in President Reagan's first term of office. Part 3 considers how and why the programme was consolidated, under harsher conditions between 1985 and 1988. Although the interest groups still worked to consolidate the programme as a whole, they were now somewhat more fragmented, not always functioning as a totality. Different factions, with differing priorities, occasionally clashed in their efforts to shape budget priorities. The debate about the future course of SDI, especially the issue of early deployment, was, as we shall see in Chapter 9, influenced by the different interest groups struggling to mould SDI.

In Reagan's second term, confusion continued about the main purpose of SDI. The President and other 'true believers' continued to present the programme in hopeful, visionary tones as 'the path to a safe and more secure future'[1] and 'the most positive and promising defense program we have undertaken'.[2] The Administration, however, increasingly justified SDI as a necessary response to Soviet activities in BMD, air defence and passive defences.[3] The argument that SDI might defend nuclear weapons and bolster 'deterrence' slowly became the main rationale cited by the Administration. Since talk of 'eliminating nuclear weapons' was never publicly rebutted, some confusion continued.

A series of high-profile experiments gives some means of charting SDI's technical progress. In September 1985, a ground-based directed energy weapon, the Mid-Infrared Advanced Chemical Laser (MIRACL), destroyed a Titan booster. This confirmed the principle that a laser could destroy a liquid propellant ballistic missile. Abrahamson dubbed it 'a world class breakthrough', and it certainly produced an impressive video sequence. But the experiment, which took 370 people and 9,000 gallons of water to operate, also drew criticism, for it was conducted in an unrealistic, benign environment on a stationary mock-up target, on the ground. One scientist at Sandia spoke of 'strap-down chicken tests, where you strap the chicken down, blow it apart with a shotgun, and say shotguns kill chickens. But that's quite different from trying to kill a chicken in a dense forest while it's running away from you.'[4]

April 1986 saw a series of successful Kinetic Energy Weapons experiments. The Flexible Lightweight Agile Guidance Experiments (FLAGE) tested guidance technologies for intercepting missiles. In July 1986 the SDI's first Particle Beam Experiment irradiated a miniature RV with a high-intensity proton beam. The Delta 180 Experiment of September 1986 provided data to develop small space-based interceptors. It studied rocket signatures during the boost phase and just before intercept. A FLAGE follow-on test successfully demonstrated guidance technologies in May 1987. The target, a US Army Lance short-range missile, was intercepted at 12,000 feet. The Delta 181 experiment of February 1988 collected data for designing sensors. A rocket was launched from Cape Canaveral with a sensor module which proceeded to deploy and then characterise fourteen test objects.

These tests indicated that, although science can slide into showmanship, progress was being made towards developing potential elements of a Strategic Defense System (SDS). Abrahamson, Weinberger and Keyworth all spoke of monumental breakthroughs, and the SDI Office distributed photographs and videotapes of 'flagship' experiments, to the alarm of the arms control community, which held that the tests eroded the spirit, or even the letter, of the ABM Treaty.

In 1986 and following years, the SDI programme was examined by a team of Senate staff members on behalf of Senator Proxmire.[5] After interviewing some forty scientists, engineers and military officials involved in SDI research, they found that the SDIO still had no specific systems architectures which could be tested against a realistic set of threat scenarios. They also noted the vulnerability of the space-based elements, which have to destroy enemy missiles in their boost phase. Failure at this stage would vastly increase the difficulty of midcourse discrimination. The SDI Office seemed still not to have addressed problems of logistics, support, co-ordination, transportation and production fully. A Defense Science Board report noted 'monumental software problems' which remained unresolved.[6]

The 'architecture studies', launched with great aplomb in 1984, were quietly concluded in October 1985. One concept had no weapons in space; another had thousands of satellites and seven separate tiers of defence. The discrepancy betokened how vague the concept of a Strategic Defense System remained.

The overall goal of a secure and reliable defence remained as remote as ever. The SDI programme showed no sign of meeting the 'Nitze criteria', established in February 1985, of being militarily effective, survivable and cost-effective at the margin. Despite the formidable problems which remained, the SDI Office did not officially revise its schedule. It still called for a development decision in the early 1990s, initial deployment in the late 1990s and effective service round about 2005.

Although SDI contracts came at a generally bleak time for research funding, US scientists showed enormous, perhaps unprecedented, scepticism about, if not hostility towards, the programme. By May 1986, close to 7,000 scientists in the academic areas most critical to SDI had pledged not to accept SDI funds. This included a majority of professors at the nation's top 20 physics departments and 15 Nobel laureates.[7] Seventy-eight per cent of members of the National Academy of Sciences in the areas most relevant to SDI research (mathematics, physics and engineering) did not believe that an SDS could be survivable or cost-effective in the next twenty-five years. Ninety-eight per cent said that SDI could not provide an 'effective defence of the US civilian population' if the Soviets employed counter-measures.[8]

The critics were helped by revived détente in East–West relations. By 1986, the Kremlin had brightened its act under Mikhail Gorbachev. The superpowers' new-found cordiality survived tense incidents, such as the US bombing of Libya (14 April 1986) and the 'Daniloff' spying affair. Regional conflicts were defused. By the end of the period, peace settlements were in sight in Namibia and Angola and the Soviets withdrew from Afghanistan. After the signing of the INF Treaty in December 1987, optimists looked towards a START Treaty, which could cut the arsenals of the superpowers by half. 'Fear of an epidemic of world peace inhibits investing in defence stocks', ran the headline in one defence journal.[9]

By 1985, the problem of federal and trade deficits began to restrict the US military budget. Although Reagan's arms build-up was over, the defence budget remained at levels about 40 per cent higher in real terms than they had been at the end of the previous decade.[10] There was thus room to expand SDI research, but the huge funds needed for an SDI deployment did not seem to be readily available. After the Democrats won control of the Senate in 1986, thus gaining a majority in both chambers, the White House had to adopt a more consensual approach. An era of 'closet pragmatism' began.

The scandal of 'Irangate' broke in the autumn of 1986 and fuelled media stories for the next year. Arms had been sold to Khomeini's Iran and the proceeds diverted to fund the Nicaraguan Contras, despite a congressional ban on support for the rebels. The revelations tarnished the Administration and implicated the National Security Council and clandestine, semi-official groups on the far Right.[11] Reagan and Bush were cornered. To admit knowledge was self-incriminating: to plead ignorance implausible.

By 1987, reform was spreading in Eastern Europe. The stock market crash of October 1987, which wiped over 20 per cent off the value of the market, nudged Reagan's Administration towards accepting minor cuts in the defence budget.[12] It entered its final year sullied by scandal, as erstwhile loyalists published 'insider' accounts.[13] George Bush, the Republican nominee, would not champion SDI with the same fervour as Reagan. Democratic presidential candidates were opposed to SDI deployment, although all but Jesse Jackson endorsed further research.

As superpower relations improved, arms control returned to the top of the political agenda, with important implications for SDI. Gorbachev launched a 'charm offensive', presenting an array of proposals which won wide public acclaim. In March 1985 the two superpowers began the Nuclear and Space Talks (NST) in Geneva. The United States sought to legitimise SDI and claimed that the Soviets had violated the ABM Treaty. The Soviets continued to denounce SDI as an impediment to arms control, and they proposed a total ban on 'space-strike arms'.

SDI was a central issue in the run-up to the superpower summit at Reykjavik (October 1986). The Soviets proposed that both sides observe the ABM Treaty for a further ten years; and insisted on retaining the traditional reading of the ABM Treaty, which would ban the testing of space-based BMD elements outside the laboratory. The US team refused these stipulations, and this the Soviets characterised as the main obstacle to an agreement.

In 1987, the Soviets effectively 'decoupled' SDI from the INF Treaty negotiations. No longer would they call for an end to the programme as a prerequisite to agreement on INF. In the September 1987 Defense and Space (D&S) talks at Geneva, the USSR modified its position to allow some ABM research in space. In November, Gorbachev told a TV audience that 'Practically the Soviet Union is doing all that the US is doing . . . But we will not build an SDI, we will not deploy an SDI and we call on the United States to do likewise.'

The superpower summit in Washington, D.C. (1987) served to cement a new relationship, and Gorbachev was lionised by the US public. On 15 January 1988, the Soviets presented a draft START Treaty protocol, which would commit both sides to abide by the ABM Treaty for ten years. In December, Gorbachev told the United Nations General Assembly that the USSR would unilaterally reduce its armed forces by 500,000 men by the end of 1990.[14]

The revival of arms control helped to create a climate in which it was much harder for SDI supporters to abrogate the ABM Treaty of 1972. None the less, they did advocate 'broad' or 'permissive' interpretations of the Treaty, in order to legitimise tests banned under the traditional reading. In the frequently recondite disputes about the hermeneutics of the ABM Treaty, there were two main areas of contention.[15] The traditional interpretation of the ABM Treaty allowed development and testing of ABM systems 'based on other physical principles'[16] only for the permitted fixed land-based systems and their components. Supporters of SDI claimed that the 1972 Treaty was open to a 'broad' interpretation, which would allow development and testing of *any ABM system* 'based on other physical principles'. By legitimising tests of such systems in space, the 'broad' interpretation would have helped testing of an early IOC and generated momentum for the programme. The reinterpretation met intense resistance from Congress, the Allies and the US negotiators of the original treaty.[17] On 11 October 1985 the President conceded that the programme would be confined to the traditional reading for the time being. In declaring that the broad interpretation was nevertheless justified, Reagan kept open the possibility of eventual US 'break-out'.[18]

A second dispute concerned ambiguities of key words in the ABM Treaty, such as 'development' and 'ABM component'. Broadly, the Administration argued that SDI complied with the treaty, since it was not developing 'ABM components'. It was merely *researching 'subcomponents'*. Consequently, SDI tests would not be conducted 'in an ABM mode' or demonstrate 'ABM capabilities'. Thus, the argument ran, SDI technologies would not be 'capable of substituting for' ABM components. This case was widely opposed as ill-advised sophistry infringing the 1972 Treaty.

Soviet aggression could have provided the pretext for contravening the 1972 Treaty, just as the Soviet invasion of Afghanistan had provided justification for the Senate not to ratify SALT II. The new image of the USSR and the fact that it was visibly seeking arms control agreements made it extremely hard for the 'hawks' to abrogate the ABM Treaty.

Given that neither strategy, technology nor international relations can adequately account for the consolidation of the SDI programme, we must now explore other explanations, notably the continued activities of SDI interest groups.

The biggest increase came in FY 1986, when the funds were nearly doubled. Although Congress made some cuts, it still authorised ample funds, for it seems that the requests included a 'cut insurance'. In February 1987, Abrahamson testified to Congress that only about $4.1 billion had been spent from the $7.3 billion authorised.[19] A total of

Table 7.1. *SDI requests and authorisations as of 1989 (in $ millions)*

| Agency | 1985 | 1986 | 1987 | 1988 | 1989 | TOTAL |
|---|---|---|---|---|---|---|
| SDIO | 1,777 | 3,722 | 4,803 | 5,463 | 6,420 | 22,185 |
| DoE | 224 | 288 | 603 | 836 | 838 | 2,789 |
| Total request | 2,001 | 4,010 | 5,406 | 6,299 | 7,258 | 24,974 |
| Total authorisation | 1,621 | 2,963 | 3,650 | 3,966 | 4,046 | 16,246 |

*Source:* SDIO figures. Quoted in David C. Morrison, 'Shooting Down Star Wars', *National Journal* (25 October 1986), p. 2544. The figures for 1988 and 1989 show the requests projected in 1987. These requests were later reduced: for the DoD portion of the budget, for FY 1988 and 1989 to $5.2 billion and $4.5 billion respectively (SDIO *Report to Congress* (March 1989), fig. 8.1). The figures for total authorisations are compiled from several sources. Figures are given in millions of dollars, at the rate current for that year.

$3.2 billion therefore remained unspent: a fact which sits uneasily beside complaints that Congress had stifled funds. Outlays indicate money actually spent: those who have already won contracts and been paid. They always lag behind authorisations, the more so in a programme such as SDI which receives large budget increases.

The SDI Contract Management Information System listed 7,467 contracting actions up to April 1988. Spread around 752 different entities, these amounted to $5,960.253 million. This sum is far less than authorisations, which again suggests that the SDIO literally had more money than it could spend.

The private sector won nearly three-quarters of funds authorised, and federal laboratories and universities accounted for most of the rest. These funds fed and rewarded the different SDI interest groups. Participation was especially alluring, first because the SDIO had plentiful funds – and indeed needed to spend them to justify its increased requests to Congress – and second because of the rich prospect of an eventual deployment. Official estimates for a Phase I Strategic Defense System (SDS) ranged from $69 billion to $150 billion. In private, contractors hoped for far more. Full-scale deployment would generate a bonanza, perhaps worth $1 trillion.

The SDI Office continued to be an effective institutional supporter of SDI, and its director, Abrahamson, remained as astute as ever in his efforts to build the programme. In 1985, the SDIO had about 80 staff, and Abrahamson told Congress he would need a few more than 150 eventually. With 230 employees only two years later, the SDIO moved from makeshift offices in downtown Washington, D.C. to more luxurious headquarters in the Pentagon.[20]

Table 7.2. *SDI outlays*

| Fiscal year | Value ($m.) | Number of contracts |
|---|---|---|
| 1985 | 1,295.547 | 1,932 |
| 1986 | 2,151.864 | 2,538 |
| 1987 | 2,212.764 | 2,032 |

*Source:* SDIO Contract Management Information System (April 1988).

The SDI Office did not obtain its own contracting authority until October 1985. In FY 1986, 83 per cent of the budget was managed by the Services and defence agencies for the SDI Office.[21] The established BMD agencies therefore continued to benefit. It seems that Abrahamson still did not trouble the military agencies about the precise, procedural details of accounting for their funds. Within the SDIO he skimmed money from each project into a central, reserve 'kitty', so that funds could swiftly be moved from one account to another.[22]

A more detailed breakdown, by authorisation, of the military agencies to gain from SDI is given below. The agencies listed stood to gain from SDI in a purely financial sense.[23] BMD had a special, further attraction for space enthusiasts in the air force and elsewhere, as a way to improve the technology base for 'space control' and space war-fighting. This faction became more significant in Reagan's second term, as the military space infrastructure grew, with, for example, the establishment of a unified Space Command in 1985.[24]

According to a Heritage Foundation Report, the former head of Space Command was instrumental in guiding six SDI projects past 'milestone I' (in 1987) and into the next stage of 'demonstration/validation':

> The important point is that the SDI Program, despite a profusion of critics, is quietly proceeding through the defense validation process. Insiders credit General Robert T. Herres, vice chairman of the JCS and former commander of Space Command, for managing the JCS acceptance of Milestone I.[25]

Support for SDI was, however, less than total in some quarters of the armed forces. According to a retired air force General: 'there's no strong support for [SDI] in the hard-core air force, the Tactical Air Command types, and there's even less in the navy, which doesn't really have a piece of this'.[26]

Added to bureaucratic support was what a former Under-Secretary of State described as 'good, free-enterprise greed':

Table 7.3. *Contracts by sector (funds authorised by April 1987)*

|  | Total | Value ($m.) | % | Number of contracts |
|---|---|---|---|---|
| Corporations | 460 | 8,000 | 73 | 2,250 |
| Federal labs. | 14 | 1,500 | 14 | 120 |
| Universities | 80 | 700 | 6 | 350 |
| Government | 53 | 450 | 4 | 375 |
| Non-profits | 16 | 100 | 1 | 100 |
| Foreign | 130 | 100 | 1 | 130 |
| TOTAL | 753 | 10,850 | 99 | 3,325 |

*Source:* Pike, 'SDI and Corporate Contractors: Momentum, Ambivalence and a Push for Early Deployment', Federation of American Scientists, Public Interest Report, vol. 40, no. 4 (April 1987).

> Firms in the hypertrophic defense industry, along with thousands of technicians, are manifesting a deep patriotic enthusiasm for Star Wars. Since they are experienced in lobbying and wield heavy influence with members of Congress who have defense plants in their constituencies, they are creating a formidable momentum for the project. Whether or not it will contribute to the security of the nation, it offers them security.[27]

One defence analyst pointed out that the traditional defence market would not grow much, adding: 'every company is on notice that if they want to be a long-term player, they can't let SDI get away'.[28]

The biggest single contractors continued to be large defence corporations, which have extensive potential for advocacy. Potentially the large corporations stood to win the biggest contracts in any eventual deployment of SDI, since they would do the production work, or 'bend tin'. In August 1988, the top ten corporate contractors for SDI were all in the top 130 of the Fortune 500 index. The annual sales of each one exceeded the SDIO's annual budget.[29] Whilst they win most in absolute terms from SDI, their revenue derived from SDI is a small fraction of their overall turnover. The company's SDI division, however, clearly depends wholly on SDI, and, in using the company's resources for advocacy, can create pressure for the programme.

The trend of previous years continued. As the large corporations invested in SDI, expanded the infrastructure or the work force, they had more at stake in SDI and became more likely to oppose any threat to SDI should one transpire. Rockwell, for example, invested $11 million in a new facility for 1,000 staff from the eight company divisions working on SDI.[30] Its new Strategic Defense Center was opened in April 1986.[31] Ford Aerospace invested $8 million of company funds in a Command

94

Table 7.4. *Share of SDI outlays to April 1988*

| Service | Value ($m.) | Number of contracts |
|---|---|---|
| 1. Army | 2,511.698 | 2,618 |
| 2. Air force | 1,646.167 | 2,850 |
| 3. SDIO | 742.878 | 185 |
| 4. Navy | 435.603 | 571 |
| 5. DARPA | 385.970 | 798 |
| 6. DNA | 237.937 | 464 |
| TOTAL | 5,960.253 | 7,486 |

*Source:* SDIO Contract Management Information System (13 April 1988).

Center Laboratory in its bid for the crucial Systems Engineering and Integration (SE&I) contract. A competing team led by General Electric won this contract, but Ford knew that their investment could also help them to win a contract to modernise the Cheyenne Mountain command centre, and to win a C³I contract offered by the Army Strategic Defense Command.[32]

General Dynamics, TRW, McDonnell Douglas, Thomson-CSF and General Electric all formed SDI offices. The Titan Corporation founded a new division, whose president was Gerold Yonas, formerly the chief scientist at the SDIO. Under Yonas, Titan acquired small firms dependent on SDI contracts, including Pulse Sciences, Aeronautical Research Associates and Spectron Development Labs. These strategic takeovers of promising SDI performers are another measure of corporate faith in the programme. Once money has been invested and new bureaucracies created, the company is tied that much more to the programme.

Some small corporations were heavily dependent on SDI. SDI contracts accounted for 75 per cent of Sparta's total revenue; 86 per cent of income at Nichols Research; and 50 per cent at W. J. Schafer.[33] These corporations had a clear interest in fighting fiercely for the programme.

SDI, however, was not devoid of problems. Corporate enthusiasm was tempered because SDI remained an R&D programme and profit margins tended to be slightly lower at this stage. 'Capital and personnel requirements are more difficult to estimate and manage. Subcontractor relationships become as complex as the systems they interface, and technical risks are obviously higher.'[34] The head of SDI work at GTE noted that 'the price of admission to this game is much higher than usual'.[35] Some SDI contracts were multiple-stage competitions. Companies knocked out in the early phases stood to gain little. Those who successfully completed these stages faced further hurdles before

Table 7.5. *Leading agencies sponsoring SDI contracts by authorisation to April 1987*

|  | Value ($m.) | % |
|---|---|---|
| *Army total* | 4,000 | 37.0 |
| Strategic Defense Command | 3,475 | 32.2 |
| Corps of Engineers | 290 | 2.6 |
| Missile Command | 125 | 1.1 |
| Other army | 110 | 1.0 |
| *Air Force total* | 3,400 | 31.5 |
| Space Division | 2,240 | 20.7 |
| Electronic Systems Division | 710 | 6.6 |
| Aeronautical Systems Division | 225 | 2.1 |
| Armament Division | 75 | 0.7 |
| Other systems command | 150 | 1.5 |
| *Navy total* | 535 | 4.9 |
| Office of Naval Research | 250 | 2.3 |
| Sea Systems Command | 230 | 2.1 |
| Space and Naval Warfare Command | 22 | 0.2 |
| Other navy | 33 | 0.3 |
| *Other DoD* | 1,080 | 10.0 |
| SDIO | 630 | 5.8 |
| Defense Nuclear Agency | 280 | 2.6 |
| DARPA | 170 | 1.6 |
| *Other government* | 1,750 | 16.2 |
| DoE | 1,650 | 15.3 |
| NASA | 85 | 0.9 |
| TOTAL | 10,765 | 99.6 |

*Source:* Pike, 'SDI and Corporate Contractors'. Some rounding errors occur.

gaining large, lucrative contracts. Some major SDI contracts such as Alpha (TRW) and Talon Gold (Lockheed) were rudely cancelled. McDonnell Douglas lost a $408.6 million contract for a particle beam weapon when the project was cancelled.[36] As a moving target, constantly being redesigned, SDI was far from perfect for the risk-averse.

In terms of geographical constituencies, California led the field with 37 per cent of SDI contracts awarded. Massachusetts came second thanks to the high-tech laboratories in Boston. Alabama's SDI contracts were concentrated around the Army Strategic Defense Command in Huntsville. New Mexico did well thanks to the national laboratories at Los Alamos and Sandia. Boeing was the main contractor in Washington. The area around the Potomac – Maryland, Virginia and

Table 7.6. *Main SDI contractors: outlays to April 1988*

| Contractor | Outlays ($m.) |
| --- | --- |
| 1. Boeing | 475.39 |
| 2. Lockheed | 393.31 |
| 3. TRW | 365.38 |
| 4. MIT | 302.34 |
| 5. Undetermined | 270.13 |
| 6. Lawrence Livermore Lab. | 224.42 |
| 7. Rockwell | 223.51 |
| 8. Los Alamos | 209.57 |
| 9. McDonnell Douglas | 191.09 |
| 10. General Motors | 169.82 |
| 11. Teledyne Brown | 140.55 |
| 12. USASDC | 124.89 |
| 13. SDIO In-house | 104.75 |
| 14. Johns Hopkins University | 100.01 |
| 15. Grumman | 82.23 |
| 16. Martin Marietta | 80.43 |
| 17. Textron | 79.19 |
| 18. Sandia Lab. | 77.84 |
| 19. GenCorp | 75.83 |
| 20. LTV | 75.63 |
| 21. Raytheon | 68.46 |
| 22. AF Weapons Lab. | 65.22 |
| 23. General Electric Co. | 62.03 |
| 24. Science Applications Intl. | 60.25 |
| 25. Flow General | 55.38 |

*Source:* SDIO Contract Management Information System (April 1988).

Washington, D.C. – accounted for $406 million. Colorado, home state of the Unified Space Command and Martin Marietta, was set to win more funds as SDI continued. Its congressman, Ken Kramer, hailed it as 'the space capital of the Free World'; founded a US Space Foundation to promote SDI; and sponsored the pro-SDI 'People Protection Act'.[37]

The rehabilitation of arms control appalled some of the most ardent BMD supporters. At a dinner on the fourth anniversary of the Reagan speech, Senator Malcolm Wallop said that the concept of BMD had been 'hijacked by the Reagan Administration's incompetent and unfaithful crew':

> They defined the job so that it could not be done. They mixed strategic defense, which was supposed to be the cure for the ravages of arms control, with the arms control process itself. Thus they gave the cure a massive dose of the disease. They managed to turn an inherently popular idea . . . into something ridiculous.[38]

97

Table 7.7. *Top states: SDI outlays to April 1988*

| State | (Value $m.) | Number of contracts |
|---|---|---|
| 1. California | 2,215.922 | 2,626 |
| 2. Massachusetts | 633.059 | 737 |
| 3. Alabama | 542.299 | 1,005 |
| 4. Washington | 477.836 | 149 |
| 5. New Mexico | 382.281 | 358 |
| 6. Maryland | 181.964 | 129 |
| 7. New York | 155.498 | 280 |
| 8. Virginia | 146.121 | 285 |
| 9. Texas | 129.377 | 158 |
| 10. Colorado | 128.812 | 173 |
| 11. Washington, D.C. | 78.602 | 150 |

*Source:* SDIO Contract Management Information System (April 1988).

The groups which supported SDI for ideological reasons were running out of momentum in Reagan's second term. The social agenda of the New Right – organised around 'moral' issues, such as abortion – was less compelling than it had been in the early 1980s. Its international agenda had been partially accomplished with Reagan's arms build-up and more interventionist foreign policy. Reforms in the Soviet Union undermined the rhetoric of hostility towards the erstwhile 'evil empire'. No longer was it so easy to blame problems with the USSR on 'arms control' and 'liberals'. As the Reagan era petered out, the selling of SDI became less intense and less effective.[39]

### CONCLUSION

During Reagan's second term, the main strategic purpose of SDI remained unclear. While it seemed that for practical purposes SDI could be understood as an attempt to defend missile silos and bolster the condition of Mutual Assured Destruction (MAD), the Administration still justified SDI at times as an attempt to eliminate nuclear weapons and the condition of MAD. There was further uncertainty about the promise of SDI technologies. Officials hailed some advances, but it seems that there were no major breakthroughs. Ninety-eight per cent of the members of the American National Academy of Sciences agreed that Soviet counter-measures could prevent an 'effective defense of the US civilian population'.

The US military budget levelled off, though at levels 40 per cent higher than at the end of the previous decade, which allowed funds for

SDI research to increase. Arms control talks resumed in Geneva and by 1987 had resulted in the INF Treaty. SDI supporters failed to modify or abrogate the agreed meaning of the ABM Treaty. Reform began to blossom in Eastern Europe. By the end of Reagan's second term it appeared that the Cold War might at last be over.

Meanwhile the SDI budget grew, along with the constituency commercially linked to the programme. The infrastructure and the constituency of interest grew together, cause and effect of each other. Some of the largest and most powerful institutions in the USA stood to gain from SDI. The Pentagon and its military agencies, the SDI Office, corporations both large and small, and 'hawkish' right-wingers combined to make a formidable coalition behind SDI. How far these groups actually influenced policy is the subject of the next chapter.

# 8 INTEREST AND INFLUENCE

Of necessity, members of the SDI interest groups helped to shape policy on SDI. This chapter assesses the extent to which they managed unduly to influence policy or override criticisms of the programme. After considering the amount of lobbying by SDI contractors, it studies the influences on the making and implementation of SDI policy in the Pentagon, within the Executive and in Congress.

As shown in the previous chapter, many corporations made a major practical commitment to SDI, through investment of material resources or expansion of the infrastructure. This suggests that they would be all the more likely to oppose any threat to SDI should one transpire.

Members of the SDI infrastructure wrote articles in favour of SDI. 'Strategic Defenses and Deterrence: A Strategic-Operational Assessment', for example, praises SDI as one of Reagan's major accomplishments and describes an array of benefits it might confer.[1] The text itself is fairly unremarkable. It outlines a 'concept of integrated offense/defense operations' and argues that, by increasing the attacker's uncertainty, SDI will stabilise the 'nuclear balance' and bolster deterrence. More revealing is the authorship of the article, which demonstrates the informal collaboration of members of the SDI infrastructure. One of the three authors, Dr Kane, was the director of Rockwell's 'Strategic Systems and Strategic Defense Center' from 1981 to 1986. A graduate of the US Military Academy and Georgetown University (which has links with US intelligence), he was in 1989 a consultant to Rockwell, then listed as the third largest SDI contractor.[2] A second author, General Meyer, had been programme manager of the US Army Ballistic Defense Program in Huntsville from 1977 to 1979. He had successfully persuaded Congress that BMD research and development should continue. 'In key congressional committees, [General Meyer] found a "strong minority" that constituted "the necessary few" who supported the program and guaranteed its continuance.'[3] General Meyer had also worked with High Frontier and been a member of the Fletcher panel, on the 'executive scientific review group'. The third author, Mr Howe, was

100

a project manager at Rockwell's Strategic Defense Center and had been a 'mission analysis task leader' in the SDIO 'architecture study'. The authors of this pro-SDI article have, therefore, a mixture of corporate and bureaucratic and 'ideological' interest in the SDI programme. General Meyer exemplifies the continuity of the BMD infrastructure and its stalwarts, before SDI and after.

The 'Marshall Report' was a more widely quoted and influential paper, which strongly favoured SDI and called for the acceleration of the SDI programme towards an early Initial Operating Capability (IOC).[4] The report, issued in December 1986, was written by six people, including three of the four directors of the right-wing Marshall Institute.[5] Two of its authors may be classified as right-wing ideologues: James Frelk, executive director of the Marshall Institute, and Robert Jastrow, author of How to Make Nuclear Weapons Obsolete. Two members come from the military bureaucracy. William Nierenberg was a member of the Defense Science Board, a past chairman of JASONS, a secret advisory group associated with the Institute for Defense Analysis, and a member of the Fletcher panel. Frederick Seitz, president emeritus of Rockefeller University, was a former chairman of the Defense Science Board and science adviser to NATO.

The two other authors of the Marshall Report, Edward Gerry and John Gardner, illustrate the links between SDI, the defence bureaucracy and profit-making companies. Edward Gerry has been 'intimately involved', as he puts it, with BMD for the past twenty years.[6] He worked at Avco Everett research laboratory and is a former assistant director for technologies at DARPA. He was a member of the air force scientific advisory board and chairman of the boost phase systems concept group for the Fletcher panel. He has been 'intimately involved in the SDI systems architecture studies since that time'. He is also the president of W. J. Schafer Associates, which had $16.417 million in SDI contracts by August 1988.[7] John Gardner designed missile defences for McDonnell Douglas, before becoming the Assistant Deputy Under-Secretary of Defensive Systems with the Reagan Administration. Whilst working in the Office of the Secretary of Defense, he was deputy director of the Fletcher panel. Simultaneously, as director of defensive systems and executive secretary of the inter-agency group on defensive technologies, he was the man directly senior to Fletcher on the organisation charts.[8] When the SDIO was established, Gardner was the director of systems there. In 1986, he returned to McDonnell Douglas as vice-president for engineering and operations.[9]

There were other relatively minor efforts to win support for SDI, such as that by the American Defense Preparedness Association (ADPA), which distributed a half-hour promotion of SDI for national television stations. Martin Marietta published a booklet – *Strategic Defense: A Martin Marietta Commitment* – which included a list of congressional swing votes and members worth 'concentrating upon'. By defence industry standards, however, these efforts, and the articles in strategic journals, are very restrained.

Public lobbying by SDI contractors for SDI was limited for at least five reasons. First, with the President of the United States as advocate, the corporations had little need to lobby. An aggressive campaign to sell SDI, on the lines of Rockwell's public relations drives for the B-1 bomber, might well have backfired on a public increasingly wary of 'defence scams'.

Second, SDI looked secure, whoever won the 1988 presidential election. George Bush would continue funding for SDI. The leading Democrat candidates, except for Jesse Jackson, were pragmatists, at pains to prove their credentials in defence.[10] Congress rarely kills a programme stone dead, and Democrats have an especially good record for funding military R&D. Although some groups saw a need to hurry the programme to procurement phase, most corporations were content that SDI would continue as R&D.

Third, SDI only amounted to about 1.5 per cent of the Pentagon budget. Whatever its prospects, SDI was not a major *present* concern for the big contractors. According to Gordon Adams:

> SDI isn't live or die for any of the big companies. They're the ones with the political clout, the access, the political will and know-how. But they aren't motivated to put their prestige on the line for SDI.[11]

Although some small companies relied on SDI for funds, they would not mount large 'up-front' campaigns, since they could influence the policy process more effectively in less public ways.

A fourth reason why corporations refrained from selling Reagan's astrodome was out of deference to the Services, which were less than enthusiastic about this version of SDI. Lockheed, for example, had won $960 million in SDI contracts by the start of 1989, second only to Boeing. Yet Lockheed's stake in SDI pales besides its interest in, say, the Trident II contract for the navy. Lockheed would not wish to offend the Services and undercut the rationale for Trident with any hard-sell SDI rhetoric about 'Mutual Assured Survival'. In practice, SDI and counter-force contracts can co-exist amicably, and profitably, within a firm.

Fifth and finally, many SDI contracts were generic and would survive the SDI programme anyhow. The absence of a major industry campaign to push SDI infuriated some of the programme's most ardent supporters: 'if industry is not more aggressive going after critics who oppose defenses – as it should – the funds are going to keep coming down and we'll never have deployment'.[12] 'Buz' Lukens, representative for Ohio, called for a campaign to build public support for space programmes in general, an action agenda and a Political Action Committee (PAC) for space:

> We get pecked to death by various roosters in the barnyard, but noone has turned loose the bull. The leaders of the space community do not come to the Congress with comprehensive, coherent and consistent action programs.[13]

Despite such complaints, there was no high-profile, aggressive campaign by the contractors to win the public over to SDI. This was partly because they could influence the policy process in more subtle fashion, through advisory panels and committees, in the Executive realm and in Congress.

Debate about SDI was, like many military affairs, conducted in the absence of crucial information. The SDI Office produced no specific systems architecture, nor did it give detailed criteria which a Strategic Defense System (SDS) should meet. It offered widely varying estimates for the cost of a Phase I SDS and no idea of the cost of a full-scale deployment. It was argued that as a 'research programme' the SDIP could not provide this information. The point of the programme was to discover it. The lack of information gave a special role to 'inside experts' and specialist advisory committees. It also introduced crucial elements of uncertainty which could be creatively exploited in discussions of SDI.

The SDIO director answered to the SDI Advisory Committee (SDIAC), established in January 1985.[14] As supervisor of the SDI programme, the SDIAC was a key committee. It gives an instructive example of coincidence of interest. Many of those on the committee and supervising the programme had a direct financial stake in it: and circumvented the rules by which this should have been disclosed.

The chairman of the SDI Advisory Committee, Frederick Seitz was, as noted above, a co-author of the Marshall Report, which called for early deployment of SDI. Like his fellow SDIAC member, Robert Everett, he had headed the Defense Science Board. Another member of the SDI advisory committee, William Nierenberg, also sits on the Defense Science Board. He too is a co-author of the Marshall Report and an advocate of early deployment. In addition, he was a member of the Fletcher panel, which recommended SDI in the first place. Dr James Fletcher himself also sits on the SDI Advisory Committee. Their

103

colleague, Edward Teller, needs no introduction as an outstanding pillar of BMD.

Table 8.1 shows only the primary institution to which members of the SDI Advisory Committee were attached; half the members of the SDI Advisory Committee were employees of SDI prime contractors. Other financial interests in SDI are not disclosed in the table. It is known that one member of the SDI Advisory Committee was a director of 1 firm doing SDI work, a stockholder in 7 and a paid consultant to 7.[15] One company in which he was both stockholder and consultant was a small business highly dependent on SDI contracts. He had filed a financial disclosure form in 1987. A year later he had still not filed any dis-qualification statement and the SDIO had not reviewed his disclosure form.[16]

Given the web of self- and corporate interest outlined above, it was all the more important that the SDI Advisory Committee should abide by the regulations of the Federal Advisory Committee Act, since, in the words of Senator Carl Levin, 'you cannot have a much riper situation for a conflict of interest'.[17]

The SDI Advisory Committee, however, broke Federal Advisory Committee Act (FACA) rules. All twelve members started work before being formally appointed, so that they were not subject to DoD's criminal conflict of interest laws. All twelve started work without the SDIO reviewing their financial disclosure forms, despite their links with firms doing SDI work. Nine had not even completed the necessary financial disclosure forms before starting work. In 1988, three years after the committee had been formed, two members had still not filed financial disclosure forms. Of the other ten, five reported that they were paid consultants for firms, schools or institutions doing SDI-related work. Six were trustees or directors of such entities and eight held stock in such firms. Two had other financial relationships with such entities.[18] The main official SDI committee, in charge of the SDIO, was therefore dominated by individuals who had extensive financial interests in SDI which were not disclosed in the proper manner.

A rather similar pattern emerges from a study of the Defense Science Board, a Pentagon board which oversees technology programmes in general and which was asked to report on SDI. In 1987, 31 of the 48 members of the board belonged to organisations profiting from the SDI programme.[19] The board's chairman, Charles Fowler, was senior vice-president of the Mitre corporation, which had $4.736 million in SDI contracts by August 1988.[20]

In a report for the Defense Acquisition Board (DAB), a Defense Science Board panel concluded that the Pentagon's SDI deployment

Table 8.1. *Members of the SDI Advisory Committee*

| Members | Institution |
| --- | --- |
| Dr Frederick Seitz (Chairman) | Rockefeller University |
| James Elms | Unknown |
| Dr Robert Everett | Mitre Corp.[a] |
| Dr James Fletcher | Burroughs Corp. |
| Charles Fowler | C. A. Fowler Associates |
| Dr Hans Mark | University of Texas[a] |
| Dr R. Montgomery | Unknown |
| Prof. W. Nierenberg | Scripps Inst. of Oceanography (University of California)[a] |
| Dr M. Rosenbluth | Univ. Texas[a] |
| Gen. B. Schriever | Schriever and McKee Inc. |
| Dr R. Sproull | University of Rochester[a] |
| Edward Teller | Lawrence Livermore Lab.[a] |

*Note:* [a]identifies SDI prime contractors.
*Source:* United States, Senate, Committee on Governmental Affairs, Subcommittee on Oversight of Governmental Management; and Committee on Armed Services, Subcommittee on Strategic Forces and Nuclear Deterrence, *Need for and Operation of a Strategic Defense Initiative Institute* (6 May 1987), pp. 75–6 [S. Hrg. 100–37].

plan was too 'sketchy' for either its effectiveness or its price to be determined. The panel therefore recommended that the Acquisition Board withhold approval for deployment 'for the next year or two', until the SDIO had filled 'gaps in system design and key technologies'.[21] These remarks were excised from the copy of the report which was given to the Acquisition Board. The chairman of the panel which had found fault, Robert Everett, apparently deleted the critical passages, without telling other members of the panel.[22] Mr Everett was also president of Mitre Corporation, an SDI contractor.[23]

The original panel was already stacked in favour of SDI. Nevertheless, its doubts about early deployment were silently removed from the report. Moreover, the facts only came to light because of sources who risked penalties by providing the *Washington Post* with a copy of the unbowdlerised version.

Interim reviews of the SDI 'architecture studies' in April 1985 exposed the inadequacy of plans for 'battle management'. In June 1985, a group was therefore convened, known as the 'Panel on Computing in support of Battle Management'. Its members renamed it the 'Eastport Group', in honour of the Eastport Raw Bar in Alexandria, East Virginia, where they had first met to mull over the concept.[24] The Eastport Group was therefore a creation of the SDI Office, a study group under SDIO. It submitted its first report in December 1985 and a second report in April 1987.

One has unusual glimpses into the workings of the Eastport Group because one of its members, David Parnas, publicly dissented from its findings. He was a computer specialist and professor of computer and information science who had provided scientific advice to the Department of Defense since 1972. Parnas told how he was invited to 'save the world from nuclear conflagration' and earn $1,000 a day by joining the Eastport panel.[25] He considered that none of the others invited were leading figures in computing science or had appropriate experience or research interests. Their presentations were superficial and 'the panelists did not distinguish between their role as advisors to SDIO and their role as researchers seeking funding'. According to Parnas, there had been little preparation for the meeting. He noted 'a lack of contact with reality' and a hidden agenda of ulterior motives. 'Many of the remarks in the Eastport Report struck me as veiled proposals of work for its members and friends.'[26]

The Eastport Group broke FACA stipulations in that it had no charter and kept no minutes.[27] Nor did it make its members file financial disclosure forms and disqualification statements. Some members were paid up to $1,000 a day, four times the FACA maximum.[28]

Two weeks after the Eastport Group published its report in December 1985, its chairman, Dr Danny Cohen, submitted an unsolicited proposal for a contract. It was on behalf of the Information Sciences Institute, ISI, a group affiliated to the University of Southern California. Dr Cohen worked for ISI, as did another of the Eastport Group's eight members, Dr David Mizell. Senator Carl Levin observed that 'ISI's unsolicited proposal, coming two weeks after the Eastport report was released, smacks of insider information. Even worse, it raises questions of self-dealing and possible conflicts of interest.'[29]

ISI sent the proposal to the Office of Naval Research for the attention of Dr Richard Lau, who, as it happened, was a third member of the Eastport Group. Dr Lau duly accepted the unsolicited proposal and became the supervising officer for the contract, which was to be worth $5.3 million over a three-year span. The contract was labelled as a naval operations research project, although the proposal made no mention of naval operations and clearly concerned SDI.

Following publicity of these questionable circumstances, the contract was terminated in July 1987. Three days later the Office of Naval Research requested proposals to follow up research on the first contract. The evaluation committee for this decision was chaired by

Dr Lau; and, although it was not the lowest bid, ISI again won the contract.

It is not clear how far the Eastport Group typifies the workings of other committees which advise the SDI Office or the Pentagon. 'Insiders' are guarded about discussing these matters. Certainly the 'Eastport Group' was atypical in that one of its members publicly criticised it. The picture it paints is of a system of mutual informal favours, conflicts of interest and cavalier contempt for federal regulations.

It was, of course, necessary that specialists, many employed by potential SDI contractors, should be consulted about technical issues concerning SDI. In their own perception, their membership of SDI panels was no doubt legitimate. There is no firm evidence that they were operating in a consciously disingenuous or cynical manner. However, in the absence of countervailing opinion on the panels, the dominance of 'defence insiders' and representatives of potential contractors functioned in such a way as to limit the scope and perspectives of SDI advice. It also led to actual or potential conflicts of interest, which were not resolved through the established means, namely, the Federal Advisory Committees Act.

Since SDI was a research programme, nearly all of the contracts sought advice in one form or another. But the SDIO avoided the FACA by contracting out requests for advice. The General Counsel for SDIO sought to characterise panels as 'technical people talking to technical people' and thus exempt from FACA.[30] He also pleaded that the SDIO had had only one person working on all personnel matters, and that person had left. The General Counsel for the SDIO excused the SDIO's disregard for FACA by referring to an interim rule of the General Services Administration which exempts 'ad hoc, unstructured, non-continuing groups' from complying with FACA, in order to encourage 'useful contacts with the private sector'.[31] Thus the SDIO's 'ad hocracy' functioned so as to circumvent acts designed to reduce conflict of interest.

Where the FACA was clearly appropriate the SDIO still avoided the spirit, if not the letter, of the law. FACA demands a 'balanced membership' on panels, which must not be 'inappropriately influenced by any special interest.' Yet the panels excluded informed critics of SDI in favour of those with a vested interest in the programme.

The SDI Advisory Committee, the Eastport Group and the Defence Science Board point to a pattern of non-compliance with the Federal Advisory Committee Act (FACA); conflict of interest; and absence of independent, impartial advice. The general picture is that the SDIO gave compliance with conflict of interest statutes such low priority that almost nothing would have been done but for congressional goading.

The large increases for SDI met strong opposition from some congressmen. A group of 46 senators (37 Democrats and 9 Republicans) wrote to the Armed Services Committee with the concern that SDI had

> received excessive and inappropriate emphasis in DoD's budget. It is difficult to conceive of a sound rationale for increasing the combined DoD/DoE SDI budget by 77 per cent while the entire DoD budget will likely be frozen at zero real growth and other vital military research programs are facing budget cuts. Not only are the goals of the research effort unclear, the need for accelerated funding for a long-range program such as SDI has not been demonstrated.[32]

The senators were also concerned that SDI was starting to 'impinge on other military research and development. The FY 1986 budget (for SDI) is twice as large as the combined Advanced Technology budgets of the three military services and is nearly as large as the Technology Base budget of the entire Department of Defense.'[33]

Some congressmen criticised SDI as a 'pork barrel':

> They want to pump enough money into the program to institutionalise it before they leave office. They hope that if they can get enough defense contractors in enough states hooked onto the program, Congress could never undo it.[34]

Ninety-two per cent of SDI contracts awarded in the first two years of the programme went to states represented by senators on the Armed Services Committee and the Defense Appropriations Subcommittee. The average amount received by these states was twenty-two times the average amount received by other states.[35] This suggests that members of the committees directly responsible for SDI had a high material interest in funding the programme, as a means of winning jobs and investment for their constituents.

It seems that contractors had at least some success in buying support for the SDI programme. In the summer of 1985, Congress voted on proposed limits to SDI growth. In three votes in the House, the top twelve recipients of Political Action Committee (PAC) money from SDI contractors voted against limits on SDI funds 83 per cent of the time.[36]

Members of the SDIO and individuals from the SDI infrastructure vigorously advocated their programme to Congress. Prominent among them, once again, was Edward Teller. With help from a working group at Livermore he produced a paper on 'Soviet SDI', for discussion with the CIA. He testified in Congress and continued to use staff at Livermore's special projects division to support his views.[37] This was criticised by Roy Woodruff, the former head of the X-ray laser programme:

> In my opinion and in the opinion of the special projects division leader, Robert Andrews, the paper 'Soviet SDI' was technically weak and unbalanced . . . The only guidance given to the special projects staff by the director, according to Andrews, was to 'support Edward, but don't go along with anything that is technically incorrect' and unfortunately this material was used to influence the Congress as well as the CIA.[38]

Lowell Wood told the House Armed Services Committee that a single X-ray laser could 'win your war, if your opponent launches all his assets at once into your field of view'. Woodruff's successor as head of the X-ray laser programme felt it necessary to modify the tone:

> It is important to understand the X-ray laser programme at Livermore is a research not a development programme . . . Our best estimate is that it will take at least five years and an integral expenditure of a billion dollars before we can actually demonstrate whether an X-ray laser weapon can be realized and what its potential might be.[39]

In that congress voted SDI large increases and adequately funded the SDI programme, the efforts of the pro-SDI lobby may be judged successful. In other respects they were less successful. Congress continued to oppose recension of the ABM Treaty and the SDIO's attempts to hasten towards a premature Initial Operating Capability (IOC).[40] Those interested only in the SDI budget and contracts were more successful than the lobby opposed to arms control.

Congress was also the forum for debate about an SDI Institute. This idea was proposed by Abrahamson in 1986. He wanted a federally funded SDI Institute (SDII) to be established to assist the SDI Office.[41] It was to have a staff of about 350, with top salaries to compete with industry. Its president would have an annual salary of $225,000.[42]

An SDI Institute could have reinforced the power of the SDI Office and the Pentagon. Critics feared that it would function to provide ostensibly independent advice in favour of early deployment, or the SDIO's preferred options. It would have strengthened the institutional base of SDI supporters. Other agencies have used outside management contractors to consolidate a programme. The Army Strategic Defense Command pays Teledyne Brown to do its programme integration. The air force used Aerospace Corporation to be management contractor for its early ICBM research. The extra level of management may serve to protect the infrastructure and ensure longevity. As the former director of DARPA, Robert Cooper, pointed out: 'FFRDCs [Federally Funded

Research and Development Centers] seldom die and fade away.' They 'last virtually forever'.[43]

It is highly unlikely that an SDI Institute of the kind proposed would have provided robust critical assessments of SDI. Those invited to form it were selected by the Secretary of Defense, Caspar Weinberger, and their identities were withheld. Critics were not invited. Abrahamson was to choose senior staff members. Staff of the SDI Office could also work at the institute. Moreover, the proposals did not include prohibitions on 'revolving door' employment. Senator Carl Levin said that staff at the institute could recommend proposals and 'six weeks later accept a job with the firm that submitted the winning proposal'.[44] Senator Proxmire said that it looked 'more like a rubber stamp than a think tank'.[45]

Plans for the SDI Institute did not promise that it would be independent. Five of the 14 on its board of trustees were also on the SDI advisory committee. This, once again, created an appearance that the programme would only be assessed by a narrow range of 'insiders':

> So the Advisory Committee for the SDIO is recommending that you get an SDII in existence. Then some members of your advisory committee end up on the SDII board of trustees. They set proposed salaries for the officers of the SDII, the full-time people. And now I take it, it's possible that some of the SDII board of trustees might also end up as officers.[46]

An SDI institute could have furthered the institutionalisation of SDI. Members of the institute, chosen by the SDIO, could have informally mobilised support for the programme. But the proposal met strong resistance in Congress. Senator Levin led the attack, saying that the nation could spend hundreds of millions of dollars only to create 'a weak but costly institute which tells the SDIO what the SDIO wants to hear. It would provide only a scientific fig leaf.'[47]

Strangely, the SDI Institute was also opposed by the representative of the Aerospace Industries Association and the 'Business Alliance on Government Competition', on the grounds that it was anti-competitive. 'From our standpoint, it appears that SDIO is seeking essentially to increase its personnel by 250 or more individuals who will be hired as professional staff to serve with SDII.'[48]

Congress effectively killed the prospects for an SDI Institute by attaching so many restrictions that the idea could never blossom in the way its supporters desired. In other respects too, Congress acted to restrain the wilder desires of SDI supporters. It stopped the SDI Office from using funds to establish a public affairs office.[49] Senator Levin spearheaded an investigation, as mentioned above, into the SDIO's disregard of the Federal Advisory Committee Act, which resulted in panels on Kinetic Energy and Lethality being terminated.[50] Deliberate congressional inaction prevented Abrahamson from being promoted to a full General with four stars.[51]

Overall, Congress was neither a 'rubber stamp' nor an independent watchdog. Its ambivalence and divisions are epitomised by the wording of decisions on testing SDI outside the traditional reading of the ABM Treaty. In 1987 and again in 1988, Congress forbade funds to be obligated or expended on space-based or other mobile-based ABM systems or components; nor could funds be spent on acquiring equipment for such tests. Simultaneously, the congressmen agreed 'that nothing in this limitation was intended or could be construed to preclude SDIO or contractor *planning activities* (including studies, design activities or computer simulations) related to any development or testing of ABM systems or components including development and testing not described in the April 1987 SDIO report'.[52] In other words, Congress permitted the SDIO to prepare a break-out from the treaty.

### CONCLUSION

In an environment less benign than that in which it had been conceived, the SDI programme was consolidated. Still no single rationale for the programme was clearly defined. It was extensively criticised for being infeasible, extremely expensive and harmful to arms control. In the superpower summits, SDI struck the main discordant note. There were no extraordinary breakthroughs in SDI technologies, and the margin of technological superiority over the Soviets did not alter enough to warrant enthusiasm about reliable comprehensive defences.

Congress was divided about SDI. It annually cut the SDIO's request, but the total of funds authorised still increased each year, until FY 1990. The key to the continued success and development of SDI was the role of powerful groups which gathered around the programme. The SDI Office, the armed forces, federal research laboratories, small consultancies and large arms manufacturers all made extensive investments in SDI. They collaborated on projects, such as the Marshall Report, which advocated early deployment. The SDI Office had little disinterested, independent management advice. The SDI Advisory Committee, the Defense Science Board and the Eastport Group all contained members with a direct financial stake in the programme they were supervising.

111

Members failed to file financial disclosure statements, in breach of the Federal Advisory Committee Act.

The large SDI contractors did not sponsor a big public relations campaign for SDI. They had no need to. They already enjoyed a large de facto role in shaping the programme. Representatives of the Pentagon and SDI contractors dominated the decision-making structures on SDI: the SDI Advisory Committee, the Defense Science Board and the Eastport panel. They supervised the day-to-day running of SDI and ensured its progress through administrative channels.

It is hard to draw any firm conclusions, of the kind made by Zuckerman, about the role of scientists in shaping SDI policy during Reagan's second term. Eminent scientists from outside the weapons' laboratories criticised SDI. However, 'in-house' advice favoured SDI. The R&D institutions were pushing ahead and shaping the programme. They harboured influential supporters of SDI, notably Edward Teller and Lowell Wood, who used their position to give extremely optimistic accounts of SDI technologies to policy-makers. More general scientific bodies showed widespread scepticism of SDI, but this was seldom translated into action and there were few resignations on the issue.

None of these factors on its own provides an adequate explanation of why and how SDI was consolidated. In terms of strategic logic or technical feasibility, it is very unlikely that SDI could ever have won congressional approval. Nor were the wider political conditions uniformly favourable to SDI during Reagan's second term. To explain the consolidation of SDI, it is necessary to focus on institutional, bureaucratic and commercial factors, and the influence exercised by SDI interest groups on the making and implementation of policy. These groups were tight-knit in their collective wish to sustain SDI in the face of criticism. They were more divided by issues concerning the detailed shaping of the programme. One such issue, the controversy about early deployment and the programmatic changes thereby entailed, is the subject of the next chapter.

# 9   EARLY DEPLOYMENT?

Previous chapters have shown why SDI was consolidated and how it acquired momentum. This chapter will examine one aspect of the *shaping* of SDI, namely, the issue of early deployment. This was a bid to change the programme by reordering and accelerating short-term projects.

Some of Reagan's keenest admirers believed that his vision had been captured by the bureaucracy. A disenchanted Angelo Codevilla, formerly aide to Senator Malcolm Wallop of the 'laser lobby', charged the SDI Office with stifling the growth of strategic defence by raising performance requirements and restricting the programme to research:

> no part of it has the task, or even the opportunity, to design and develop any weapons system or any part thereof. Such things would require integration of work in all five program elements . . . Severally and jointly, the parts do not necessarily have any connection with the reality of weaponry . . . SDI is in effect a decision to postpone until the 1990s any serious consideration of what, if anything, the United States shall do to prevent Soviet missiles, once launched, from landing in the US.[1]

In late 1986, important SDI factions started to urge deployment of SDI, with an early Initial Operating Capability (IOC) for a partial defence, to be followed by a fuller system. In the short term and for practical purposes SDI would become a defence of some 'point' sites, rather than being what Reagan envisaged, a comprehensive protection for the nation.

Some supporters of an early IOC were motivated by anxiety about the future of SDI after the Reagan presidency. They wanted to hurry SDI into the lucrative procurement phase, to expand the programme and cement it institutionally. This prospect alarmed the arms control community, for an early IOC would consolidate the SDI programme and break the ABM Treaty. A letter to President Reagan on 1 October 1986 called for 'employment in the very near term of the most modern

113

defensive means'. It was signed by key SDI supporters, including Edward Teller, Lowell Wood and senior congressmen:

> We believe that imperfect but significant defensive options have already been laid before the American leadership by the SDI, and that they must not only be continued toward perfection but also prudently exercised, while the political will to do so undeniably exists.[2]

Later in October, the Heritage Foundation proposed that, over the following five years, 100 upgraded missile interceptors should be deployed, at an estimated cost of $3.5 billion. The Heritage proposal would primarily have benefited Lockheed, the holder of the ERIS missile interceptor contract. Lockheed made its own proposal for an early Initial Operating Capability (IOC). If the go-ahead were given to deploy 100 ERIS interceptors, Lockheed would have reopened the former Safeguard site at Grand Forks; upgraded the ground-based radar there for early warning and battle management purposes; and accelerated work on its Functional Test Vehicle (FTV), to develop ground-launched, non-nuclear interceptors.[3]

Also in October 1986, High Frontier published its own plan, also involving ERIS interceptors. Daniel Graham lobbied Capitol Hill, calling for a new Strategic Defense Development and Deployment (SD³).[4] It added a post-boost defence layer with space-based kinetic kill weapons. High Frontier put the cost at $30 billion over seven and a half years.

In December 1986, the George C. Marshall Institute proposed a more ambitious deployment of 13,000 ground-based interceptors (10,000 ERIS and 3,000 HEDI) and 11,000 space-based interceptors (SBKKVs). Their bullish report, 'Missile Defense in the 1990s', put the cost for an IOC at $54 billion and for Full Operating Capability (FOC) at $121 billion over seven years.[5] Deployment of the first layer could start in 1992 and of the three-layer defence in 1994.[6] The panellists 'calculated' effectiveness at 'greater than 90%'.[7] Marginal cost ratios could favour the defence (by roughly 2:1 in the space-based and HEDI layers).[8] Battle management requirements would be 'substantial but not stressing'. Finally, there were always Soviet ABM activities which were described in intelligence reports as 'ominous'.

The Press reported that a classified 1987 joint chiefs of staff (JCS) document had called for near-term deployment of a system to stop about 30 per cent of Soviet warheads. The four-page document reportedly justified the partial system as a further deterrent to Soviet attack. A review of SDI by the Defense Acquisition Board in 1987 recommended that six elements of the initial (Phase 1) system move into the Milestone 1 demonstration and validation phase. Normally speaking, the next phase would be full-scale development (FSD), but with SDI this was complicated by the need for tests in space, which might infringe the ABM Treaty.

The call for an early IOC commanded support from senior officials. Weinberger hinted at such a system in testimony to the Senate Armed Services Committee on 12 January 1987. Two days later, the Attorney-General, Edwin Meese III, urged early deployment of SDI, 'so it will be in place and not tampered with by future Administrations'.[9] Weinberger returned to the theme in a speech at Colorado Springs on 22 January 1987:

> Today, we may be nearing the day when decisions about deployment of the first phase can be made. We are now seeing opportunities for earlier deployment of the first phase of strategic defense than we previously thought possible . . . our bags are packed.[10]

Weinberger insisted, however, that any near-term deployment must be 'an integral first phase of our whole tiered defense'. It seems that he desired a limited defence rather than 'a point defense, as some have urged, to protect missile fields'.[11] The reasons for this seem to be a mix of military, political and programmatic considerations. According to Weinberger's Colorado speech:

> An early deployment of defensive components that protected only some military assets and was not part of a global defence, would weaken our SDI program and rob us of limited resources. Phase 1, whatever form it takes, must be one piece of the entire system that provides a thoroughly reliable defense for the free world.[12]

The projected cost of a Phase 1 deployment was a major criterion in deciding whether the programme would actually be funded. It was therefore a crucial political issue. There was a huge degree of uncertainty in the 'guesstimate', since a strategic defence system could take many forms and no one can safely predict Soviet responses, technological surprise, the extent of espionage, and so on. This leaves plenty of scope for 'creative accountancy'. The historical record is that successful programme managers proffer an initial bid which grossly underestimates costs. Costs can then be revised upwards once Congress has committed funds, on the grounds that Congress is unlikely to axe a programme once it has been started.

In September 1988, the SDIO reduced its estimate by 40 per cent, creating a new figure of $69.1 billion: not much more than other programmes such as the Advanced Tactical Fighter (ATF) and the B-2 Bomber. It produced this remarkable reduction by cutting the proposed

Table 9.1. *Cost estimates for a Phase 1 Strategic Defense System*

| Date | Estimate ($bn) | Source of estimate |
|------|----------------|--------------------|
| March 1987 | 40–60 | Abrahamson |
| September 1987 | 70–100 | Abrahamson |
| February 1988 | 75–150 | Abrahamson |
| June 1988 | 115.4 | SDIO |
| September 1988 | 69.1 | SDIO |

number of weapons. Space-Based Interceptors (SBIs) were reduced by 51 per cent and the Ground-Based Surveillance and Tracking Systems (GSTS) by 42 per cent.[13] Reductions in technical capacity and the use of different cost models were said to justify these hefty cuts. The General Accounting Office pointed out that the $69 billion estimate would rise by $20 billion to allow for inflation, and by $2.8 billion annually for operating expenses.

An early IOC would be a good staging post to a fuller defensive system. The criteria for a partial SDS were less demanding, in that it would rely less on space-based elements (to intercept enemy missiles whilst still in the boost phase of their flight) and the software task would also be less ambitious. It was easy for critics to show that a 'full' SDS would be vulnerable: less easy to argue that a partial SDS might not stop some missiles. By redefining the goal of an SDS, the SDI Office could at least make the programme look more technologically feasible.

Proponents of an early IOC had to acknowledge that a partial system held no hope for making nuclear weapons and deterrence strategy obsolete. In place of a secure area defence, they adduced an array of strategic arguments. Lockheed's manager of the ERIS asserted that a 'fast track' decision offered 'collateral safety' or 'preferential defence', meaning that 'a small number of ERIS interceptors can be used preferentially to defend a specific area of the United States – either for population defense or to protect the deployment routes of Midgetman or the rail-mobile MX system as examples'.[14] The Lockheed manager also proposed that a near-term deployment would be an insurance against accidental launch and rogue attack. He said that 'the most important thing' would be to provide infrastructure, learning and operational experience: 'if you had this system in place, had the industrial base, I think then that you are not that far away from being able to do something in a real "war-fighting" standpoint'.[15] Finally, as ever, a near-term deployment would be 'a hedge for a breakout'.[16] Although the Administration increasingly justified SDI as a response to the 'Red Shield' of Soviet military space preparations, supporters of an early IOC made little attempt to substantiate their case in terms of a specific Soviet programme.

If deterrence is taken to mean 'deterrence by denial', even a faulty defence would remove an attacker's certainty of destroying a target and force the attacker to dedicate several warheads to each target. However, a deployment consistent with the ABM Treaty of 100 interceptors around Washington, D.C. and North Dakota would be of only marginal importance to a potential aggressor. Nor would a wider deployment have much effect on an enemy's plans to attack. There is already a massive realm of uncertainty and risk in any planned nuclear attack. Leaving aside factors such as the international opprobrium which the USSR would incur, the USA could counter-attack with any configuration of its arsenal of more than 10,000 nuclear warheads and wreak havoc far beyond that of the Second World War. Many of the US missiles are submarine based and virtually invulnerable. A partial SDI programme would involve a huge price for a small (and uncertain) amount of increased Soviet uncertainty. Moreover, deployment of BMD would jeopardise the measure of predictability and confidence central to strategic stability. A side which deployed BMD would probably also have a substantial ASAT capability which would threaten the reconnaissance, verification and communication satellites of the other. To the extent that the threatened party (or perhaps both parties) felt vulnerable to a 'blinding' first strike, they would have an incentive to 'go first' in a crisis.[17] As well as decreasing crisis stability, a partial BMD might be seen as backing up a pre-emptive strike capability, since it could be used to 'mop up' any remaining enemy warheads after a first strike.

SDI contractors had a demonstrable interest in hurrying the programme to a point of no return: beyond the R&D phase and into full-scale procurement, where the large profits are reaped. An R&D programme worth some $16 billion over five years could metamorphose into the largest strategic mission ever – one to the value of $1,000 billion, by some accounts. The longer deployment was delayed, the greater the risk that public support would collapse. A Democrat president might curtail, or even cancel, Reagan's project. The programme would be safer if it were already 'up and running', gathering an ever larger constituency of dependants.

In their letter to the President, Edward Teller, Lowell Wood, Jack Kemp and other supporters of early deployment expressed their anxiety about domestic politics and programmatic momentum:

> We are deeply concerned that a SDI Program which has no definite consequence for defense of America within the next ten years will not be politically sustainable.[18]

The SDIP's acting chief scientist was blunt in his assessment:

> Like it or not, we see a political reality staring us in the face. If we don't come up with something specific, people are not going to let us play in the sandbox for ten years.[19]

To the extent that an early IOC would increase the programme's budget, nearly all SDI contractors would gain from it. Proportionately, more would go to large companies with established assembly lines and a proven record in supplying the Pentagon. These corporations would benefit directly from 'bending tin'. Their work might well generate a 'spin-off' of further problems and unforeseen challenges, so that the smaller research corporations, the 'beltway bandits', could also expect to do well. Thus the entire BMD constituency could benefit and remain united.

Lockheed, suppliers of ERIS and the probable main beneficiary of an early IOC, lobbied openly for such a decision, as mentioned above. Lockheed also supply BSTS, a component of an early IOC Strategic Defense System (SDS). Other beneficiaries would include McDonnell Douglas (HEDI), Boeing (AOS), LTV (ER-HIT), Grumman (BSTS), Raytheon (TIR) and Hughes/General Motors (IR sensors).

The motive to push for a rapid IOC decision clearly existed: the evidence of lobbying is less plentiful. There are obvious reasons why this should be so. A partial system, the antithesis of what the President had promised, would come as a disappointing anticlimax to swollen public expectations. It would be easy prey to critics and hard to push through Congress. Whilst rendering nuclear weapons obsolete was crusading material, a leaky 'umbrella' was not. It is therefore not surprising that most advocates of an early IOC did not run a high-profile public campaign. Well-placed telephone calls would be more appropriate than full-page advertisements in the national papers. In so far as the media reported the issue of early Initial Operating Capability, they were responding to the alarm of the arms control community as much as the desires of early IOC advocates.

Ground-based terminal defence would have a central role in early IOC and in 'point defence' of missile silos. This would benefit the army, for the Strategic Defense Command at Huntsville had long been researching these concepts. Rapid budget growth in this area might reduce funds for space-based DEW in the short term. The air force, which dominates space-based BMD, might win proportionately less for some years. However, SDI would have indubitably arrived at deployment phase. Research on space-based weapons would continue and there would be more chance of their being deployed in the longer term.

No evidence suggests that any one Service was pushing strongly against the others in favour of an early IOC. Since a limited IOC did not extend the promise of a world free of nuclear weapons, it may have appeared less embarrassing to the Services, whose traditional deterrent or counter-force role was theoretically jeopardised by the Utopian rhetoric of the early SDI. Some groups may have been concerned that if SDI funds were increased for an early deployment, whilst the overall Pentagon budget levelled off, other programmes might have to be curtailed. However, that was a long-term anxiety, not an immediate problem. In so far as an early IOC furthered SDI, the Services as a whole would be reasonably contented at the prospect.

Although it looked in 1986 and early 1987 as if the SDI Office might soon win official endorsement for the early deployment of a Strategic Defense System, this did not occur – for several reasons. Firstly, technologies did not mature as fast as SDI supporters had hoped:

> Yesterday we were pursuing this with the head guy in the Pentagon for C[3]I and we were told yesterday that there is absolutely no way that we can provide the command and control to support any kind of an early deployment. Even if we had the dollars, we were technology limited in the C[3]I area. The one that I feel would give SDI a black eye is a premature deployment where we spent $3, $4, $5, $10 billion and had something that was relatively easy to counter.[20]

Secondly, congressmen were wary of premature deployment of SDI. By their careful attention to the issue, they discouraged covert plans for an early IOC or a fait accompli.[21] Liberals, arms control supporters and the original negotiators of the ABM Treaty put up a spirited defence of the traditional, restrictive reading. Furthermore, the international and domestic political climate was turning against new military adventures.

The SDIO did not in the 1980s win official endorsement to build an early IOC Strategic Defense System. None the less, rumours abounded on Capitol Hill that a secret 'black' programme was investigating near-term deployment architectures. Certainly the SDIO did modify the programme to encourage the near-term option. This was apparent in a number of changes made in late 1986 to the FY 1987 SDI budget.[22] The alterations were ordered by Lt-Gen. Abrahamson, and it is reasonable to suppose that Weinberger (and perhaps the President) were aware of their implications.

119

The main change in this and subsequent years was that money was deducted from the budget for essentially far-term Directed Energy Weapons (DEW). Funding for Kinetic Energy Weapons (KEW), which could be built and deployed much sooner, increased. The restricted 'Program Descriptive Summaries' explained that 'milestone changes' in DEW and KEW 'reflect fact-of-life slippages resulting from the FY 1987 budget reductions and from a change of relative emphasis away from countering the responsive threat and to support early deployment options'.[23]

There were also cuts to the Innovative Science and Technology (IS&T) directorate, which engaged in longer-term research. The original aim was that IS&T should have 3 per cent of SDI funds. But in FY 1989, Abrahamson cut the IS&T budget from $111 million to $76 million, which was less than 2 per cent of the SDI budget.[24] The SDIO strived to reduce the estimates for the programme, pressurising contractors to lower their costs. The manager of the ERIS programme described Lockheed's proposed system as 'only a very cheap – if I can use that word – version of what HOE [Homing Overlay Experiment] was. The name of the game is to make it affordable.'[25]

## CONCLUSION

The issue of an early IOC was crucial to the future of SDI. Early deployment was proposed by a number of SDI supporters, principally Lockheed, the Heritage Foundation, the Marshall Institute and High Frontier. The SDI Office made several reorganisations consistent with an attempt to hasten deployment. Funds were switched away from long-term research and into short-term demonstration and development.

A limited defence of the kind envisaged for an early IOC would have provided operational experience for a fuller system. It would have increased an attacker's uncertainty, though to a questionable degree and at a high price. A partial defence was also justified as an insurance against the possibility of an accidental or 'rogue' attack. These potential benefits had to be weighed against the negative implications for the ABM Treaty and for arms race stability. Overall, the strategic arguments for an early IOC were less than compelling. The idea also had less public appeal than Reagan's original vision.

The motivation for an early IOC Strategic Defense System was mainly political, programmatic, ideological and financial. An early IOC would have set the production lines running and helped to cement or institutionalise the programme. Both the army and the air force would stand to gain. Although much less demanding than in a full system, technical specifications were still a major reason for the failure to achieve an early deployment. In particular, the problem of command and control remained intractable for even a partial system.

The arms control community and critics of SDI staunchly opposed early IOC and defended the traditional reading of the ABM Treaty. The vigilance of Congress foiled premature deployment, whilst the growing mood of détente increased the political cost of an early, unilateral SDI deployment to unacceptable levels. That said, the SDI Office was perhaps the ultimate victor, in that it has continued in the 1990s to shift funds towards early options. In its funding request for FY 1991, funding for near-term technologies represented 34 per cent real growth over the previous year, whilst funding for far-term technologies was only 13 per cent real growth.[26] GPALS, announced in early 1991, could be seen as a realisation and culmination of proposals for early IOC. It envisages early IOC dates in the first half of the 1990s for theatre defence elements: Patriot, the Extended Range Interceptor (ERINT), the Arrow ATBM and the Theater High Altitude Area Defense (THAAD), being developed by the army. Deployment against long-range strategic ballistic missiles is then due to be phased in during the late 1990s.[27] Although the idea of countering limited strikes from the Third World differs from SDI, in programmatic terms the new plan is very much in line with calls in the latter part of the 1980s for an early IOC.

# PART 4
# CONTEXTS AND CONDITIONS

# 10 EUROPE

The original plan for SDI offered nothing specific to the Allies. How, then, should they react? One response, which came to prominence in late 1985, was for a programme to provide SDI-type capabilities for Western Europe: a European Defence Initiative (EDI). More detailed and less ambitious proposals for Anti-Tactical Ballistic Missiles (ATBMs) and Extended Air Defense (EAD) also won considerable support. As these ideas gathered momentum in early 1986, it looked as if NATO might embark on a major new programme to parallel SDI.[1] In examining European responses to SDI – including EDI, ATBMs and EAD – this chapter seeks also to explore and illuminate the course of SDI. The EDI subplot reflects and refracts the themes of the main history.

The immediate reaction in Western Europe to Reagan's speech of 23 March 1983 was one of surprise, falling short of consternation. Many suspected it was an electoral ploy or a passing presidential whim. The West German Defence Minister, Manfred Worner, later the main proponent of EDI, dismissed SDI at the time as 'absolute Zukunfts-musik': pie in the sky. Only after the reports of the SDI 'advisory panels' and Reagan's re-election (November 1984), when it became clear that BMD was going to remain a major policy issue, was there some deep alarm.

The President had not consulted with the Allies about the ramifications for East–West relations and arms control. His insistence that the programme was intended to eliminate nuclear weapons not only appeared to rebut the declared basis for deterrence, 'flexible response', and for the cruise missiles and Pershing II, which the Allied governments were still trying to persuade their public to accept, but also seemed to impugn the rationales for British and French nuclear forces. Even the British government, proud of its 'special relationship' with the US, offered only qualified support. In December 1984, Mrs Thatcher persuaded Reagan to tone down the radical appearance of SDI with the 'Camp David Accords', which stated that: (1) the aim of SDI is to maintain balance, not to achieve superiority over the Soviets; (2) in light of treaty obligations, deployment of SDI would be a matter of negotiation; (3) the aim was to enhance, not undercut, deterrence; (4) negotiations should continue, aimed at reducing offensive weapons of both sides.

The SDI Office desired access to some European technologies, as well as the political endorsement implied by European participation. In March 1985, Weinberger therefore invited eighteen Allied nations to perform SDI work:[2] that is, to compete with US firms for the less sensitive contracts.[3] To establish the terms under which firms in Allied nations could perform SDI contracts, the SDI Office sought to negotiate Memoranda of Understanding (MoUs).

West German businesses, with expertise in fibre optics, optical sensors, space technology and high-frequency technology for radar and signal processing, were well placed to further some SDI projects. The large arms manufacturers – Sperry, Messerschmitt-Bölkow-Blohm and Dornier Systems – could all participate. The main French centres of excellence were in Aerospatiale and Thomson CSF. British companies with SDI potential included British Aerospace, Short Brothers, Plessey, Racal, Thorn EMI, Royal Ordnance PLC, Rolls-Royce and GEC-Marconi. Contracts could be awarded, it was hoped, to government research laboratories: the UK Atomic Energy Authority at Culham, the Atomic Weapons Research Establishment at Aldermaston,[4] the Royal Signals and Radar Establishment at Malvern, the Royal Armaments Research and Development Establishment near Sevenoaks and the Royal Aeronautical Establishment at Farnborough.[5]

Although many in European military circles were wary of SDI and the disruption it might entail, they believed it could produce significant military spin-offs, as noted by one West German arms magazine. 'In particular this will be the case in the development of sensors, information technology and lasers. Taken together the military benefits from the SDI research programme will advance conventional military technologies in such a way that new, revolutionary weapons systems will result.'[6]

Apart from strategic and political matters, the Allies also had to weigh the economic and technological consequences of joining SDI. Some thought SDI offered little to civilian industry: Europe would never play a lead role and would reap little benefit. SDI could enable the US to 'hoover' promising technologies out of Europe, classify them as secret and then exploit their commercial potential. According to this view, which prevailed in Paris at least until 1986, Europe should spurn SDI in favour of indigenous technological initiatives.[7]

Others thought SDI could produce major breakthroughs and hoped to use SDI funds to improve their own technology base.[8] They wanted to join in, having negotiated safeguards on intellectual copyright, patent rights and commercial spin-off.[9] This approach prevailed in Bonn and London.

There were major barriers to European participation in the SDI programme.[10] First, the ABM Treaty forbids each party to transfer to other states 'ABM systems or their components' and 'technical descriptions or blue-prints specially worked out for the construction of ABM systems and their components limited by the Treaty'.[11] Second, the Pentagon follows a 'Buy American' policy. Federal Acquisition Regulations prohibit R&D contracts with foreign entities if a US source is equally competent and less expensive.[12] The Defense Appropriations Acts for 1986 and 1987 prohibited set-asides for foreign firms, ordering that SDI funds must go to US firms unless that would harm research. US laws ensured that the US would retain unlimited rights to information provided by foreign contractors. According to the Memoranda of Understanding on SDI, which the US signed with individual Allies, the USA is guaranteed to receive 'the royalty-free rights to use, duplicate or disclose this information, in whole or in part, in any manner and for any purpose'.[13] Foreign contractors' rights to use the results of their SDI research, or take out patents, depend on 'security considerations' as defined by the US.

The Allies' responses were complicated by the emergence of the 'European Defense Initiative' (EDI): plans for a European counterpart to SDI, which would defend Europe against fighter aircraft, cruise missiles and short- and intermediate-range nuclear weapons, especially the SS-21, SS-22 and SS-23.[14] It would use upgraded technologies for air defence, Surface to Air Missiles (SAMs), a modernised Patriot missile, and Anti-Tactical Ballistic Missiles (ATBMs). It might also involve more exotic technologies, directed energy weapons and satellite-based remote sensing. The idea was proposed in September 1985 by the West German Defence Minister, Manfred Worner, who discussed it with other NATO defence ministers at the end of the year.[15]

By April 1986, Worner had modified his position.[16] Instead of space-based elements and a separate BMD, he called for non-nuclear Anti-Tactical Ballistic Missiles (ATBMs) and Extended Air Defense (EAD), The idea of EDI, a true counterpart to SDI, complete with ground-based Directed Energy Weapons (DEW) and space-based or pop-up satellites and mirrors, then became a more marginal concern, linked to 'High Frontier Europa'.[17] The sponsors of EDI never agreed on a specific architecture or cost estimate. The idea was shaped by politics and presentation. It was a strategic political initiative which, like SDI, presented diverse opportunities to different interest groups.

Some of SDI's original supporters saw EDI as their chance to lock otherwise reluctant Allies into the US programme, so presenting a united front at Geneva and starting to integrate space and air operations for Europe and the USA. Hard-liners thought that EDI would strengthen the Alliance in a military sense, by exploiting the West's comparative advantage in high technology.[18] It offered some potential for more mundane improvements in alliance-wide air defence, and it complemented the campaign to increase 'survivability'. Atlanticists hoped that divisions about the deployment of 'Euromissiles' and Star Wars might be healed by a new programme to unite Europeans and Americans. A number of right-wing Germans thought EDI would strengthen the Bundeswehr and provide US endorsement for West German rearmament.[19] EDI could also appeal to pro-Europeans who wanted the military, political and industrial integration of Europe, as distinct from the US. This group saw European co-operation and self-determination in strategic affairs and procurement as a virtue in itself. EDI might be one of a series of measures to defend the European technology base.

Supporters of EDI also supported ATBMs, since these were a component of EDI. A campaign for ATBMs gathered pace within NATO through 1985 and 1986, winning the support of the US Secretary of Defense Caspar Weinberger, the West German Defence Minister Manfred Worner, NATO Supreme Allied Commander General Rogers, and the Konrad Adenauer Foundation.[20]

The case posited for ATBMs was that Soviet medium-range missiles (SS-20, SS-21, SS-23, SS-23) might attack key NATO targets with conventional or chemical warheads. This would force NATO to respond with *nuclear* weapons, unless it had ATBMs to destroy the Soviet missiles. Even some ATBMs would raise the cost and uncertainty of a Soviet attack and therefore contribute to deterrence. ATBM was also presented as a response to equivalent Soviet efforts. The Soviets had deployed two new surface-to-air missiles, the SA-10 and the SA-12, which might be allocated for the defence of point sites against cruise missiles and, perhaps, Short-Range Ballistic Missiles (SRBMs). The Pentagon reported that the SA-12 might be able to intercept Lance and Pershing missiles, although no definite evidence to support this was offered in public and independent analysts were sceptical.[21]

Proposals for ATBMs won more support than EDI because they were both technologically and financially more viable. Whereas EDI envisaged grandiose concepts to intercept missiles in the boost phase,

ATBMs involved already existing terminal and midcourse technologies. Confidence in ATBMs was boosted by the highly publicised intercept of a Lance surface-to-surface missile by the army's Patriot air defence system in September 1986.[22] Whilst EDI was clearly associated with 'Star Wars', an object of suspicion in Europe, ATBM could pass as an unrelated programme justified in its own right, or as an extension of the INF modernisation, plus being politically more saleable as 'defensive'.

ATBMs could also contribute to established military missions, such as defence of command and control posts and airports. Mobile versions might defend fronts or armies on the move. The research would improve Tactical Ballistic Missile (TBM) offences and fit into the Counter-Air '90 programme, which aims to improve NATO capabilities for ATBMs, air defences, 'survivability', offensive counter-air operations and (pre-emptive) attacks on Soviet missile launchers and airfields.[23] Furthermore, ATBMs would complement programmes related to Counter-Air '90, notably the Joint Surveillance and Target Acquisition Radar System (JSTARS), an airborne radar to detect targets at stand-off ranges and direct attacks at them: and the joint Tactical Missile System for air-launched stand-off weapons. These benefits of ATBMs made the idea popular in NATO circles.[24] ATBM seemed a way of delivering something concrete from the otherwise nebulous SDI.

In the USA, some SDI supporters wanted ATBMs as a staging post to a fuller Strategic Defense System. The Hoffman Report of 1983 had already identified ATM as an 'intermediate option', which could be pursued 'within ABM Treaty constraints', combining advanced midcourse and terminal components. This 'should reduce Allied anxieties that our increased emphasis on defences might indicate a weakening of our commitment to the defences of Europe'.[25] ATBM also offered a chance to circumvent the ABM Treaty, which forbids the signatories to hand over to other states technical descriptions or blueprints of ABM systems. But the text refers only to *strategic* missiles, not Anti-*Tactical* Ballistic Missiles (ATBMs).[26] Since there is an approximately 60 per cent overlap between ABM and ATBM R&D, the SDIO might test even a multi-layered system in the guise of an ATBM.

Successful ATBM demonstrations would reinforce public faith in the feasibility of SDI. A European programme would help US institutions with their 'rich reservoir of experience' in the area.[27] Advice given on ATM and ATBMs was not wholly disinterested. AT&T Bell Laboratories produced a report for the Pentagon called *ATM Independent Assessment*, which, perhaps not surprisingly, found in favour of ATMs. AT&T had $9.463 million in SDI contracts by August 1988.

Subcontractors for the report included Arvin/Calspan ($580,000) and BDM Corporation ($350,000). All these considerations weighed with Congress. In 1985, the Senate ordered the SDIO to work with the DoD and 'in close coordination with our allies' to improve ATBMs.[28] In 1986, Congress directed that $50 million from the SDI budget should be dedicated to ATBMs 'with a view towards deployment in the early 1990s'.[29] In the summer of 1986, the Pentagon established an 'ATM steering committee' to study options for European defence.[30]

For the Allies, ATBM offered a way of consolidating existing research. A large number of European contracts (and most British ones) for SDI were related to ATBM studies.[31] The German arms industry, in particular, had been working hard on ATBMs, led by Messerschmitt-Bölkow-Blohm. The French were designing an advanced surface-to-air system called Aster, as anti-aircraft and ATM, to provide site defence for the *force de frappe*. Proposals for a Europe-wide ATBM would be an opportunity to expand Aster, make economies of scale and foster a genuinely European effort.[32] The French invited the Germans to participate. Britain was also interested, thinking that Aster could defend airfields or be a follow-on to the Seawolf as a defence of ships.[33] In addition, ATBM offered an entrée into the new SDI market.

In sum, ATBMs had some tactical support from numerous factions for divergent reasons. But its adherents lacked organisation, commitment and influence. More support was garnered by proposals for Extended Air Defense (EAD), which might include ATBMs, but would focus on intercepting aircraft and bombers.[34] EAD would upgrade existing air defence systems, to enable them to deal with Short-Range Ballistic Missiles and cruise missiles. Like ATBM, EAD was proposed by Manfred Worner, the West German Defence Minister, who promoted the idea in NATO circles.[35] EAD involved no space-based elements and could be presented as a simple improvement of conventional forces, far from images of Star Wars. At the same time, EAD would benefit from some of the generic technologies developed by SDI, for sensing, target acquisition, interception and command and control.

In the mid 1980s, air defence was a major concern in NATO circles. NATO was designing a unified command and control for Allied Air Forces in Europe and its maritime approaches;[36] creating a new Command for early warning;[37] and upgrading air defences in West Germany, France and Spain.[38] France was improving the Roland short-range air defence missile and the Mistral low-level SAM. It was also building a medium-range SAM, the SA-90, which had a potential ATBM capability.[39] Britain was on the verge of a massive upgrading of UKAIR defences, intended to counter aircraft and cruise missiles, but not ballistic missiles. Some £5 billion was earmarked for an Improved United Kingdom Air Defence Ground Environment (IUKADGE), along with enhanced early warning, ground radars and Tornado F-2 interceptors.[40] A total of £2 billion was being invested in improving the Rapier low-level surface-to-air (SAM) missile.[41] Another British SAM, the Bloodhound, was also being upgraded, as well as the Seawolf mentioned above.[42]

The Patriot air defence system, deployed by the Dutch Air Force and by German and American units in West Germany, was also being upgraded. It consisted of an early warning system, command and control, and a long-range surface-to-air missile (SAM). Its surveillance radar was being modified in order to track ballistic missiles and its interceptor was being improved to destroy conventionally armed short-range missiles. It was hoped that the Patriot might acquire a limited ATBM capability against conventionally armed SS-21s and SS-23s, so as to provide limited 'point defence' of specific sites. Meanwhile, the Independent European Program Group (IEPG) was looking for a successor to the Hawk surface-to-air (SAM) missile, which might defend against cruise missiles as well as bombers.[43]

The US was also upgrading its own defences. It planned to invest $9.3 billion in Forward Area Air Defense Systems (FAADS).[44] NORAD was being modernised and there was a new line of radars called the North Warning System. The US was also deploying Over-The-Horizon Backscatter (OTH-B) radars. The Pentagon's Air Defense Initiative (ADI) was smaller and less glamorous than SDI.[45] The 1988 budget request for ADI was only $78 million. Although this is a comparatively small amount, it did involve significant changes, with some programmes being restructured,[46] and others newly started.[47] The scope of these programmes would be greatly increased by a European initiative.

All of these plans offered lucrative contracts for the European aerospace industry. Extended Air Defense (EAD) would consolidate order books well into the 1990s. It offered the opportunity of incorporating SDI-type technologies without being taken over by the SDIO. In this respect, it was an example of strategic incrementalism or of Kurth's 'follow-on imperative', as described in Chapter 1.

### THE FALL OF EDI (AND RELATED PROPOSALS)

As early as April 1986, the main proponent of EDI, Manfred Worner, distanced himself from the idea, reassured, he said, by US guarantees to consider the tactical missile threat to Europe.[48] By 1988, EDI had slipped off the agenda. There was no likelihood of a large procurement programme, though research on ATBM and EAD continued, beyond the realm of publicity. The collapse of the Warsaw Pact in 1989 made it unlikely that NATO would embark on an ATBM initiative.

The failure of EDI was to some degree inscribed in its very inception. The proposals for EDI lagged two years behind SDI. In that time, wider conditions became much less favourable to a new weapons programme. Had EDI been proposed in 1980, when NATO budgets were due to grow at 3 per cent per annum in real terms, or even 1983, it might have fared better. But by 1986, when EDI was squarely on the agenda, East–West relations had greatly improved and NATO defence budgets had levelled off.

By late 1986, the superpowers were approaching agreement on banning intermediate-range nuclear forces in Europe. This would reduce the threat on which the strategic case for ATBMs had been predicated. At the talks on Mutual and Balanced Force Reduction (MBFR), the Soviets also proposed to limit Short-Range Ballistic Missiles (SRBMs) with a range of up to 1,000 km and to withdraw SRBMs from East Germany and Czechoslovakia. The INF Treaty (December 1987) freed Europe of all land-based intermediate-range nuclear missiles with ranges from 500 to 5,500 km. The very missiles ATBM was supposed to counter – Soviet short- and intermediate-range nuclear forces, especially the SS-20 and SS-23 missiles – were now to be eliminated. The 'double zero' solution re-established the credibility of arms control. Thereafter, the politics of the 'third zero' made it politically counter-productive to play up the threat of SS-22s. If they were so dangerous, the new prospects for arms control suggested that they should be negotiated away.

The scientific debate about EDI revealed the immense technical difficulties of the project. A full-scale EDI would have all of the problems of SDI: prohibitive cost, susceptibility to counter-measures (underflying, overwhelming, spoofing and decoys), vulnerability of space-based elements and need for faultless software. These problems would be compounded by the short flight times of missiles before reaching their target. The Soviets would have a wide choice of counter-measures: stealth technology, decoys, depressed trajectories (to shorten flight time), elevated trajectories (to increase the region to be searched), use of stand-off missiles or pre-emptive attacks on early warning sensors.

The strategic consensus which emerged from the ATBM debate was that the objectives of an ATBM – to protect key NATO installations – would be better met by other measures: dispersal of nuclear weapons and storage sites, mobile air defences, alternative runways, the ability to repair air strips quickly, and hardening of command installations, aeroplane hangars and munitions bunkers.

The armed forces were less than enthusiastic about EDI and the radical disruption to traditional roles which it would entail. A new EDI budget might threaten other commitments to, for example, first-echelon lead forces and short-range targeting. Nor was there any powerful European military space bureaucracy to lobby for a European space war-fighting capability.

The elements of Extended Air Defense (EAD), however, were compatible with established military roles. Improved air defence would not complicate traditional procedures. Airborne Early Warning (AEW) might enhance strategic reconnaissance, targeting for 'deep strikes', and monitoring of enemy air activity and Electronic Intelligence (Elint). Research into improved air defences could contribute to the Counter-Air '90 programme, designed to improve air defences, ATBMs, and capabilities for offensive counter-air operations and (pre-emptive) attacks on missile launchers and airfields.[49] It could also complement the doctrines of Follow-On Forces Attack (FO/FA), Air–Land Battle and Deep Strike, as well as other projects for 'interdicting' Soviet launchers before they can fire.[50] Perhaps for these reasons, European air defences continued to be upgraded, as planned before the EAD debate. This did not constitute, and was not presented as, a major initiative, parallel to SDI.

At the political level, EDI never commanded sufficient loyalty. SDI supporters in the US were preoccupied with establishing the programme in their own country. Plans to protect the Continental United States were ambitious enough without adding a European dimension. Once formal European support had been achieved through Memoranda of Understanding, the need to push EDI fell away for US supporters of SDI. It became clear to Atlanticists in Europe that EDI was a poor form of Alliance management, likely to divide NATO. Most European policy-makers remained committed to the ABM Treaty, believing that it symbolised the validity of arms control, restrained the arms race in space and guaranteed that British and French nuclear forces could strike Moscow. Centrists noted that ATBMs would not replace aircraft, missiles or any other offensive forces. They would merely supplement them.

EDI could consume enormous resources in an area of relatively little commercial spin-off. It would mean accepting as the ground for competition the very areas where the US excelled: advanced BMD and space technology. By contrast, other initiatives, especially EEC ones, offered definite European control. The Airbus consortium was challenging US dominance in manufacturing civilian aircraft.[51] Space exploration could be carried out through collaborative ventures with the United States and the Soviet Union, or through the European space programme.[52] Other EEC projects, which could compete with SDI and provide more direct commercial benefit, included ESPRIT, BRITE, RACE, SPRINT, and BRAIN.[53]

The Eureka programme, established in 1985, co-ordinated projects in information technology and telecommunications, robotics, materials, advanced manufacturing, biotechnology, marine technology and lasers.[54] The French promoted Eureka first as an alternative, then as a supplement, to SDI. It was a form of damage limitation which sought to stem the 'brain drain' to the USA and 'create a sort of common co-ordinated technological front'.[55] By 1986, Eureka, funded at £1.4 billion,[56] and other EEC projects were a serious alternative source of R&D funds to military programmes such as ATBM. They undercut the rationale that military technology would produce significant spin-off.

The main differences between EDI and SDI, which explain why the one has withered while the other still flourishes, may now be summarised. SDI was steadfastly backed by President Reagan and the White House. It was announced and established, whilst EDI was merely proposed and debated. The challenges to EDI were more daunting than those to SDI, for the former required close Alliance co-operation, in the face of firm opposition from some NATO members.

The US interest in EDI was quite transient. Apart from some technological benefits, EDI offered opportunities for alliance management with respect to SDI and a means of gaining Alliance support to bolster the authority of the SDI Office in Congress. Once this was achieved, US interest in EDI faded. The advocates of EDI and ATBM lacked both power and staying power. They failed to persuade their governments to provide the necessary funds and they were too easily marginalised and fragmented by the changing political climate.

'Perfect defence', 'space shields' and 'making America lead in space' were all tailor-made for the ten-second sound bite. In comparison, the esoteric discourse in which EDI was presented offered nothing to the public. Whilst the Right held sway in the US, with overt antagonism towards the Soviets, the electoral consensus in Europe was more social-democratic, with greater commitment to arms control, dialogue and the ABM Treaty.

SDI benefited from the 'Pentagon system' which, in the absence of a civilian industrial technology policy, subsidises advanced research in the US. The spin-off argument was less compelling in Europe, since commercial progress could be made more efficiently through direct

Table 10.1. *Foreign contractors for SDI by 1991*

| Country | Value ($m.) |
| --- | --- |
| Israel | 218.73[a] |
| United Kingdom | 92.06 |
| West Germany | 74.55 |
| Netherlands | 22.24[b] |
| Italy | 14.84 |
| France | 13.00 |
| Canada | 7.43 |
| Japan | 3.83 |
| Belgium | 0.30 |
| Denmark | 0.03 |
| TOTAL | 447.01 |

*Notes:*
[a]Includes $47.1 million contribution by Israel.
[b]Includes $7.0 million contribution by the Netherlands.
*Source:* 'Status of Allied Contracts', SDIO viewgraph (March 1991).

investment in civilian projects. In the States, a steady BMD research programme had continued since the 1950s. Strategic defence enjoyed firm support from a well-entrenched infrastructure: Space Command, sections of the army and air force, federal laboratories and corporate contractors. EDI lacked this solid foundation. It was, in the final analysis, a strategic concept which offered political benefits but lacked a sound material or financial base.

Whilst EDI failed, SDI slowly won tacit, limited European endorsement. Six allied states expressly ruled out a formal agreement on SDI.[57] Some of these, however, were keen for industry to participate on a nongovernmental basis. By the end of 1989, none of the European Allies had won the large amounts quoted in 1985 and 1986, when the MoUs were being negotiated. In fact they had won just under $303 million.[58] Israel had won $142 million in SDI contracts, over twice the amount won by West Germany, the next largest foreign SDI contractor. Israel's funds are to flight test and manufacture the Arrow ATBM, to counter Short-Range Ballistic Missiles.[59]

The British had won barely 4 per cent of the $1.5 billion hoped for by the then Secretary of State for Defence when the UK signed its Memorandum of Understanding (MoU). Although the Ministry of Defence established an SDI Participation Office,[60] commercial interest declined. In 1987 a symposium for UK defence contractors met with indifference. 'Despite a very comprehensive programme, some expert speakers and a Cabinet minister as guest of honour, we did not attract a single delegate from industry and had to cancel the event.'[61]

In early 1991, the picture was much the same. Overall, the Allies had won contracts worth just under $400 million.[62] The countries which did participate in SDI helped to endorse a concept which they disliked. However, as participants, they argued that they had more influence to steer the programme to appropriate goals; and they gained a chance to learn of SDI advances. For the British in particular, SDI represented a cheap way to keep abreast of advanced military and space technologies. Whether the Europeans or Americans gained some overall advantage over the other is hard to assess.

Europeans are not likely to win substantial contracts in further SDI work. The British, with their SDI Participation Office in the MoD, may be best positioned to win funds if SDI moves into procurement phase. The German Defence Ministry maintained interest in ATBMs and EAD, in the belief that technical progress would revive the issue of procurement in the mid 1990s: a prospect inimical to the German Foreign Ministry.[63]

## CONCLUSION

By 1991, the allied nations had won just under $400 million in SDI contracts, a token figure in terms of international trade and far less than some had initially expected. For the US Administration, however, this could be seen as 'value for money', since, as well as providing some useful R&D work, it precipitated political endorsement of SDI by the Allies.

Ambitious plans for EDI or ATBMs never materialised. As East–West relations improved, the strategic threat on which the call for ATBMs was predicated receded. The INF Treaty and the renaissance of arms control increased the domestic political cost of embarking on a major military programme in this area. The changes in Gorbachev's Russia undermined the case that Europe had somehow to imitate or emulate SDI. European policy-makers continued to respect the ABM Treaty, and EEC high-technology initiatives provided a civilian alternative to SDI research. The European armed forces could achieve their defensive objectives through cheaper 'passive' means, such as hardening runways and dispersing targets. There was no powerful Space Command to push EDI in Europe, or a charismatic president to sell the idea. Whilst modest efforts at improved air defence continued in Europe, and SDI consolidated itself in the USA, EDI petered quietly away.

# 11  MILITARY ECONOMY

## MILITARY SPIN-OFFS

The Strategic Defense Initiative, christened and presented as immaculate defence, has always had potential to produce spin-offs for 'conventional' weapons, military space weapons and anti-satellite (ASAT) weapons. The connections between SDI and related programmes officially excluded from it suggest why SDI could win support even from those who scorned Reagan's vision of perfect defences; and how SDI may be modified now its original rationale is discredited.

The crusading rhetoric about SDI was always eschewed in the restricted literature, such as the Pentagon's 'Program Descriptive Summaries', which spoke instead of advancing aerospace science in quite general terms: 'the mission of the SDI is to advance aerospace science and technology, apply it to aerospace development and improvement, and plan for acquisition of qualitatively superior aerospace systems and equipment needed to accomplish the SDIO mission'.[1] In practice SDI was intimately linked to the modernisation of the very offensive weapons which it was supposed to supersede. Table 11.1 shows 'near term defense program areas' which the Pentagon 'identified as having potential for utilization of SDI technology or that may perhaps provide "spinbacks" of technology for SDI use'.[2]

The Air Defense Initiative (ADI) was created in 1985 as an adjunct to SDI, though ADI has a much smaller budget. SDI, ADI and North American Air Defense (NORAD) are connected in that they are elements of what should logically be a single system:

> we have a program that integrates strategic defense initiatives, the so-called SDI, North American Air Defense and space defense as one integrated strategic defense program. It makes no sense to have an SDI if you let bombers and cruise missiles in for free. So we have this SDA-2000 [Strategic Defense Architecture 2000] which pulls all that together as one integrated strategic defense program.[3]

137

Table 11.1. *Programme areas related to SDI*

Air Defense Initiative Programs
Balanced Technology Initiative Programs
Tactical Defense Programs
Strategic Forces Modernization Programs
Defense-wide Communication and Information Programs
Science and Technology (S&T) Programs
Space Systems Programs
Hardening/Survivability of Conventional Systems
Test Facilities, Resources and Instrumentation

*Source:* United States, Department of Defense, Strategic Defense
Initiative Organization, Office of Technology Applications, 1987.

Table 11.2 shows associated research not officially included in SDI
when the programme was formed. This overlapping work continues
today, providing much scope for 'relabelling' SDI projects according to
the exigencies of budgetary politics. Other programmes to overlap with
SDI are the army's Anti-Tactical Missile Program; air force R&D on
advanced weapons, survivability, laser applications, surveillance, command and control; and the Advanced Military Spaceflight Program.[4]

SDI-related technologies should apply to 'smart' weapons in general,
to the Advanced Tactical Fighter, the F-16 aircraft and other naval, air
and surface weapons. Research into expert systems, survivability and
computer-controlled multi-target fire control systems could produce a
wide range of 'conventional' military innovations. Electro-magnetic
gun technology is being incorporated in new artillery. Advances in
capacitor storage capability have a potential for ship and aircraft power
systems. Lightweight, rapid-fire hyper-velocity gun technologies could
improve fleet defence, anti-armour and anti-aircraft abilities. Many SDI
technologies are also needed for the strategy of 'Deep Strike': sensors
for target acquisition, novel explosives and missiles, and information
processing for command and control.

Some of the many military spin-offs expected from SDI were listed by
the Institute for Defense Analysis, as shown in Table 11.3. Each of the
five main SDI Program Elements (PEs) has other military applications.
The Surveillance Acquisition Tracking Kill Assessment (SATKA) PE
and the Systems Analysis/Battle Management (SA/BM) PE should
lead to advances in sensing, subsurface imaging, air defence, surveillance, command, control, communications, electronic intelligence and
counter-measures. They could precipitate breakthroughs in the intelligence and counter-intelligence wars. The Survivability Lethality Key

138

Table 11.2. *Associated research not included in SDI funding*

| | |
|---|---|
| 64406F | Anti-satellite (ASAT) R&D |
| 63226E | Air Defense Surveillance Warning (Teal Ruby) |
| 63401F | Research on Satellite Power and Survivability (Advanced Spacecraft Technology) |
| 63605F | Advanced Radiation Technology |
| 62707E | Particle Beam Technology |
| 62307A | Laser Weapons Technology |
| 63424F | Missile Surveillance Technology |
| 65806A | DoD High Energy Laser Facility |

*Source:* United States, Congress, Congressional Budget Office, 'Analysis of the President's Strategic Defense Initiative 1985–1989' (May 1984), pp. 15–19. Also in SDIO Report to Congress, 1985, C-23.

Table 11.3. *Potential military spin-offs from SDI: IDA study*

New technologies for tactical air defence include: air-to-air, surface-to-air applications; weapons, energy sources, pointing and tracking; and detection, identification, battlefield, surveillance, multi-sensor correlation.

Structural materials: fatigue-resistant metal composites; ceramic matrix composites with high fracture resistance; and personnel protection and vehicular applications.

Reliable high-efficiency rocket fuels.

Anti-tactical missile systems: kinetic and/or directed energy technology.

The technology of cooling windows (for SDI terminal interceptors) will materially improve the performance of guidance systems for missiles used by tactical forces. Also this may be of critical importance to the development of hypersonic commercial aircraft.

Most optical and infrared detectors are designed and used in relatively benign environments. SDI has forced consideration of highly adverse environments and methods to cope with them. These methods are just as seriously needed for tactical purposes, but are not being pursued.

*Source: Congressional Record* (12 June 1985), E2709, 'IDA Study results supplied by Dr B. Balko to SDIO/IST'.

Technologies (SLKT) PE has obvious applications in hardening and will enhance C³I, satellites and research into materials science. The Kinetic Energy Weapons (KEW) PE has ASAT spin-offs.

The trend of nuclear weapons development has long been towards greater accuracy and precision. 'Smart' counter-force missiles, with a Circular Error Probable (CEP) of tens of metres, can destroy specified

Table 11.4. *Abrahamson cites military benefits of SDI research*

A new miniaturised inertial navigational unit designed by Draper Labs could be fitted into the M1A1 tank land navigation system.

Another such device would make it possible to upgrade the Trident and MX missiles.

Advances in pulse power technology could enable detection of covert North Korean tunnels under the demilitarized zone in Korea.

Miniaturised linear accelerator technology developed at Los Alamos could produce new non-destructive techniques to inspect rocket engine seal mechanisms or to locate structural fatigue in aircraft.

*Source: Jane's Defence Weekly* (2 April 1988).

targets such as missile silos. None the less, nuclear warheads still produce collateral damage in the form of radiation fall-out, which prevents a really precise or 'surgical' nuclear strike. In the SDI programme, the Directed Energy Weapons PE develops laser and particle beams which could prove more accurate and 'usable' than present-day weapons. They therefore have greater strategic and coercive potential.[5]

Although the SDI Office usually portrayed its programme as 'purely defensive', it also argued on occasion that SDI would improve offensive weapons in general. Since this entailed an apparent contradiction, the SDI Office wielded this subsidiary rationale in a tactful, tactical way, using suggestion more than statement. Thus, Abrahamson reminded Congress that the Israelis' use of SDI technologies to manufacture an anti-tank rail gun 'is also an illustration of how research on the SDI can and will be applied to a very broad range of conventional applications as well'.[6] Abrahamson indicated some of the military benefits to support his budget request (see Table 11.4).

This line of argument could reassure risk-averse contractors, who wanted to focus on generic technologies immune to programmatic reorganisations. Thus a Lockheed executive confided that:

> We are consciously trying to do those SDIO activities that will survive a presidential transition, like BSTS [Boost Surveillance Tracking System]. We've also made heavy investments in battle management/$C^3I$, AI [artificial intelligence] and surveillance systems, all of which are going to be needed in any case.[7]

The president of Grumman's space systems division spoke likewise of survival through adaptability:

> The surveillance market is a good market. We'll always need surveillance. Of course, we never dreamed of handling the kinds of targets

SDI is talking about. That shows where SDI has pushed us, but even if SDI funds disappear, there are other buyers. The company strategy is to develop other applications so we'll survive most circumstances . . . As far as space-based radars, we decided a long time ago that some day there will be a need for a SBR in this country. First we did work for the air force, then DARPA, and now SDI. But, if not SDI, then it will be someone else.[8]

Abrahamson's adroit gesturing towards 'conventional' military spin-off also appealed to 'traditionalists': a crucial group in Congress. Preferring recognisable weapons to new-fangled notions of 'space shields', they needed sound subsidiary rationales to back SDI. Their concerns were met by Congress, which, in 1987 and subsequent years, mandated the SDI Office to report on the contribution of SDI technologies to other military missions.[9] Keen to maximise such spin-off, the SDI Office formed a panel on Joint Defense Technology Applications Initiative, to share SDI technologies among programme managers, operational commands, the Defense Acquisition Board committees and the Defense Science Board.[10]

### SDI AND 'SPACE CONTROL'

Apart from 'conventional' applications, SDI could contribute to broader strategies for the military control of space, as emphasised by the SDI director in a talk entitled not the 'Strategic Defense Initiative', but the *'Space* Defense Initiative'. After outlining some of the technologies which SDI uses, Abrahamson emphasised that 'the important thing is not simply what these technologies can do for SDI today and in the future. We must link them to a space station that will help us to achieve a permanent, manned presence in space.'[11]

The US Air Force, Army and Navy have long been competing for the mission of 'space control'. In the 1980s each of the Services activated its own Space Command and a unified Space Command was opened in 1985 at Colorado Springs. The First Space Wing was activated in 1983 to run a world-wide network of missile warning and space surveillance sensors. Two years later, a Second Space Wing was opened to run satellite and shuttle control activities from the Consolidated Space Operations Center (CSOC) in Colorado. A Third Space Support Wing was added in 1986.[12] The growth of the military space infrastructure is exemplified by the Air Force Space Command (AFSPACECOM), established at Colorado Springs in 1982. By 1987, it employed some 30,000 military and civilian personnel.[13]

In future, any Strategic Defense System (SDS) will be integrated with

141

operations for the overall military control of space, centred on US Space Command.[14] The distinction between the 'shield' and the 'sword' is somewhat academic, a fact not lost on Lt-Col. Barry Watts and Major Lance Lord, from the Office of the Secretary of Defense:

> We will therefore argue that a major US defense effort should be undertaken, at the earliest possible date, to locate outside the atmosphere permanent manned military forces able to carry out the following missions:
> - *ballistic missile defense* of US (and Allied) territory against attacks with ICBMs and SLBMs of the kinds now deployed by the US, USSR and China;
> - *space to earth offensive operations* against any area of the globe;
> - and *space superiority* (that is, the ability to engage and defeat enemy space forces) from near-earth orbit out to lunar distances.[15]

Talk of SDI in the context of 'space to earth offensive operations' and the deployment of counter-force nuclear weapons suggests that SDI could complement a first-strike capability. Although a partial strategic defence system would be overwhelmed by the full Soviet arsenal, it could mop up the remnants if the Soviets had been 'decapitated' by a devastating first strike. Soviet scientists argued that space-based weapons could be used to strike at the opponent's airborne $C^3$, and perhaps against some ground-level structures.[16] In effect, the Soviets were worried about their own 'window of vulnerability': larger than that of the USA, because most of the Soviet arsenal is based on land.

The official Air Force Space Systems Architecture (SSA 2000) – a document marked 'secret' – pays little attention to what it calls 'the president's Strategic Defense Initiative'.[17] SSA 2000 notes the principles of SDI (most of which are deleted), adding that these 'have not traditionally been tenets of US space policy and are therefore susceptible to shifts in national direction'.[18] SDI is subsumed under more general strategic objectives, which include:

> Deter attacks on the US, its vital interests world-wide and its allies.
> Terminate a conflict on terms favorable to the US.
> Facilitate post-war reconstruction.[19]

The 'Space Systems Architecture' claims that the National Aeronautics and Space Act provides the 'legislative basis' for 'the development of a warfighting capability in space'; and that SDI and current policy 'strongly suggest' that a 'warfighting capability in space' will be 'fundamental to military space policy in the year 2000'.[20]

The distinction between attack and defence capabilities, assiduously maintained in much pro-SDI literature, is extremely tenuous in this context. SSA 2000 shows that the air force views SDI as just one more 'combat function', qualitatively no different from the others.[21] The army too looks to space as a 'combat multiplier': an aid to the tactical commander, maximising the effectiveness of ground-based weapons. When asked how he hoped to 'leverage' SDI, the army's director of space and special weapons listed precision navigation equipment, such as fibre optics and gyroscopes; sensors; miniaturisation; and 'real-time' information processing for the tactical commander.[22] SDI's role in furthering the military 'control' of space and the improvement of conventional weapons wins it the support of a powerful military and ideological constituency.

## ANTI-SATELLITE WEAPONS (ASATS)

The space race took off in earnest after the launch of Sputnik 1 in October 1957. In the next twenty-five years, 2,114 military satellites were launched, three-quarters of which had some military application.[23] Of the two superpowers, the US is marginally more dependent on satellites, because of its far-flung military bases.[24] The satellites are used for photographic reconnaissance, electronic reconnaissance, ocean surveillance, navigation, meteorology, verification of treaty compliance, and communications. These satellites provide early warning and reassure each side that it is not under attack and that it would be able to respond if it were. They are thus defensive, to the extent that they enhance deterrence and stabilise crises.

Nuclear missiles depend on meteorological, geodetic and other satellites for accurate targeting and missile guidance. Communications, reconnaissance, navigation, weather and other satellites would be needed to support an attack.[25] In this respect, satellites aid an attack and assist counter-force strategy. This leads each side to research ASATs in order to neutralise an enemy attack, and hinders ASAT arms control.

Questions of strategic defence and ASAT are inextricably linked by technology, strategy, politics and history. The generic needs of an ASAT system are similar to those of BMD, since both need to locate, track and then destroy objects in space. ASAT is simpler than BMD in that satellites make an easier target and have more vulnerable parts, including sensors, solar panels and communications antennae. Whereas a BMD system might have to destroy thousands of warheads, the ASAT would only have to shoot down a few crucial satellites. Since satellites have predictable orbits and are exposed in space for long periods, an ASAT attack can be prepared well in advance. This gives

143

ASAT the advantage of surprise, whereas surprise would normally work against a BMD system.

A Strategic Defense System (SDS) would depend on space-based weapons to destroy enemy missiles in the boost phase. These space-based elements are themselves vulnerable to attack by ASATs. If the USA deployed strategic defences, the Soviets might use ASATs as a relatively cheap counter-measure. To protect its satellites, the USA would then have to deploy its own ASATs, defensive satellites (DSATs) or Anti-anti-satellites (AASATs). ASATs would thus take a central part in any serious attempt to deploy strategic defences.

Because the technologies for BMD and ASAT are so similar, strategic defence programmes have always had the potential either to be modified into ASATs, or to further the development of ASATs. This is borne out by the history of ASAT development. In the late 1950s and early 1960s 'Project Defender', run by the Advanced Research Projects Agency (ARPA), simultaneously researched BMD and 'satellite inter-ception'. Between 1963 and 1975, the air force researched ASAT under its programme 437, with tests called SQUANTO TERROR. The facilities and missiles for this programme were also used for BMD testing.[26]

The army's ASAT capabilities were an outgrowth of research into ABM. In the early 1960s the army called for Nike-Zeus ABM to be given an ASAT capability, which led to the Nike-Zeus ASAT (programme 505), based at Kwajalein Atoll and codenamed 'Mudflap'. At the end of the 1960s, the proposed Safeguard ABM system had a dual capability for BMD and ASAT, as confirmed by the director of defence research and engineering: 'The Safeguard ABM system when deployed beginning in early FY 1974, will have an anti-satellite capability against satellites passing within the field of fire of the deployed system.'[27]

In the budget submissions for 1990, when all three of the Services requested ASAT funds, three of the candidates for the ASAT mission had been funded under SDI. They were the Exoatmospheric Re-entry vehicle Interceptor System (ERIS), an army Lockheed programme; the Free Electron Laser (FEL), a promising technology for ASAT in the longer term; and the Mid-Infrared Advanced Chemical Laser (MIRACL), originally a navy programme to research defences against aircraft and cruise missiles, taken over by the SDI Office and then dropped in favour of the Alpha chemical laser. Other options for ASAT were Neutral Particle Beam Weapons, X-ray lasers and the Chemical Oxygen–Iodine Laser (COIL). These technologies under research in the SDI programme would contribute more to offensive ASATs than to 'defensive' BMD.[28]

SDI's adherents underplay the programme's links with ASAT out of deference to the near-consensus that ASAT would be strategically destabilising. President Bush's national security adviser, Brent Scowcroft, was one of many hard-liners to acknowledge that the unrestrained development of ASATs would jeopardise US national security: 'all scenarios involving the use of ASATs, especially those surrounding crises, increase the risks of accident, misperception and inadvertent escalation'.[29] If both sides had an operational ASAT system, they would come under intense pressure to fire first, creating an unstable 'hair trigger' situation in space. Both sides would have an incentive to strike before the other:

> Pre-emptive attack would be an attractive countermeasure to space-based ASAT weapons. If each side feared that only a pre-emptive attack could counter the risk of being defeated by enemy pre-emption, then a crisis situation could be extremely unstable.[30]

This 'use them or lose them' crisis would increase the risk of accidental war. The initial report of an attack might be due to accident, computer malfunction or impact with a meteoroid. A satellite might thus become the Arch-Duke Ferdinand of the Third World War.

There are, therefore, organic links at nearly every level between strategic defence and ASATs. Their inherent overlap ensures that ASAT will be one of many 'offensive' applications of a supposedly 'defensive' programme.

### SDI AND US INTERVENTION OVERSEAS

If, as this chapter has proposed, SDI generates significant military spin-off, this would increase the military power of the United States and its ability to intervene, directly or indirectly, overseas. In this respect, SDI could help to maintain or expand US economic power, in the interests of the US ruling elite as a whole.

Such a conclusion gainsays the conventional academic wisdom that military expenditures weaken the domestic economy, by draining investment from civilian industry. Liberal analysts have long argued (to little avail) that the production of weapons is counter-productive. Their favoured illustrations, Japan and (West) Germany, out-perform the USA by concentrating on the export of consumer goods. The USA should therefore repair its economic base and rebuild domestic prosperity, since these measures are, ultimately, the true foundation of national security.[31]

The liberal orthodoxy tends to ignore US dependence on overseas markets (for cheap labour and to sell products); profit repatriated from abroad; debt servicing; and foreign military sales. It neglects the steady, significant growth in US overseas investments. Direct investment by US companies in overseas plant and facilities has risen from $12 billion in 1950 to $200 billion in 1980. In 1977 the Commerce Department reported that 3,540 US companies had 24,666 foreign affiliates.[32] Much of this investment is in parts of South-East Asia, the Caribbean and Central and Latin America, which offer a high yield on investments because of cheap, non-unionised labour, tax concessions for foreign investors, strict wage control and scant provision for health, safety and the environment. These areas are also vulnerable to radical nationalist movements.[33]

Direct intervention, 'low-intensity operations' or mere coercion safe-guard US investments; secure access to strategic factors of production (rare minerals, oil, etc.); ensure the smooth repatriation of profit; encourage the servicing of international debt; and deter wild thoughts of nationalisation or asset seizure. Military power thus serves to 'ensure the unimpeded flow of critical resources to the West' and 'protect sea lanes'.[34] It is calculated that between 1945 and 1978, the USA used its armed forces to protect its interests abroad in some 36 'dramatic confrontations' and 180 less serious incidents.[35] Study of US coercion shows that 'discrete uses of the armed forces are often an effective way of achieving near-term foreign policy objectives'.[36]

Although common sense suggests that space-based lasers are inappropriate as a response to Third World radicalism, SDI-induced advances in electronic intelligence, satellite technologies and sensing and tracking capabilities could be applied to 'search and destroy' operations against nationalist guerrillas. 'The low intensity threat is not necessarily a low technology threat.'[37] More importantly, SDI spin-off in generic military technologies – $C^3I$ and materials technology – should spur rapid redesign of 'conventional' weapons. It might entail modernisation in fighter aircraft, missile systems and communications networks: all profitable markets for US Foreign Military Sales (FMS), which have direct and indirect value.[38] Politically, they establish regional gendarmes for the USA. For example, improved air defences and ATBM, resulting from SDI, might be sold to Israel and Saudi Arabia. Since the client has further needs for spare parts, servicing and training, this nurtures within the state concerned a powerful group dependent on and friendly to the USA. The initial sale thus provides continuing leverage within the region. Economically, the client may share R&D and overhead costs; and the larger production runs which result from FMS usually reduce unit costs, thanks to economies of scale and learning curves.

146

SDI therefore provides opportunities to market improved weapons and accessories, instruments of intervention and dependence, beneficial to the US balance of payments. It is one symptom of the over-riding concern, especially prevalent in the 'New Right', to maintain global hegemony. SDI should keep the US on the 'leading edge' of military research and reinforce its ability to 'police' or intervene in the defence of US interests.[39] Many policy-makers probably came to accept SDI on these cogent, if Machiavellian, grounds. Their views might be balanced against those of the liberal tradition discussed earlier. Whilst the US economy gains short-term rewards from its foreign-orientated character, in the long run this makes it precariously dependent on foreign politics, over which the US can have little (legitimate) control. The sweetmeats of Empire may have bitter, cumulative poison.[40]

### INDUSTRIAL TECHNOLOGY POLICY

With its investments in electronics and hi-tech industries, SDI must affect wider technological development.[41] The official Air Force Space Systems Architecture (SSA 2000) says that a main peace-time objective of the USA is to **'maintain a technological lead in space'**, since this 'enhances US international prestige and promotes economic prosperity'.[42]

SDI is a direct subsidy for R&D, in a state-of-the-art area. It forms part of the 'Pentagon system': the pattern of military investment in US high technology, which offers volume production, price premiums and protectionist 'buy American' safeguards. Whilst SDI supporters were coy about offensive military applications, they were quick to proclaim its potential civilian spin-offs.[43] The SDI Office established a formal network to encourage commercial entrepreneurs: its Technology Applications Information System (TAIS), modem-accessible to approved US citizens.

In practice, the amount of spin-off from SDI is constrained in important ways. First and foremost, the Pentagon classifies research for secrecy and security. It cannot simultaneously keep information secret (necessary for a secure strategic defence) and disseminate the infor-mation (necessary for commercial spin-off). The extreme performance requirements of Strategic Defense Systems and their esoteric weapons-orientated goals diverge widely from commercial needs. SDI spin-off is most likely to be derived from basic, generic research performed by the Innovative Science and Technology directorate at the SDIO.[44] This is the very area which has been cut in efforts to achieve an early Initial Operating Capability (IOC). The IS&T budget has been reduced in favour of short-term (early IOC) hardware demonstrations and proto-type development.[45]

Apart from these constraints on spin-off, SDI is far from ideal as Industrial Technology Policy (ITP), because of its opportunity costs. It deprives the civilian sector of high-technology venture capital and employs engineering talent at the expense of commercial projects.[46] The DoD practice of non-competitive 'sole-source' contracts and 'cost-plus' contracts can be a subsidy for inefficiency.

SDI's impact on technology policy should not be exaggerated. The USA spent about $120 billion on R&D in 1985. This amounted to half the world's R&D.[47] Half of that $120 billion was federal investment. A total of $34 billion went to military R&D. SDI therefore accounts for about 2 per cent of US R&D. If SDI is Industrial Technology Policy (ITP) designed to stimulate high-tech innovations for US industry, it compares poorly with Japanese ITPs co-ordinated by MITI, or even EEC high-tech projects. SDI is more the result of the relative absence of a genuine ITP in the US, which permits the Pentagon to act as a rather inefficient substitute.

### THE 'BAROQUE' THEORY

The structure of R&D and the process of technological innovation are also at issue in the theory of the 'baroque arsenal', now to be considered, although it is less about the 'arms economy' than the institutional shaping of technology.

Modern weapons are created, according to the theory of the 'baroque arsenal', by a conjunction of 'the capitalist dynamic of the arms manu-facturers and the conservatism that tends to characterise armed forces and defence departments in peace time'.[48] This 'distorts' technological growth, since it encourages 'elaborate custom-built product improve-ments that are typical of industries on the decline, instead of simpler mass-market process improvements which tend to characterise indus-tries in their prime'.[49] 'Baroque' weapons assimilate high tech beyond a point of saturation: they then become militarily ineffectual, 'incapable of achieving limited military objectives'.[50] The classic (Clausewitzian) link between war and policy is rent asunder.

In the early 1980s the 'baroque' theory had some plausibility. The peasant-based militia in Vietnam had defeated a modern army, which was over-reliant on high technology. The Shah of Iran with all his US weapons had proved powerless against Khomeini's Islamic revolution. Operation Eagle Claw, the attempt to rescue the hostages from the US embassy in Teheran in April 1980, ended in technical ignominy. There

148

Table 11.5. *Possible civilian and commercial spin-off from SDI*

Supercomputers
    automation and expert systems
    artificial intelligence
    neural networks
    fault-tolerant computing (pattern recognition and learning)
Robotics
Electronics
    electro-optics
Telecommunications
    communications satellites
    robust optical fibres (mining and petrochemical factories)
Advanced materials
    high-strength, light-weight materials
Space technology
    low-cost space transportation
    satellite repair
Directed energy
Pulse power for oil-well drilling
Food irradiation
Biotechnology
Medical lasers

*Source:* Nozette (ed.), *Commercializing SDI Technologies.*

were some counter-examples: the Israeli/Syria conflict demonstrated the success of sophisticated air-to-air missiles (AIM-9) and fighter planes (Israel's F-15s and F-16s against Syrian MiG-21s). In the Falklands/Malvinas War, Britain and Argentina proved the military worth of Seawolf, Seadart, Blowpipe and Exocet missiles.[51]

Since then, the Gulf War conclusively demonstrated the capabilities of high-tech weaponry. The many military successes included 'smart' bombs,[52] Tomahawk cruise missiles, Stealth bombers, Tornadoes and the Patriot anti-missile.[53] The Iraqis were driven from Kuwait with perhaps 80,000 casualties, whilst the Allied forces sustained fewer than 150. The subsequent Iraqi crushing of the Kurds provides further refutation, if any were needed, of the baroque theory.[54] The events of 1991 suggest that technological superiority confers a huge military advantage, and may achieve immediate political goals; though perhaps, in the longer term, with tragic repercussions.

Military innovation entails the risk of (passing) unreliability or even spectacular absurdity, but to propose this as a *defining characteristic* is a huge error. The proponents of the baroque theory are probably, like other anti-nuclear analysts, opposed to weapons innovations on quite other grounds: that they are a horrendous diversion from the pressing

149

social and environmental problems we should face. That would be a simple, humane and honourable case – the 'idealism' of which would curtail dialogue with professional decision-makers. Rather than making this case, the theorists contort it into an ultimately misguided, academic argument which apparently subscribes to the presuppositions of professional military discourse. In evading the fundamental (moral) issue, in enumerating modern instances and finer elaborations, the theory of the baroque itself becomes somewhat baroque.

Originally intended for conventional weapons, the baroque theory may be more applicable to SDI. Reagan's initial conception of SDI could be seen as the crowning glory of the rococo: the epitome of a technologically super-sophisticated, prohibitively expensive, militarily unreliable system. The Bush Administration has apparently rejected this 'astrodome' concept. If it presses ahead with Global Protection Against Limited Strikes (GPALS), this might represent a transformation, a bursting beyond the baroque, a radically new 'process' improvement, rather than the accumulation of 'product' developments associated with the baroque. The effect of SDI spin-off will provide the evidence on which to judge. If the US decides that GPALS or a partial SDI would also be 'baroque', the key issue of the other military applications for SDI R&D – the extent to which it is 'baroque' to other military goals – will move to the top of the agenda.

### DEEP TECHNOLOGICAL CHANGE

Underlying the theory of the 'baroque arsenal' is the idea of 'long waves' in the capitalist economy of the kind outlined by Schumpeter and Kondratiev.[55] Kondratiev's theory of cyclical oscillation about every fifty years in the capitalist economy, beginning in about 1780, is elaborated by Carlota Perez, who states that each cycle is associated with a new 'technological style' and 'socio-institutional style'.[56] Whilst economists dispute the merits of the Kondratiev theory and whether it can be used as an analytic or predictive tool, it does at least provide a rough descriptive approximation of broad changes.

Roger Hutton has attempted to situate SDI within the theories of Kondratiev and Perez.[57] He identifies the fourth Kondratiev cycle (1930–80) with US hegemony, 'the mass production of discrete identical units made with energy-intensive materials' and 'the sharp separation of management and administration from production'. The fifth Kondratiev cycle, from about 1980, sees the pre-eminence of electronics and information technology, with a shift from the USA towards Japan. SDI could be a way of sustaining fourth Kondratiev structures (the US

150

arms industry) by judiciously introducing a measure of fifth Kondratiev technology, as a result of deliberate policy or unintentional processes. SDI would be one manifestation of the wider assimilation of information technology into weapons systems. It could mark a transition from the fourth to the fifth Kondratiev cycle: the way in which the US invests in and gains access to the fifth Kondratiev. SDI might be linked to a sixth Kondratiev cycle, based on the exploitation of space. However suggestive such speculation, it only relates to SDI in the broadest sense and cannot be verified.

### THE 'PERMANENT ARMS ECONOMY'

The final 'arms economy' model is probably the best known and most professedly 'radical'. It holds that (capitalist) economies need high military expenditures to maintain demand, or, as Mandel would put it, absorb surplus value. Although the terminology is Marxian, the argument is, undercover, a Keynesian underconsumptionist one.

Marx's reproduction scheme had identified two sectors: (1) the means of production and (2) consumer goods. Mandel posits a third department, producing 'means of destruction'.[58] Its massive expenditure creates a 'permanent arms economy', analysed by Mandel in terms of the 'struggle' by 'late capitalism' 'to increase the rate of surplus value, to cheapen the cost of constant capital, to reduce the turn-over time of capital, and to achieve the valorization of surplus capital'. By buffering or transmuting these pressures towards crisis, the permanent arms economy 'contributed substantially to the accelerated accumulation of capital in the "long wave" of 1945–65'.[59]

Mandel criticises Michael Kidron, who had also claimed that mass arms production 'tends to offset the [capitalist] system's inbuilt bias towards declining rates of profit'.[60] The details of their disagreement are less significant than the dubious premises which they share: the labour theory of value and the tendency for the rate of profit to fall. Both are attacking the reformist belief that high military expenditure is a distortion, which reduces productive investment and undermines the civilian economy; and which therefore ought to be remedied through arms control and arms conversion, in the interests of social welfare and economic competitiveness, within a capitalist framework. Both Mandel and Kidron portray inflated arms expenditure as so integral to the very structure of modern capitalism that it could only be slashed by revolution. This simple (im)practical implication is a key to their complex theoretical explication. But the crisis of capitalism, which both relish, seems not so much terminal as interminable. Although Mandel and

Kidron provoke creative questions about the military role in the economy, they can do almost nothing to elucidate SDI.

## CONCLUSION

SDI will generate multiple military spin-offs and forward the weaponisation of space. It will therefore retain its strong support among the military space enthusiasts, who see an assault on the 'high frontier' and the development of space war-fighting capabilities as an extension of deterrence and a means of maintaining strategic, psychological and political supremacy. For them, SDI is a publicly acceptable way of subsidising their military space agenda.

SDI may also come increasingly to rely on its contribution to strategic *offensive* capabilities; and to be valued for its position on the 'cutting edge' of military technology. Now that the INF and CFE Treaties have constrained some quantitative aspects of the arms race, there is an increased premium on high-tech and high-quality weapons. The 'conservative' view, embedded in the Bush Administration, willingly contemplates deep reductions in some nuclear forces, providing that it can win funds to develop the technologies most critical to advance the weapons of the future. SDI's military spin-offs will matter more than its civilian applications. Although the research touches on many state-of-the-art technologies, dissemination, a prerequisite for commercial spin-off, is incompatible with the military desire for secrecy. As industrial technology policy, SDI rates poorly beside those of the EEC and Japan. But in that it furthers military, technological and political hegemony, SDI will also contribute to US economic power.

# 12  THE CULTURE OF 'STAR WARS'

If the course of 'Star Wars' has often baffled observers, this may be due to its strange mingling of science and culture, expertise and popularisation. From its very inception SDI was both a high-tech programme *and* a popular idea, a mélange of physics, psycho-politics and metaphysics, attuned to the drives and dissatisfactions of the American people.[1] Its secret strength lay in its emotive connotations, its capacity to motivate people by mobilising culture, discourse, emotion and fantasy.

## AVOIDANCE

The imagination could hardly comprehend the sheer megatonnage of the nuclear arsenal. The horror can, however, be distanced or absorbed by the specialised language of evasion and euphemism which has been refined in 'expert' discussion of nuclear matters.[2] The resulting discourse, sometimes called 'nukespeak', fosters group identity; its acronyms create a secret world of privilege and expertise. SDI has its own subdialect, replete with characters such as AMOS (Air force Maui Optical System), TOM (Threat Object Map), SAM (Surface to Air Missile) and SPOCK (Special Purpose Operating Computer Kernel). At the operational level, computer language homogenises the issues into a 'colourless world of files, records, fields, reports, updates and processing'.[3]

There is good reason for 'professional' fora to prefer the technocratic style of nukespeak, since their aim is negotiation and management, rather than self-disclosure or demagoguery. But, in focussing on techno-strategic details, the 'experts' usually disregard the presuppositions underlying debate. The unspoken consensus has been that the Soviets pose a greater threat than the arms race itself. Many 'liberals' disagree. The absence of genuine dialogue on this or other fundamental questions feeds veiled hostility and covert aggression in 'expert' fora.

Disagreements are seldom pursued and arguments settled less on their merits than by relation to entrenched positions.

In straining to be hard-headed, 'nukespeak' tends to dull the imagination and numb the mind into accepting the balance of terror and the terror of balance. It abstracts and absolves, quantifying humans and humanising weapons.[4] For it even to consider the human impact of using the weapons being procured creates an aporia, a disturbing dissonance, which both shows the limits and strains the coherence of 'expert' debate. Four rare occasions, in which the phantom prospect of destruction troubles the gentility of congressional hearings, are discussed below:

> It seems to me that there is a middle ground that I would like for us to look at, that if we could preclude the area of surprise attacks, we would say, 'Hey, you know you can't come down in New York City. You can't come down on a command control area', that this might be more within our reach. Would you comment on that? Instead of providing an entire blanket.[5]

'You can't come down on New York City' makes nuclear attack sound like an aeroplane crash. Catastrophe is concealed in a cliché. Space weapons are metamorphosed into an 'entire blanket' – the metaphor itself a blanket against clear thought.

> MONAHAN. Here you see the effects of a munitions canister being dropped from an F-16.
> DR COOPER. This one will ruin your whole day if you are in the way of it.
> MONAHAN. 202 bomblets, which have armoured penetration capability, antipersonnel fragmentation capability and incendiary – you will see them all hit. They fuze on impact. That one canister covers an area a little bigger than a football field.
> MR BATTISTA. That is CBU-87.
> MONAHAN. Combined effect munitions. Thank you. Just two charts to wrap this up.[6]

Monahan, who later became director of the SDI Office, seems to enjoy numbering and describing the 'bomblets'. The orotundity of 'antipersonnel fragmentation capability' is far more congenial than plain talk of mangled corpses. The 'bomblets' all hit. The scale is impressive, yet also familiar, 'a little bigger than a football field'. One can sense a shared excitement – the flip side of anxiety – and an irony, which lightens tension and accommodates destruction. Like the slide they are watching, the perspective of the discussion is from on high, from the perspective of those bombing, so far removed from the explosion that any victims are rendered invisible. They are annihilated by a discussion which overlooks them.

Apart from slight inhumanity, much congressional discussion is internally muddled, with issues never fully resolved.

> But how do you address the C[3]I [Command Control Communication Intelligence] issue when it comes to the – I am talking about now looking at this in a total system context, because there is no doubt in my mind you are going to field this successful interceptor – but then I am talking about 3,000 RVs [Re-entry Vehicles] coming in. I mean that's his SS-18 force with several thousand more RVs in reserve, recognizing he's got fratricide problems and everything else, still if he goes to contact salvage fusing, I'm in deep trouble.[7]

The thought is 'in deep trouble' for there is little idea of who the 'enemy' is. It is just 'he', 'his' RVs and 'his' 'fratricide problems'. What passes as 'reason' is not very 'rational' at all. Even as emotional reaction is being excluded, it returns in altered forms, in the illogical syntax, the evasive expressions, the gaps between words.

The final example comes from John Gardner, who has worked in the Pentagon and for McDonnell Douglas, and who was also the systems director in the SDI Office:

> According to this investment house, the asset value of the United States is some $25-plus trillion. That is if you take a look at the entire investment houses, plants, communications, facilities, transportation, the entire thing, its value is something like $26 trillion, $25 to $30 trillion. That entire value structure right now is exposed to destruction, so another way of looking at this problem is, is it possible that we could reduce the exposure of that value structure to destruction?[8]

SDI is evaluated through a techno-strategic style, superficially objective and value-free, but in a deeper sense value-confused or value-less. It is a triumph of empiricism over wisdom, a triumph reinforced throughout the SDI literature:

> The Brilliant Pebbles navigation system is based on a novel, already-demonstrated real-time stellar navigation module and standard miniature angular rate-sensing and linear accelerometers, backed by a high precision clock.[9]

The celebration of cleverness – 'Brilliant Pebbles', real-time, novelty, high precision, 'smart rocks' – avoids fundamental questioning: is this expenditure a wise use of resources? What purpose does it serve? What will be the results? Energy and effort, pride and intellectual competition crowd out wider or deeper reflection. 'Star Wars' exemplifies a society which divorces the 'positive' from the 'normative', teaching knowledge

155

and power at the expense of wisdom, extremes of brilliance which are heights of folly.

The culture of ethical avoidance and contrived innocence is formalised in the work-place, where 'need-to-know' policies explicitly forbid enquiry about a product's final use.[10] Compulsory product ignorance, enforced on pain of clearance revocation or the sack, creates a collective alienation, in which workers resort to the private ploys of resignation or fantasy. In their 'cloistered' surroundings, the thousands of researchers and executives who comprise the SDI infrastructure have taken vows of ignorance as well as obedience. Like other military electronics workers, they can therefore pursue their work with scant concern for any harmful consequences.

## TRANSFERENCE

The arms race and SDI are emotional subjects, bound to arouse intense feelings in sentient people. Open expression of these reactions is precluded by the etiquette of professionalism and the codes of 'nuke-speak'. As feelings are repeatedly ill expressed or repressed, the line of thought is likely to become warped or dissociated in its emotional dimension. Emotions – such as hope, powerlessness, and frustration – which pass unacknowledged in their original form may be transferred and redirected. Denied in their proper context, they return elsewhere. That which is dispossessed becomes demonic. Fear of holocaust reappears as phobia about the Soviets. Group aggression may be projected on to the 'Enemy'. Guilt about self-complicity is shifted into an anxious quest for strategic vulnerabilities. Doubtless there are far more complex transferences too. This may explain why so much 'expert' debate, proud of its 'professionalism' and purporting to be above emotion, produces little but ill-feeling.

A discourse which routinely blocks expression of feeling systematically encourages emotional transference. The principal transference is that which shunts negativity on to the 'Enemy', which conjures up an Evil Empire, thus offering a blank cheque in the currency of moral justification. People may be predisposed to believe in an 'Enemy' as lethal as the Bomb itself, as a way of accepting or making sense of nuclear terror. Until the late 1980s the USSR was the perfect scapegoat. Fear of the Russians seemed a sine qua non of SDI and the arms race itself. The extent of this fear was hard to overestimate, its cause open to interpretation. A former US Ambassador to Moscow noted an 'anxious preoccupation' with weapons of mass destruction combining with irrational fear of the Russians. 'So wildly overdrawn is this view that I

156

can see it only as the product of some mass neurosis, and a highly morbid one at that – a neurosis I can only assume to be rooted in the effort to repress some sort of inner insecurity to the unreal image of an external danger.'[11] According to Herbert York, the Director of Defense Research and Engineering (DDRE) under Eisenhower and Kennedy, 'the majority of the key individual promoters of the arms race derive a very large part of their self-esteem from their participation in what they believe to be an essential – even a holy – cause'. York identifies other motives: 'patriotic zeal, exaggerated prudence and a sort of religious faith in technology', stimulated 'sometimes by a desire to go along with the gang, sometimes by crass opportunism and sometimes by simple fear of the unknown'.[12]

By activating the twin currents of patriotism and anti-Communism, SDI could cut across party lines and bind diverse groups. Naive or disingenuous views about the Russians extended to the first director of the SDI Office, Lt-Gen. Abrahamson: 'the Americans struggle against obstacles imposed by nature, while the Russians struggle against men. The Americans combat the wilderness and the savage life; the Russians, civilization itself.'[13] Abrahamson could then present his programme as a simple morality play of good guys and bad guys. 'However, don't forget that in the movie, the good guys won, because the Force was on their side. I am convinced that the Force is with us.'[14]

Some of the 'Star Warriors' in Lawrence Livermore's 'O' Group mixed prejudice with contempt and anxiety:

> As far as I'm concerned the Russian people have had dictators for a thousand years now. I think it's something in their culture. They also have a much higher tolerance for suffering than I consider rational or sane. To me that labels them as people who can take adversity very well, but who are never going to produce anything.[15]

It remains to be seen whether the collapse of the Warsaw Pact will finally undermine phobia about the Russians, the visceral foundations of strategic defence programmes.

### FANTASIES

One facet of US patriotism is faith in technology, especially military and space technology. Space is seen as America's destiny and the 'pre-eminent military environment of our time'. This configuration is illustrated by a booklet called *Space: America's Frontier for Growth, Leadership and Freedom*, published by the major space weapons contractor, Rockwell, in the early 1980s. The booklet's cover displays some of the icons of US hegemony: the globe, orbited by a satellite, a satellite dish, a telescope, a tank, a diagram of an atom, a dollar sign, all dwarfed by the Stars and Stripes banner. The introduction aptly remarks that the collection of symbols 'describes well the importance of space to America's future'.

SDI is sometimes conveyed as progressive and exciting, a dramatic assault on the final frontier. High Frontier is a pro-SDI pressure-group; Air Force Space Command has the motto 'Guardians of the High Frontier'. The metaphor of the frontier invokes American history to 'naturalise' the weaponisation of space, implying that space is just the latest in a series of geographical constraints to be conquered. This quest may have a compulsive, obsessive quality, a feeling that the challenge must be met, lest the virility of the nation be impugned. The frontier theme reworks a myth which can be traced back to the first US frontier: Nature and the natural limits which were cast as the USA's Manifest Destiny to conquer – in the face of rival imperial powers and the native inhabitants obstructing human progress. Like its predecessors a tale of innocence and embattled self-reliance, the new frontier adventure also blurs the distinction between self-defence and offence: thus a weapon which facilitates fantasies, or even realities, of a nuclear first strike takes the form of an exciting display of self-defence.

The submarine, the steam warship, the torpedo, the strategic bomber and thermo-nuclear missiles have all been presented in their time as purely defensive means of ensuring the peace.[16] The myth of a super-weapon recurs in films, cartoons, comic strips and science fiction. Reagan himself had once had to defend a wonder weapon from the enemies of the United States who were trying to steal it. That was in his 1940 Brass Bancroft film, *Murder in the Air*. The superweapon, an 'inertial projector' which could bring down aeroplanes by knocking out their electrical systems, was credited with properties which Reagan might later have wished on SDI: it will 'make America invincible in war and therefore be the greatest force for peace ever invented'.[17] Four decades later, one congressman noted how Reagan 'has made repeated comments including the phrase "once we develop this weapon", suggesting that he honestly believes that the SDI is comprised of a single powerful defensive technology – such as the X-ray laser as presented to him by Dr Teller'.[18]

Others too see SDI as principally an attempt to design the weapons of the future:

> People talk about SDI, whether we need it or not, whether it is prac-
> tical, defensive, offensive and other related questions. When it comes
> right down to it, we can look at this fiction story and see – call it Star

Trek now, but back in the Buck Rogers days they had a beam they shot out there and shot down all kinds of space ships. Now it is the Star Trek kind of thing, but it is coming. Some say it is too far off. Some say you cannot defend against it, but when you come right down to it, that is what we are talking about.[19]

The near-magical aura of advanced lasers and supercomputers can glamorise and blur discussions of SDI. The images of science fiction short-circuit debate by suggesting easy, convenient responses. The assumption that science fiction prefigures actual scientific advance implies that the development of futuristic space weapons is now pre-ordained. It is merely a question of hastening their inevitable evolution and ensuring that our side comes in, to use Abrahamson's words, 'firstest with the mostest'.

The fantasy of the superweapon is part of the wider myth of the 'technological fix'. Edward Teller has apparently devoted his life to a quest for technical answers to political problems. After two superweapons which he had promoted, the A-bomb and the H-bomb, failed as panaceas, Teller turned to the third-generation nuclear weapon. It was named after the Arthurian superweapon, Excalibur – only it was 'Super Excalibur' – in a tradition of legendary BMD heroes: Nike-Zeus, Nike-Ajax and Nike-Hercules. Teller wrote that we cannot 'put the atomic genie back in the bottle. But technology can provide something of a solution. The Genie should contribute to the shield. The Genie can make the shield stronger than the sword.'[20]

The new superweapon was presented as being inherently defensive: a notion which, according to a former US Secretary of Defense, appeals to something peculiarly American:

> Russia, both Soviet and Imperial, has been repeatedly invaded, has suffered grievous damage, and has survived largely through its own efforts. But the United States throughout its history has been secure here in the Western hemisphere. The American psyche believes that perfect defense *should* be attainable. In that we differ from all other nations. It is this unique belief that underlies the current hope for the SDI.[21]

Reagan's offer of a 'shield', 'blanket' or 'umbrella' to 'eliminate the threat of nuclear weapons' had a wider resonance, to all who yearn for security, or subconsciously hope that the Absolute Bomb should be matched by an Absolute Defence.

SDI's offensive potential could also be seen as a panacea, as in cartoon book (but serious) form by one writer for the *Washington Times*: 'if we had gone ahead and put some of that space-based artillery up

above the ozone back when Ronald Reagan and the gang were pushing
. . . we'd be frying ol' Saddam Hussein with a couple of shots of laser
technology'.[22]

Star Wars is about power: technological power, economic power and
military power. The most powerful supercomputers and the most
powerful weapons confirm the United States as the most powerful
superpower ever. The rhetoric of SDI is a language of power, real or
imagined. Those who identify with it presumably have some stake in
that power. The cognoscenti may savour a sense of vicarious might by
talking about a Hyper Velocity Gun (HVG) or SPEAR (Space Power
Experiments Aboard Rockets), by playing with the idea of a Space
Based Nuclear Particle Beam Weapon (SBNPBW) or the Multiplanar
Organic Scintillator High Energy Detector (MOSHED).

Power is exciting. According to a former Hertz fellow at Lawrence
Livermore National Laboratory, the 'Star Warriors' in the elite 'O'
Group are on a power trip, perhaps the biggest ever: 'what they're
doing could save or destroy the world. They deal with that by enjoying
it.'[23] Some of the Livermore scientists, themselves avid science fiction
readers, express their excitement in briefings like 'A Technological Race
for the Prize of the Planet' or 'Pillars of Fire in the Valley of the Giant
Mushrooms'.[24] The fantasies are also available to the ordinary citizen in
the home. Inestimable hours are spent on board games, videos and
fantasy role-playing games about Star Wars:

> Star Warriors puts you at the control of the TIE fighters, X-wings and
> other starfighters from the Star Wars Universe. You'll jink, roll, loop,
> angle deflectors, dodge lasers and return fire – pushing your ship and
> yourself to the limit as you battle to decide the future of the galaxy.[25]

'To appreciate the benefits of video games', President Reagan
remarked at the Walt Disney Epcot Center two weeks before his SDI
speech, one need only 'watch a twelve year old take evasive action and
score multiple hits, while playing Space Invaders.'[26] The games, like
Star Wars itself, allow us to play the hero, to position ourselves as
spectators, participants or victors, rather than victims. Fantasies of
simulation assimilate the idea of annihilation and recapture in imagination a control absent in reality. They make the exceptional mundane
and the destructive enjoyable. Anyone can call the shots or press the
button:

> Blasting the whole world to bits
> Was too like slamming a door
> Too like dropping in a chair
> Exhausted with rage

160

> Too like being blown to bits yourself
> Which happened too easily
> With too like no consequences.[27]

The power and excitement of the nuclear world appeals to a particular form of masculinity. Opinion polls indicate that markedly more men support SDI than women: the fact that this 'gender gap' is common to other weapons programmes makes it all the more significant. Nearly all of those working on SDI are male and some, it seems, are 'turned on' by the hardware itself:

> I have indicated the Israelis always ask the question, 'Can we put these rail-guns on tanks?' They have already found a way, and they are converting this by removing the breach and putting an electron gun in the back end to a hybrid form of rail gun and doubled the velocity of the projectile already [sic]. It is just fascinating.[28]

Before becoming director of the SDI Office, Major-General George L. Monahan Jr testified to Congress. Apart from the word 'unclassified' his first chart had five terms, in bold capital letters: '**MUNITIONS, THRUSTS, PRECISION, STANDOFF, NIGHT CAPABILITY**'.[29] Perhaps 'thrusts' and 'night capability' elicit a snigger from his male audience, or perhaps the Major-General is just groping for words. 'Precision' is an interesting association: the wish to have things clean, exact, precise.

Hints of displaced sexual fantasies surface in some of the artists' animations of SDI – phallic rockets, potent lasers and 'wargasmic' explosions in the voluptuous depth of space – and in some primarily technical texts:

> Hardness against nuclear attacks, for instance, is further leveraged by the interceptor's maneuvering capabilities, conferred by its restartable, high-specific-thrust engines.[30]

Whilst the above passage is in one sense a neutral description of operational considerations for 'Brilliant Pebbles', 'hardness', 'maneuvering capabilities' and 'restartable, high-specific-thrust engines' suggest that there is a different subtext. The desk of a liberal congressman and critic of SDI sported numerous 'freebies' from the Pentagon: certificates that he had flown in the B-1B, a signed photograph from the pilot, little model planes, more model tanks and armoured vehicles, all to pick up, finger, play with.

In that it thrives on the acquiescence of a disenfranchised majority, Star Wars may be symptomatic of a wider culture of apathy, alienation and aggression (passive, covert or direct). It could be studied in terms of general theories of violence: Melanie Klein's 'object relations theory', for instance. Whilst girls are 'mothered' into caring, boys are 'othered' into a competitive, adversarial fixation on power – increasingly brain-power. Obsessed with beating others, males cultivate a detached, 'schizoid' mentality, until it seems not unnatural to sit all day at a console, poring over missile guidance systems, little troubling about the consequences. Leboyer surmises that both girls and boys are 'brutalised' from birth. The mass psychology of obedience, investigated by Reich (the 'armoured character') and Fromm (the 'authoritarian character'), yields clues about the human and inhuman underpinning of SDI.[31]

SDI, in its cultural form of 'Star Wars', could be seen as part of a male bonding process; an obsession with 'strength' (physical, technological, economic and military); a quest for political or personal 'muscle'; a boffin's dream; a 'sexy' idea; a fantasy of frontiers and fighting, with an underlying sublimated eroticism:

> 'Hang on buddy', you call 'I'm coming in!' You lean your A-wing through a gut-wrenching loop and come up behind the enemy ship. You trigger your laser as the TIE swoops in for the kill.[32]

It is indeed a question of taking the toys from the boys. The neat designs, the smart exteriors, the gleaming metal and ceramic weapons systems and the fantasy of infallible hardware amount to a vision which transcends the grubbiness of reality, or at least subordinates human relations to a higher realm of brilliant gadgetry.

The metaphors of SDI are about distance, height and superiority: high technology, the 'high frontier', 'riding high', 'standing tall', 'reaching for the stars'. As Reagan put it in his autobiography: 'there is no left or right, only an up or down. Up to the maximum of individual freedom consistent with law or order, or down to the ant heap of totalitarianism.'[33]

The images of SDI are distant, clean, fast, romanticised. It is a designer programme – a challenge to devise a 'smart' architecture – and a baroque example of the 1980s cult of conspicuous consumption. It has the effect of *fictionalising* war, offering celestial images far more fetching than hibakusha in Hiroshima, traumatised GIs in Vietnam, or even tanks in Iraq. Instead, a laser shoots down a gleaming battle station against the dark background of space; a neat surgical strike, removed, beyond ordinary human control, the province of high tech.

SDI, Star Wars, is a Hollywood version of conflict and the 'life beautiful': a delightfully innocent yarn, with superb special effects. It transforms anxiety into excitement, exorcising the sombre earnestness

162

of 'Threads' and 'The Day After'. It sanitises war, playing down mass destruction and personalised death in favour of a pleasant electronically mediated experience. Man is in love with war, and Reagan's vision allowed the romance to blossom. It became the user-friendly, faintly ludicrous face of genocide.

SDI was the epitome of the politics of spectacle, as if designed for the ten-second sound bite or news clip. The French Minister of Defence commented how he had 'been struck by the way that screens the world over have been invaded by highly evocative multicoloured sketches and animated cartoons spliced with lengths of film of real life experiments carried out on earth and in space'.[34] These animations, which typically showed a clean line sliding through space for a smooth interception, fostered the idea that Star Wars systems are already a feasible option.

How far did this appeal to popular culture translate into direct public support for SDI? The evidence of opinion polls is ambivalent, but three general points may be inferred. First, there is a good deal of volatility, ignorance and uncertainty about SDI. Second, answers are highly influenced by the context of the question and the terms in which it is framed. Many polls are commissioned by interest groups with ulterior agendas, and even if questions are not deliberately 'loaded', it is hard to find neutral, value-free wording. Third, allowing for the above caveats, US public opinion has been divided roughly evenly for and against Star Wars, with men backing the project more than women. Two pollsters noted that:

> As long as Star Wars was described as a war fighting system, introducing war fighting capability to outer space, the public tends to oppose it. When it is depicted as the Strategic 'Defense' Initiative, capable of defending the United States from outside attack, it gains public support.[35]

In so far as the *name* 'Star Wars' is linked with danger and aggression, it damages the image of SDI. To the extent that the *culture* of Star Wars is seen as exciting and entertaining, it gains support for SDI.

### CONCLUSION

The techno-strategic style, predominant in 'expert' discussion of SDI, blocks the open expression of feeling and encourages a series of unacknowledged emotional transferences. These serve to reinforce the image of an enemy, on to which negative feelings are projected, taking the collective form of militant anti-Communism. The masque of rationality is often animated by a hidden play of unrecognised motives: self-interest, sympathy, pride or careerism. Other feelings, such as fear, anger, grief or aggression, may be more assiduously repressed. Prevailing emotions are often hard to identify: bizarre amalgams and complexes, derived from repeated disavowal of primary emotions. The SDI debate was all too often estranged from direct feelings, emotionally disturbed, ignorant of its fundamental premises and blind to alternative uses for the money.

Although US popular culture contains some themes which are oppositional to SDI – the 'Strangelove' myth of the mad scientist, or fears of technology as a modern Frankenstein's monster – these were in a minority. 'Star Wars' was reinforced by other motifs from mass culture: US nationalism, the ideology of anti-Communism, faith in space and 'technical fixes', myths of the frontier and the superweapon, and fantasies about American power and benevolence. The images of 'Star Wars', seen by millions on news clips and in magazines, have the effect of distancing, sanitising, beautifying and fictionalising war. They flatten and screen, domesticate and dehumanise, stimulate and sedate. The configuration of power, fun, alienation and machismo gratifies a masculinity preoccupied with competition and domination. To the population as a whole SDI promised a different kind of emotional reward, an end to fear and vulnerability. The genius of Reagan was his sensitivity to the cultural and symbolic dimensions of strategic defence and his unsurpassed skill in tapping popular motifs for the purposes of mass politics. The President and his acolytes transcended intellectual argument, as they tapped deep and hardly explored roots in US popular culture, linking their project to popular motifs and drawing on its full symbolic potential to win popular support.

# 13  THE SELLING OF SDI

The main features of SDI's marketing, to which it largely owes its budgetary success, are visible in its inaugural presentation of 23 March 1983. The President began by hinting at 'a decision which offers a new hope for our children in the 21st century'.[1] After a rhetorical denial,[2] he went on to imply very powerfully that the Soviet Union was a menace and was planning to wage war. The bulk of his address catalogued frightening Soviet activities in Cuba, Nicaragua, El Salvador, Costa Rica, Honduras, Angola, Ethiopia, South Yemen, Vietnam, Afghanistan and Poland.[3] 'They are spreading their military influence in ways that can directly challenge our vital interests and those of our allies.'[4] Reagan showed aerial photographs of Soviet hardware in Nicaragua and Soviet facilities in Cuba, places whose historical connotations would automatically worry Middle America. 'The rapid build-up of Grenada's military potential', the President stated, 'is unrelated to any conceivable threat to this island country.'[5] He wished he could show more 'without compromising our most sensitive intelligence sources and methods'.

Reagan's many statistics were selected to put the worst imaginable gloss on approximate strategic parity. He was especially disingenuous about intermediate-range nuclear missiles, but he passed it off with a grim humour: 'So far, it seems that the Soviet definition of parity is a box score of 1,300 to nothing in their favour.'

Reagan also capitalised on verbal ambiguity. In an adroit subordinate clause, he raised the fear of a 'window of vulnerability' through which the USSR might launch a pre-emptive strike: 'the Soviets . . . have enough accurate and powerful nuclear weapons to destroy virtually all our missiles on the ground'.[6] He said nothing of the sea- and air-based portions of the nuclear triad, which carry most US nuclear missiles and which could obliterate the Soviet bloc on their own.

The speech repeated variations on a theme which couples 'they, the Soviets' with a menacing active verb and a quantity of hardware and 'us' with a negative verb or a form of inaction. Thus 'they'

> built . . . strengthened their lead . . . are still adding . . . have built up . . . [have] built . . . upgraded . . . continue to develop . . . built . . . produced twice as many . . . increased their military power . . . have been emboldened to extend that power . . . spreading their military influence.[7]

Meantime 'we'

> haven't built . . . already retired . . . had none . . . still had none . . . still had none . . . still have none . . . so . . . we decided . . . will begin . . . are willing to cancel.[8]

The repeated 'we' embraces the viewers, creating a sense of belonging and national pride. 'We' is elided with 'free people', to conjure up an opposite category of aliens: 'they', 'them', 'not free people'. The techniques are not specific to the SDI speech, but are all the more significant for being so widespread.

Reagan hinted that there was an 'enemy within': 'liberals' responsible for 'poor morale' and 'lost years of investment', who even now were trying to restrict defence increases to 2–3 per cent.[9] The tale of Soviet cunning and American vacillation strongly implied, without quite stating, that liberals were to blame. Reagan created an image of a weak liberal naively opposed to every new American weapon.[10] One opposed the speech at the risk of confirming oneself as precisely the kind of misguided ignoramus whom it so cleverly sketched.

By devoting four-fifths of his speech to 'threat and fear', Reagan anchored his audience in a state of acute vulnerability, conducive to accepting his new proposal.[11] Skilled salesman as he was, Reagan ignored the small print of reality: cost, feasibility, counter-measures, arms control and threat to crisis stability. Instead he ran euphorically through the potential advantages of BMD. In entertaining the President's idea, his listeners could themselves experience the pleasure of anxiety melting into hope. It was then only natural to expect that, if the idea were collectively acted upon, the same agreeable transaction – anxiety turning into hope – might ensue.

When announcing their Ballistic Missile Defence (BMD) programmes of the 1960s, McNamara and Nixon had publicly acknowledged the risks of such a course. Most of McNamara's speech was a cogent summary of the arguments *against* BMD. Nixon too stressed that 'the question of ABM involves a complex combination of many factors'; and that 'it might look to an opponent like the prelude to an offensive strategy threatening the Soviet deterrent'.[12] Reagan's style was different, as might be expected from a former salesman for General Electric, the salesman president *par excellence*, steeped in the world of

166

'motivation analysis' and 'conformity enhancement', whose electoral success was attributed to clinical psychologists hired from the Behavior Sciences Corporation (BASICO).[13] Reagan avoided the tricky issues. He knew that the best evidence for a proposition is the listeners' own prejudices. There was no dallying with debate, doubt or nice distinction. The President delivered a congruent, carefully crafted, speech. He sold an idea, to considerable effect.

Reagan demonstrated that he cared about SDI as he continued to sell the programme in the best possible light to the American people. He was aided by the first director of the SDI Office, who was, in the view of the then chairman of the joint chiefs, 'as much an advocate and a salesman as he was a project director'.[14] Abrahamson was a high flier, who had flown forty-nine combat missions in the Vietnam War and was also skilled in nurturing controversial weapons programmes. As director of the $24 billion F-16 programme he had been responsible for a budget equivalent to the seventieth largest US corporation in the Fortune 500. Moving to NASA in 1981, he was dealing with a budget equivalent to the sixty-sixth largest US corporation in the Fortune 500, with about 8,000 civil servants and over 80,000 contractor personnel.[15]

Whilst the SDIO was nominally supposed to be investigating the potential for BMD in order that a future Administration might make an informed decision, it seems that Abrahamson and others saw his job as primarily that of a salesman for SDI:

> Specifically, the Director and his staff: manage the aerospace systems equipment development programs [sic]; *act as the primary OSD agent for technical advocacy of development programs* to provide the technology and capability to fulfill known or anticipated OSD operational requirements.[16]

The interim charter of the SDIO said that the director was to be responsible for 'communicating the objectives of the programs of the SDIO to congress and to the public'.[17] This Abrahamson did with skill, charm and charisma. For the most part, he ignored criticisms by eminent scientists outside the DoD, adroitly refusing to be drawn into debate.

'Abe', Reagan and fellow supporters presented SDI as 'the greatest peace initiative of our time', heralding a new era of 'mutual assured survival'. The new 'peace shield' was sold on its winsome simplicity, its good intentions, its innate attractiveness to all who desire security and protection. SDI budgets always included token funds for medical research. Its adherents linked it to transcendent themes. Edward Teller

167

spoke of SDI, freedom and world history. 'Reagan's epochal proposal has not borne fruit as yet. It may be seen by posterity to be as important as the liberation of slaves by Abraham Lincoln.'[18] One Republican likened SDI to Columbus's search for the New World, urging Congress to 'play the role that Ferdinand and Isabella played'.[19] Few other weapons systems are justified in humanist, even millenarian, terms.

Such verbal flamboyance, such hyperbole was in a tradition of American 'tall talk': a language without inhibition, of breezy magnificence, which blurs the edges of fact and fiction.[20] In 1817 an English traveller remarked that the Americans often use 'the present indicative instead of the future subjunctive . . . what may be is contemplated as though it were in actual existence'. SDI partook of the proleptic tendency, this habit of anticipation and innocent overstatement, intended to be vaguely clairvoyant.

SDI was also marketed by the advertising professionals. A High Frontier commercial features a child-like animation of stick-people, the sun, a house and a dog with the voice of a little girl drifting over the dulcet tones of a toy piano.[21] The girl says: 'I asked my Daddy what this Star Wars stuff is all about.' A dome-like arc comes over the scene. 'He said that right now we can't protect ourselves from nuclear weapons, and that's why the President wants to build a peace shield.' The sun and the stick people frown as plump red missiles bounce against the arc, pop like bubbles and vanish. 'It would stop missiles in outer space so they couldn't hit our house', the girl continues. 'Then nobody could win a war.' And the missiles stop coming. The advertisement was devised by Mr Don Ringe of Ringe Media Inc., the original doodles done left-handed by his right-handed girl-friend, a computer analyst. It cost $50,000 to make and became the flagship of High Frontier's $1.7 million strategy to sell SDI to the people. Of the twelve other agencies consulted, National Media proffered a housewife-with-baby-facing-holocaust vignette, whilst Hal Larson Etc presented SDI as 'The New Freeze'.

From about 1985, the Administration increasingly sold SDI in negative, reactive terms, as a response to Soviet activities. Although his original speech had not mentioned any Soviet BMD or military space threat, Reagan now began to invoke a 'Red Shield' as justification for SDI. 'The Soviet defense effort, which some call "Red Shield", is now over 15 years old and they have spent over $200 billion on it – that's 15 times the amount that we have spent on SDI.'[22] According to a former CIA analyst, the statement was 'seriously misleading'.[23] Whilst the US figure was for SDI alone, the Soviet one was a crude estimate for all BMD, air defence against bombers and cruise missiles, plus estimated anti-satellite research. The figure was repeated as fact by high-ranking officials.[24]

The Deputy Director of the CIA warned of 'an intensive world-wide propaganda campaign', against SDI, run by 'the same Soviet covert action structure that was used against the enhanced radiation weapon in the late 1970s and the deployment of intermediate range nuclear weapons in the early 1980s'.[25] Critics of the Pentagon were cast by this time-honoured innuendo as fellow travellers or dupes of the Kremlin.[26] They were wrong by association. From about 1986, however, Gorbachev's foreign policy belied efforts to portray the Soviets as ruthless manipulators, or critics of SDI as tools of international Communism.

On Capitol Hill, SDI was sold in more sophisticated fashion: as a defence of missile silos, a response to Soviet BMD research, or a bargaining chip.[27] This variety of rationales entailed a risk, noted by a presidential science policy aide: 'if the message isn't totally coherent, then the sales force is less coherent internally'.[28]

A semi-organised incoherence allowed a double message to be sent: about partial defences to the educated and about a faultless astrodome for the public. Abrahamson was an accomplished salesman in his own right. Before SDI, he had negotiated Foreign Military Sales (FMS) worth over $8 billion with Iran, Israel, Egypt, Norway, Denmark, the Netherlands and Belgium.[29] He proved an excellent spokesman for SDI, aided by his congressional liaison officer, a Lieutenant-Colonel with a master's degree in communications and public policy who, by his own count, had visited at least 120 House members and 45 senators by August 1985.[30]

Abrahamson and other Administration officials made numerous visits to advocate SDI in the capitals of Europe.[31] They presented SDI not as a 'space shield', but as a prudent research programme offering lucrative contracts for Europe. They played on European fear of being left behind by new technological developments: an anxiety which was probably greater than fear of the Soviets.

Much of the lobbying for European participation was through informal contacts and is, therefore, hard to document. A confidential report on a conference of June 1985, which passed otherwise unreported, shows how US officials tried to involve the Europeans.[32] The event was sponsored by the 'Center for Strategic Concepts Ltd', a subsidiary of BDM International,[33] and the 'German Strategy Forum', an association of high-ranking former government officials. It was hosted by the German Air Force Logistic Command Headquarters. After a 'highly polished' speech by Lt-Gen. Abrahamson, Lou Marquet of the SDI Office described Soviet BMD and stressed that 'SDI research is worthwhile even if no actual Ballistic Missile Defense results.' The SDI Office would seek to expedite binational co-operation. Richard Perle stressed that the Soviets might be 'creeping out' of the ABM Treaty. Edward Teller emphasised theatre defence, of special interest to the Allies. He brought a white paper by Greg Canavan of Los Alamos Laboratory on 'Theater Applications of Strategic Defense Concepts'. Ex-Ambassador Bob Ellsworth said that 'the US congress strongly desires European moral involvement and help for SDI, even though it still wants to protect US industry'. But the participant, an American, reported that 'the conference did not alter German scepticism'.

In 1986, the US Administration organised eight seminars to convince Allied governments and industrialists that SDI could generate major spin-offs.[34] It was emphasised that SDI technologies like the rail-gun could become new-generation anti-tank weapons; and that electro-magnetic energy weapons and laser-beam riding technology could have similar applications. The obvious application for the Allies was in countering the Short-Range Ballistic Missile (SRBM) threat and devel-oping Anti-Tactical Ballistic Missiles (ATBMs).

In the negotiations preceding the signing of joint agreements on SDI, US officials gave misleading estimates about the prospects for SDI contracts in Europe. Abrahamson forecast that 'contracts worth billions of dollars could eventually be won by British companies'.[35] A senior Pentagon official told a British MP that 'he thought that there should be little difficulty in exceeding Michael Heseltine's $1.5 billion expendi-ture over five years for the UK. However this last assessment turned on the degree to which the United Kingdom was successful in competition situations and he felt that it would be impossible to guarantee expendi-ture on this count, without overwhelming legal, political and practical difficulties.'[36]

After five years, Britain had won a paltry 4 per cent of the $1.5 billion sum quoted. Either British industry was disastrously less competitive than had been thought, or British policy-makers had been misled. Only four days after the signing of the British MoU, the chairman of one congressional committee observed:

> We promised them 'substantial' and we gave them the wink with the word 'substantial' that could lead them to believe they might get $1.5 billion, when in reality European companies might get about $30 million in the near future and maybe $300 million over a 5-year period . . . My point is we might be building ourselves up for a fall. In other words, in an attempt to build up political support – assuming we do want to proceed on the Strategic Defense Initiative – that is creating

170

false hopes and is going to undermine whatever support might be created on a short-term basis.[37]

In signing 'Memoranda of Understanding', with the Allies, the SDIO won implicit endorsement of SDI and access to European technologies. Some efforts to build European support for SDI continued. The SDI Office awarded European firms contracts for research into 'theater defense'. It directed a Western Pacific Architecture Study (for Japan), a UK Architecture Study for the European area and a Theater Missile Defense Architecture Study (TMDAS) for the central region of NATO. The sums involved were not large enough to offend any US interest group, but sufficient to encourage Allied firms to link up and explore the opportunity.[38]

There were sporadic, relatively trivial attempts to garner mass support for SDI in Europe. In 1986, just after the Reykjavik summit, Britain's *Sun* newspaper gave '10 REASONS WHY WE MUST STICK WITH STAR WARS'.[39] Six of these were variations on a single theme of anti-Communism. 'We cannot trust the Russians', who seek 'world domination'. If they oppose SDI, the logic runs, it must be a good thing. Three of the reasons harp on the idea that 'Star Wars is solely defensive'. The remaining one is economic: 'a good deal of the work will go to Britain'.

### SDI AND THE DOMESTIC POLITICAL DEBATE

'The real purpose of SDI', said the French Minister of Defence, is 'to create a consensus within American society':

> Thanks to the project, President Reagan has managed to pull together most currents of public opinion behind him. In the first place, the SDI matches an expectation of the American people, who see Soviet ICBMs as the only real threat. It satisfies the peace movements and the churches who are opposed to nuclear policies but are patriotic. It slots in with the concern of the military and industry to step up America's defence effort and strengthen its superpower image. Finally it throws down a challenge like that of the 'New Frontier' when America decided to put a man on the moon. All these themes are guaranteed to rally support and mobilise American society.[40]

Although the extent to which SDI forged a consensus is overstated here, SDI did have a significant impact on the popular debate about defence and, particularly, on the fortunes of the 'Freeze' movement, which, in the early 1980s, had surged through the United States, winning over professional organisations, churches and unions with its

171

urgent, almost a priori call: 'There are too many nuclear weapons! Freeze the arms race!' A million people took to the streets in New York under the Freeze's banners. The Catholic bishops issued a pastoral letter, which challenged the morality of nuclear weapons.[41] By April 1983, a Harris Poll indicated that 81 per cent of Americans favoured the Freeze, with only 15 per cent against it.[42] The collapse of the Freeze, synchronous with the rise of SDI, may be attributed to the internal dynamics of the movement: the difficulty of holding together a coalition of disparate groups with different agendas. The Freeze had relied heavily on fear (which does not long sustain action), and by the mid 1980s the atmosphere of imminent menace had passed.

SDI also 'put the heat' on the Freeze. 'The new policy announced by the President went one step beyond the Freeze', according to a member of the Scowcroft Commission. It worked by 'joining the Freeze proponents in being against nuclear weapons (as everyone is) but then proceeding to the next step and proposing that we use US technology to help get rid of them'.[43] The Freeze could no longer claim a monopoly of good intentions. To ignore Reagan's hopes might seem endorsement by default, but to criticise them looked churlish or cynical: anti-technology, anti-Progress, anti-American. The Freeze had mobilised against solid artefacts (such as cruise, Pershing 2 and MX missiles). It was harder to generate equal urgency against less 'tangible' research, which was not, for the foreseeable future, due to be sited in anyone's 'backyard'.

Popular debate had coalesced around a number of simple scripts (sets of roles and emotions which people adopt when tackling or evading a problem). Against resignation and cynicism, the Freeze projected fear, urgency and protest. Reagan's intervention was a new public philosophy; a rhetorical peristrophe which reframed the pet themes of the Freeze; and an inspired political bricolage which 'drew freely from orthodox cold war mentalities and from anti-nuclear critiques of deterrence, popular exhortations about the horrors of nuclear war and the perceived need for radical change in an intolerable status quo'.[44] A pledge of transformation and deliverance, it flattered the best intentions of many Americans with a brand new 'rescue script': that the USA could eliminate nuclear weapons and save the day. Wittingly or not, Reagan out-flanked the Freeze, which relied on fear, anger and grief, by mobilising a breezy, can-do, never-say-die optimism, conforming to an emotional division of labour between 'warriors' and 'worriers', in which peace activists express anxiety, freeing others to be vectors of excitement. Reagan's sun-belt-style positive thinking drew on the popular psychology which has evolved alongside supercharged salesmanship. SDI was a package of unimpeachable intentions and a product of emotional Realpolitik.

Amongst those to appreciate the mind-altering potential of strategic defence was John Bosma: a defence consultant associated with the High Frontier, editor of the market intelligence newsletter *Military Space* and author of a plan aimed 'at keeping the BMD program alive in 1984 and to make it impossible to turn off by 1989'.[45] The front page of the 'Plan' is written on Heritage Foundation notepaper, across which is scrawled 'Not for Release'. Bosma said that he submitted the paper to High Frontier in February 1984 when he was finishing full-time work there.[46]

Bosma's 'Plan' gives unguarded insights into pro-SDI thinking and sketches some of the differing priorities and covert agendas which converged around SDI. He wanted the US to move ahead 'forcefully and *unilaterally*' whilst representing BMD as a bilateral effort. 'The project should unambiguously seek to recapture the term "arms control" and all of the idealistic images and language attached to this term.' Once confused, the critics might be co-opted. 'It is very likely that the freeze movement, paradoxically, represents the best mass constituency for an early-IOC BMD system – but only if an unorthodox and radical approach to selling BMD to peace groups is undertaken by someone or some group.'

Many of Bosma's goals were attained to some degree:
'seek to recapture the term "arms control" for BMD'.
'play freely on high-road ethical themes'.
'converting or otherwise neutralizing peace groups'.
'broaden the support for BMD'.
'get an "off-shore" constituency, particularly the governments of major US allies'.
'get an early-IOC BMD programme underway as soon as possible'.

In particular, the aim of redrawing the defence debate was achieved. The Coalition for the SDI noted that 'anti-defense elements are having difficulty fighting SDI, since they must in essence argue for a continuation of the MAD policy, which relies entirely on the destructive power of offensive nuclear weapons. The obvious contradictions involved in opposing a non-nuclear SDI effort have caused serious erosion in public support for the freeze movement.'

Through High Frontier and the Heritage Foundation, Bosma would have had some access to senior policy-makers, but there is no way to aggregate the influence of his plans. Others had similar ideas independently. In an internal talk to researchers at Livermore in 1982, Edward

Teller said that 'our answer [to the Freeze movement] can be and should be that we have a third generation of nuclear weapons . . . The Third World War can be avoided if the people preaching the Freeze will not succeed . . . I think we have come dangerously close to a third catastrophe. It yet may be averted, and if it is, I am certain that this laboratory will play no small part in it.'[47]

In the same speech which announced SDI, the President chastised sympathisers of the Freeze:

> I know that all of you want peace and so do I. I know too that many of you seriously believe that a nuclear freeze would further the cause of peace. But a freeze now would make us less, not more, secure and would raise, not reduce, the risks of war. It would be largely unverifiable and would seriously undercut our negotiations on arms reduction. It would reward the Soviets for their massive military build-up while preventing us from modernizing our ageing and increasingly vulnerable forces.[48]

The Hoffman Report, which recommended SDI, noted as a 'supporting rationale' that 'the public in the United States and other Western countries is increasingly anxious about the danger of nuclear war and the prospects for a supposedly unending nuclear arms race'.[49] In the literal sense, therefore, SDI was introduced in the context of the Freeze. To infer that SDI was a response to the Freeze is a logical leap, but not an unreasonable one.

### SDI AND PRESIDENTIAL ELECTIONS

SDI can be seen as a strategic electoral initiative, which contributed to Reagan's re-election in 1984. The Republicans campaigned in favour of a 'space shield' to defend the people and restore American greatness. They implied that SDI would be good for America and that the Democrats were 'soft on defence'. It enabled them to set the agenda and added to the optimism and benignity of their candidate. Positive thinking triumphed over doubt and fear.

The Democrats failed to present a coherent, united front on SDI. Although sometimes they lambasted the idea, they also endorsed limited research, without clarifying the precise limits. This reduced the extent to which SDI could be used against them, but also produced an appearance of contradiction: why research a system that would supposedly be so dangerous to deploy? The Democrats' response to SDI lacked simplicity, conviction and congruence. They were once again cast as pessimistic nay-sayers, as SDI reinforced the gloomy, trouble-spotting image which was Mondale's downfall.

By the mid 1980s SDI was diminishing in novelty value and depreciating as an electoral asset. The easy optimism on which it flourished was undermined by the continuing deficits, the Challenger space shuttle disaster of January 1986, Chernobyl in April 1986 and a growing public scepticism about Reagan's idea. In the 1986 mid-term Senate elections, Reagan campaigned vigorously on the issue of SDI, but this did not prevent the Democrats from winning control of the Senate.

SDI was less significant in the 1988 presidential elections, in which the Republicans again linked defence (and SDI) with the Stars and Stripes, jobs and prosperity. Although Bush was not a 'true believer', he used SDI and defence in general to insinuate that his rival was 'weak on issues that strike emotional chords in voters – patriotism, crime, gun control and the environment'.[50] Bush's pugnacious campaign attacked the Democrats' record, mixing Dukakis's opposition to SDI deployment with his equivocation about some other military programmes, his membership of the American Civil Liberties Union[51] and the issue of furlough for prisoners. It made 'liberal' a dirty word. Whereas in 1984 SDI had been presented as a great peace initiative, in 1988 it was used negatively, to provide extra 'knocking copy' against Democrat 'weakness'.

### CONCLUSION

Most people ignore most nuclear debate because most nuclear debate ignores most people. The critics of BMD were often stuck in an esoteric, techno-strategic discourse, of little meaning to ordinary people. By contrast, Reagan's SDI speech was simply inspirational. The President's followers adopted the popularist style to side-step complexities and sell SDI in terms of vision, humanity and global defence.

Like so many other programmes SDI was presented in terms of chronic anxiety about the Russians. Unlike them, it was also sold as a shield, a blanket or an umbrella: a promise of ultimate protection. In more informed circles, SDI was depicted as a means of bolstering deterrence and hedging against the Soviets. To Europeans it was described as a research programme, which promised technological spin-off, lucrative contracts and leverage for arms control.

Although ABM supporters in the 1960s argued their case vigorously, they never marketed the idea with the passionate conviction accorded to SDI. ABM had had the official support of the Administration. SDI enjoyed much more. The difference is exemplified by the contrast between McNamara's thoughtful but troubled speech on Sentinel and Reagan's simple, skilful announcement of SDI. It serves to explain in part the relative success of SDI.

The early advocates of strategic defence were its first salesmen and Reagan their customer. General Graham's sales talk included wildly optimistic schedules for deploying 'High Frontier'. His 'off-the-shelf' product came to sound rather shop-soiled and humdrum compared with Teller's more imaginative sales pitch: the high-tech, hush-hush Super Excalibur laser. Although more suited to an ASAT mission, and thus diametrically opposed to SDI, this product was successfully presented as a centre-piece of the President's vision. 'Our work was many orders of magnitude short of the advertisements', an X-ray scientist at Lawrence Livermore said later.[52]

Whilst efforts by Reagan, Abrahamson and SDI supporters to market the idea had less than total success, they undoubtedly won over some groups who would otherwise have spurned BMD. Without its marketing, SDI could not have established itself as it did. Abrahamson's replacement, George Monahan, lacked his predecessor's skills as a salesman, which may have exacerbated SDI's problems at the end of the 1980s. The latest version of BMD has a chummy acronym, GPALS: Global Protection Against Limited Strikes. 'Global Protection' retains Reagan's appeal to our deepest anxieties and desires. 'Limited Strikes' tempers that with a more modest pragmatism. It remains to be seen if GPALS, more feasible than SDI and equally attractive, can reinvigorate the image of strategic defence in the 1990s.

# PART 5
# CONCLUSIONS

# 14 INTO THE 1990s

Since 1988, SDI has had its budget cut and both its design and rationale transformed. In early 1991 it was refocussed into a Global Protection Against Limited Strikes (GPALS).

The new détente threatened the most fundamental rationales for SDI. Although the Soviets were concerned about space weapons, their desire for arms reductions was now paramount. They undercut the argument that SDI would be a good 'bargaining chip' by declaring, in September 1989, that SDI would no longer block a START Treaty.[1] The fall of the Berlin wall and the domino-like collapse of state socialist regimes across Eastern Europe was endorsed, or even encouraged by Gorbachev. Leninism was de facto buried. The Soviets were reducing their forces and redeploying them in defensive positions: a process formalised by the Conventional Forces in Europe (CFE) Treaty, signed in November 1990. In July 1990 the USSR began to raze the phased array radar facility at Krasnoyarsk, thus underlining a commitment to the ABM Treaty.[2] SDI looked increasingly vulnerable to demands for a 'peace dividend'. The new international climate, coupled with federal and budget deficits in the USA, ruled out the large budget increases, envisaged in the early SDI requests, for full-scale RDT&E and deployment in the 1990s. In 1987 the SDIO had planned to request $8 billion in FY 1991; in the event, the Administration asked for $4.66 billion and was granted $2.89 billion.

The programme as a whole showed little sign of fulfilling the basic criteria of military efficacy, survivability and cost-effectiveness at the margin. Individual projects were blessed with success,[3] and beset by failure.[4] There was no substantial evidence (in open sources at least) that the *margin of technical superiority* over the Soviets widened significantly. As Administration claims about the maturity of SDI technologies were proven optimistic and Congress cut SDIO requests, deployment schedules began to slip.[5] This gave the Soviets more time to devise counter-measures such as decoys, underflying, overwhelming, shortening the boost phase or interfering with SDI software.[6] The

179

prospect of a secure Strategic Defense System could therefore recede, even though the technologies were advancing.

After Reagan's retirement, SDI was no longer sheltered from technical, political and fiscal realities. Although George Bush publicly endorsed SDI, he did not see it as a way of 'eliminating the threat posed by nuclear ballistic missiles'. Lt-Gen. Abrahamson also left with the outgoing Administration. His successor, Lt-Gen. George Monahan, was a pragmatist, lacking in fervour, whose appointment marked a further step from Reagan's original aims.

With 'true believers' gone, officials no longer needed to genuflect to the vision of a population defence. More and more, they publicly acknowledged what the critics had long been castigated for saying. Even while Reagan was still in office, his Secretary of Defense admitted that SDI could not provide an 'impenetrable shield'.[7] President Bush's new Secretary of Defense, Dick Cheney, called Reagan's original idea 'an extremely remote proposition'.[8] He said that 'oftentimes, during the Reagan administration, it was sold in terms which I think, frankly, oversold the concept'.[9] Vice-President Dan Quayle was also candid: Reagan 'talked about this impenetrable shield that was going to be completely leak-proof . . . I believe that, in the semantics of let's say political jargon, that [sic] was acceptable. But it clearly was stretching the capability of a strategic defense system.'[10]

In June 1989 the Bush Administration formally defined SDI in terms of creating 'options for strengthening deterrence and stability through the deployment of strategic defenses based on advanced technologies'.[11] The vice-chairman of the joint chiefs of staff called for 'the minimum capability required to begin making a contribution to deterrence . . . the least militarily significant capability'.[12] At Bush's accession, six SDI technologies had reached demonstration/validation phase:

> BSTS, Boost Surveillance Tracking System
> SSTS, Space Surveillance Tracking System
> GSTS, Ground-based Space Tracking System
> SBI, Space-Based Interceptors
> ERIS, Exoatmospheric Re-entry vehicle Interceptor System
> BM/C³, Battle Management/Command Control Communication

In January 1990 the Pentagon added a further concept to Phase 1: 'Brilliant Pebbles'. This was a transformation of the SDIO's original design for space-based defence, which had envisaged clusters of large satellites capable of launching ten interceptor rockets each. The satellites would contain radars and scanners to guide the rockets to

Table 14.1. *SDI authorisations under President Bush*

| Fiscal year | Total SDI funds ($m.) |
| --- | --- |
| 1989 | 4,046.424 |
| 1990 | 3,820.000 |
| 1991 | 2,890.000 |
| 1992 | 4,150.000 |

their targets. These space-based assets had always looked especially vulnerable. The Space Surveillance Tracking System (SSTS) satellites – eighteen in number – intended to guide the Space-Based Interceptors, were, in Monahan's words, 'fat, juicy targets' for the Soviets.[13]

The proposed solution, 'Brilliant Pebbles' (BP), would dispense with the vulnerable space platform (the satellites) and disperse and miniaturise the interceptors. They would therefore be much harder to attack. Each new interceptor, or 'pebble', would, it was conceived, weigh about 45 kg and orbit the earth, controlled by its autonomous computer, perhaps as small as a packet of cigarettes.[14] Supporters of the BP concept claimed that it would be relatively cheap, perhaps $275,000 per interceptor.[15] They originally envisaged several thousand pebbles, but by 1991 this had been reduced to one thousand.

The new BP design, devised at Lawrence Livermore by Gregory Canavan, Edward Teller and Lowell Wood, won early support from Vice-President Dan Quayle and Lt-Gen. Abrahamson.[16] Another scientist at Lawrence Livermore reported, however, that the pebbles 'would be easy targets for fleets of far cheaper anti-satellite weapons launched swiftly by an enemy from the ground'.[17] In order to respond rapidly to any Soviet missile attack, it is intended that the pebbles would largely operate automatically, requiring only a minimum degree of control and coordination from the ground.[18] This raises concerns about crisis stability, as well as enormous technical problems. BP is still only a design concept. It could prove to be much heavier and more expensive than has been claimed, as the necessary capabilities for target acquisition, guidance and 'brilliance' are incorporated. US Air Force officials believe that continuous ground control is necessary. This would generate its own problems, as extraordinarily complex computer software and communications systems would have to be developed. It seems unlikely that BP would be cost-effective at the margin: a BP defence 'could be nullified or destroyed at a cost much lower than what it might cost to expand or replace the BP defense'.[19]

Many suspected that the smartly packaged Pebbles were another instance of haste and hype.[20] One senator, who had voted against cuts to SDI, spoke of 'a seemingly endless search for near term deployment possibilities, silver bullets or brilliant pebbles or genius dust, whatever this year's fashion in SDI designer systems happens to be'.[21] 'It's time we stopped listening to snake oil salesmen in white lab coats', another congressman opined.[22]

No longer a popular cause or badge of fealty to Reaganism, but just another means of enhancing deterrence, SDI now had to compete on equal terms with programmes such as the B-2 'Stealth' bomber, the MX-rail garrison and the Midgetman ICBM. Though no longer granted a privileged status, essentially superior to other efforts, SDI did retain a special appeal as a way of sponsoring research to further the commercial and military exploitation of space. Its budget contained, for example, a secret item, codenamed 'Timberwind', for developing nuclear-reactor-powered rockets to haul very heavy payloads – perhaps large weapons or satellites – into space orbit.[23] Allusions, often veiled, to such 'secondary' benefits weighed heavily with the 'pragmatist' constituency. The chairman of the joint chiefs of staff from 1985 to 1989 suggested later that SDI was accepted for its contribution to the broader technical agenda. 'There is evidence that the Soviets have not been doing as much as we thought. There's been a lot of hoopla about this stuff which I think has been misleading. Frankly we have done a lot of positive experiments and development. However, that doesn't mean we have SDI.'[24] He went on to praise the more sober approach to SDI which prevailed after Abrahamson's departure as being 'eminently good sense'. 'On the other hand the whole conservative clique behind SDI got mad as hell about it.'

In the mid 1980s, the SDI programme was a safe haven for generic technologies which might not otherwise have been funded. In the interval between the fall of the Berlin wall and the outbreak of the Gulf War, this changed as SDI became a target for deeper cuts. The Pentagon was increasing its funds for the technologies most critical to weapons' advances and seeking to protect these allocations from expected cuts to the SDI request.[25] In the FY 1991 budget, the Boost Surveillance Tracking System, which accounted for $265 million, was moved from SDI to an air force programme for tactical warning attack assessment.[26]

Though many SDI contractors were resigned to cutbacks, to have slashed the budget much below $2.5 billion, without providing alternatives, would have antagonised powerful forces. The contracts remained broadly distributed, with strong concentrations in California, Washington, Alabama and Massachusetts.

By the end of the 1980s about 28,000 US citizens were working

Table 14.2. *Top states: SDI contracts to January 1989*

| State | Total ($m.) |
|---|---|
| California | 3,847 |
| Washington | 1,150 |
| Alabama | 1,089 |
| Massachusetts | 980 |
| New York | 740 |
| New Mexico | 409 |
| Texas | 349 |
| Colorado | 331 |
| Maryland | 251 |
| Virginia | 221 |
| Florida | 163 |
| Missouri | 133 |
| Connecticut | 126 |

*Source:* SDIO data, January 1989. The total includes prime contracts and subcontracts.

directly on SDI.[27] Fear that the big SDI contractors might flex their political muscle was expressed by former President Carter. Calling 'Star Wars' a '$5 billion slush fund', he warned that 'money that goes to senators and congressmen legally will overcome unorganized concern expressed by ordinary citizens'.[28]

In January 1990, *Investor's Daily* reported that SDI's congressional supporters 'are readying an intensive lobbying campaign' for a first-phase SDS deployment.[29] Public advocacy was in fact restrained, for interest groups continued to exert influence in more sophisticated ways, through official advisory bodies. The American Institute of Aeronautics and Astronautics produced an 'independent' report in favour of SDI. Of the 80 participants in the review, 70 came directly from SDI contractors and others were connected.[30] The main advocacy was private and high level, focussing on ways to modernise SDI's rationales in the post-Cold War era. The SDI die-hards revived the spectre of accidental or unauthorised launch, terrorist attack and 'rogue' Third World states. Because such attacks would involve only a few missiles, a strategic defence would be much more feasible. By redefining the threat scenario, SDI could resolve the problem of being 'survivable' and 'cost-effective at the margin'.

These rationales were not entirely new. The possibility of accidental launch was mentioned by both McNamara and Nixon in their respective announcements of Sentinel (1967) and Safeguard (1969).

183

Table 14.3. *The top twenty SDI contractors to 1991*

| Contractor | Value ($m.) |
|---|---|
| 1. Lockheed | 1,618.6 |
| 2. Boeing | 1,295.8 |
| 3. TRW | 983.8 |
| 4. McDonnell Douglas | 947.6 |
| 5. Rockwell | 834.5 |
| 6. GM Corp. (Hughes) | 628.1 |
| 7. Teledyne Brown | 559.2 |
| 8. Raytheon | 459.1 |
| 9. Martin Marietta | 386.7 |
| 10. MIT | 324.6 |
| 11. Aerojet | 321.8 |
| 12. General Electric | 319.4 |
| 13. LTV | 285.5 |
| 14. Grumman | 279.5 |
| 15. Applied Physics Laboratory | 243.8 |
| 16. Nichols | 228.9 |
| 17. SAIC | 213.6 |
| 18. Los Alamos | 181.3 |
| 19. Ford Motors (BDM) | 179.3 |
| 20. Lawrence Livermore | 170.4 |

*Source:* SDIO information, as of 11 February 1991.

Reagan also had alluded to both this fear and that of 'lunatic' attack. 'This threat hangs over all of us worldwide and some day there may come along a madman in the world someplace – everybody knows how to make 'em anymore – that could make use of these [nuclear weapons] [*sic*].'[31]

In January 1988, Sam Nunn, head of the Senate Armed Services Committee, proposed that SDI be converted into an Accidental Launch Protection Scheme (ALPS).[32] Accidental launch had long been a special concern of peace activists, to whom Nunn's idea (like SDI) had a strong, superficial attraction, even though they mostly rejected it. Although his plan also appealed to centrists and pragmatists who sought a tangible return on investments made, it had a surprisingly lukewarm response from the Pentagon. Dismissing the likelihood of an accidental launch as 'very very low', the chairman of the joint chiefs of staff told a Senate panel to bear in mind 'that a system of this type would have to deal effectively with random and unforeseen events and achieve nearly 100 per cent effectiveness to be worthwhile as an investment'.[33] Critics feared that ALPS could be a 'stalking horse' for a full SDI system. Its declared objectives might be better met by direct measures to prevent accidental launch, such as arms limitation or equipping operational missiles with a command-destruct link, of the kind fitted in tests, which enables a range safety officer to destroy a missile that goes astray.[34]

High Frontier exploited some of the popular potential of an Accidental Launch Protection Scheme (ALPS) in their film *One Incoming*, which showed the President hustled from the White House one rainy night on to Air Force One, where he is notified of an accidental missile launch by the Soviets. 'The president: "we can't stop it? We can't even stop one damned missile! All I can do is watch a million people die, or start blowing up the whole world. That's my only choice? How did we ever get into this?"'[35] Overall, however, the SDIO missed an opportunity to promote ALPS as a popular cause.

According to an article in the *Wall Street Journal*, George Bush, once agnostic over SDI, 'began getting more enthused one day in 1988' when Edward Teller walked into a National Security Council meeting, bearing a model of 'Brilliant Pebbles'.[36] Bush's seedling interest was cultivated by his Vice-President Dan Quayle, an evangelist for both SDI and 'Brilliant Pebbles', with a particular concern about theatre defence. The article described Quayle as 'the key behind-the-scenes player in the evolution of the Bush Administration's surprisingly robust advocacy of SDI'.[37] Encouraged by Quayle, Secretary of Defense Dick Cheney toured the Lawrence Livermore Laboratory in September 1989. He returned a more vocal supporter of SDI, even though the Warsaw Pact was crumbling at the time. 'Technology is no barrier to deploying', Cheney informed the National Security Industrial Association. He hailed 'Brilliant Pebbles' as one of the 'major technological discoveries of the decade'; and justified SDI as a means both of deterring a Soviet first strike and of guarding against attack from the Third World: 'a second class power can become a first class threat'.[38]

In November 1989, after Congress had again slashed the SDIO's request, 'Quayle convened a meeting of about 20 sympathetic lawmakers in the Executive Office Building to develop more effective arguments for SDI spending.'[39] The chosen option was apparently the 'rogue state', which was increasingly cited over the next year.

In an article published in April 1990, Edward Teller and Gregory Canavan added the Third World rationale for SDI in a postscript headed 'Recent developments'.[40] The case was more fully outlined in a report the following month for the Center for Strategic and International Studies. SDI should be redirected towards facing the growing menace of tactical ballistic missiles in the Third World. R&D should be concentrated on 'five critical combat needs', including reconnaissance, long-range strike systems, battle management and survivability. In

185

addition the US should 'exploit space for conventional combat with kinetic energy weapons'.[41] The same threat was underlined by the head of the Army Strategic Defense Command, which specialises in ground-based and theatre defence.[42]

In July 1990 the Pentagon's announcement of Henry Cooper as the new director of the SDI Office delighted the programme's supporters. A former ambassador to the defence and space talks in Geneva, Mr Cooper was known as a 'true believer', committed and pugnacious, more in the mould of Abrahamson than Monahan. He believed that 'the importance of a plan that could lead to the deployment of an effective defense cannot be overstated'.[43] On his appointment he said that he hoped to 'move toward deploying defenses as soon as the program can demonstrate they are feasible'.

Iraq's invasion of Kuwait in August 1990 dramatically illustrated the theory of 'rogue states' and prompted speculation in the US media about refashioning SDI.[44] The US Senate responded quickly, voting by 97 to 1 that $300 million of SDI funds should be channelled into defence against short-range, tactical ballistic missiles, of the kind used by Third World powers.[45] The *Reader's Digest* helped to disseminate the new case for SDI: 'weapons of mass destruction are getting into the hands of Third World tyrants and Middle East madmen. The technology to defend us is at hand – if congress will act.'[46] *Fortune* too heralded the resurrection of SDI, with its new short-range focus, 'good news for Army contractors, such as Lockheed, McDonnell Douglas and LTV'.[47]

Meanwhile the SDIO was both reorientating its mission and reducing its estimates for costs. By December 1990 it had devised the GPALS acronym – Global Protection Against Limited Strikes; according to its director, the concept would cost $40 billion to implement. The new rationales were a patchwork of old and new. GPALS could provide leverage in the Geneva arms talks; blunt a Soviet counter-force strike; and guard against accidental, unauthorised or limited launch from the USSR or anywhere else.[48] According to congressional supporters, a GPALS programme would be a continuation of SDI in terms of projects and technology. 'Programmatically, you are not doing anything different whether you are going to do a PALS or a more robust system.'[49]

In December 1990, thirty leading conservatives urged President Bush to announce deployment of a partial BMD by the year 2000. This, their letter said, could 'help prevent a future nuclear Pearl Harbor'. Without SDI, 'every tinhorn dictator who gets his hands on reasonably accurate ballistic missiles with chemical and eventually nuclear warheads will be able to paralyze Western nations and hold them hostage to this threat and aggression'.[50]

The Gulf War itself and the success of the Patriot anti-missile in shooting down Iraqi Scuds gave a further boost to the GPALS concept and theatre defence. Dan Quayle was quick to draw conclusions. 'SDI's critics say it doesn't work. I say to them – watch CNN.'[51] The comment had a Reaganite ingenuousness in that no SDI systems were deployed, let alone used against Iraq. The connection between SDI and Patriot was more tenuous than Quayle implied. Patriot anti-missile was not and never had been part of the SDI programme. It destroyed some Scud missiles and missed others, but this scarcely compared with countering a full-scale Soviet attack, as envisaged by SDI. Patriot is land-based and counters relatively slow, low-flying missiles, whereas SDI, partly space-based, is aimed at faster intercontinental ballistic missiles. By demonstrating the efficacy of low-flying cruise missiles – a threat entirely neglected by SDI – the war might be construed as evidence against strategic defence.[52]

None the less, though not programmatically linked to SDI, Patriot did incorporate similar software. Pictures of Patriot and 'smart' bombs had currency from their familiarity after 'Star Wars'; and SDI in turn gained credibility from them. 'If someone had asked me to go out and execute an advertising campaign to get the point across to the American people and the rest of the world . . . I couldn't have done it any better than the television has done', said one SDI official.[53] As laser-guided 'smart' missiles steered down the ventilation shaft of a bunker, the commentary emphasised the 'astonishing accuracy' of the 'pin-point targeting'. Operation Desert Storm was metamorphosed into a 'surgical strike': the theatre of war mediatised into a medical theatre, cleansed of casualties. The resulting spectacle repopularised 'Star Wars', with the President as the supreme spectator/player and surgeon/manager. 'We have a game plan and we've stayed with the game plan and we're on target.'[54]

The 'superweapon' in the Gulf was high technology itself: whether incarnate as a Stealth bomber, a Tomahawk cruise missile or a Patriot anti-missile. 'Smart' weaponry and Allied command of the skies guaranteed quick victory with 'acceptable' casualties;[55] and sound implications for the order books. '"You have to sell the connections between billion dollar technology and minimal casualties", according to one business end of the American industry.'[56] Dan Quayle specified what others implied: that the war vindicated the high-tech principle exemplified by SDI. On Capitol Hill, Quayle's logic may well hold sway: the images of the war, reprocessed by the pundits, absorbed into popular debate and reinvoked in budget battles, are likely to justify further funding.

187

The emotional and political capital so long invested in anti-Communism was readily transferred to a new 'enemy'. It was not merely that Baghdad had replaced the Kremlin. The new 'threat' was more flexible and diffuse: a mélange of Middle Eastern 'Hitlers', 'rogue states', Third World nationalists, stateless terrorists and Muslim fundamentalists.

These new fears fast began to reshape the SDI programme. In the second week of the war, Bush announced that SDI would be revamped into a new scheme, intended to provide 'protection against limited ballistic missile strikes whatever their source'.[57] Though this merited barely a paragraph in a wide-ranging 'State of the Union' address, it may prove as significant in the long run as Reagan's more crafted presentation of SDI. With the new brand name came an increased budget request: $4.58 billion for fiscal year 1992, as against an authorisation of $2.89 billion the previous year. The programme was reorientated towards more mature technologies for tactical defence. The X-ray laser project, Teller's original 'Star Wars' concept, was cancelled. In the words of the head of Britain's SDI Participation Office, the programme 'moved away from the fringes of science fiction to something credible, real and concrete'.[58] The day before Bush announced GPALS, the SDIO had achieved a much-needed success with its Exoatmospheric Re-entry vehicle Interceptor System (ERIS), which flew more than a hundred miles into space to collide with a mock warhead from a Minuteman ICBM launched from California.[59] This was a timely demonstration of the principle of SDI, or GPALS.

Apart from its increased funds, the SDI Office would oversee a new 'Tactical Missile Defense Initiative', whose funding request totalled $603 million in FY 1992 and $723 million the following year.[60] This consolidated programme would include the Arrow Anti-Tactical Ballistic Missile, being jointly developed with Israel (but not used against Iraqi missiles), as well as the Patriot missile, to be funded at $170 million. For the first time, therefore, the new budget would programmatically tie SDI to Patriot. The new institutional plan follows the imaged presentation of Patriot/Star Wars links and lends some retrospective validity to Quayle's comment. Winning lead role for theatre defence was a coup for the SDI Office, facilitated by bureaucratic fumbling between potential competitors within the army, notably the Strategic Defense Command and the Missile Command.[61] These agencies may try to win back this increasingly important mission for themselves.

Was GPALS a fair, sensible revision of SDI; an unscrupulous attempt to salvage it; or both? Will GPALS make friends in Congress? By definition the new plan is technically and financially more feasible than its precursor. That said, its declared objectives might better be met in more direct and efficient ways. Any renegade state should already be deterred by the threat of the massive nuclear arsenal. GPALS would be an extra military outlay, which is not envisaged to replace any other weapons. The threat of stateless terrorists (whose absence of territory could not be threatened) might be better met by improving covert operations, security at nuclear installations and surveillance at Customs. Terrorists, whether state-sponsored or stateless, who were determined to attack the USA would find it hard to design, finance and operate nuclear-tipped ballistic missiles. Rather than going to the trouble of firing a bomb from an identifiable spot on a costly ballistic missile, it would be much simpler to resort to conventional terrorist means, to attack US citizens with nerve gas, or to plant a nuclear device in a locker at Grand Central Station.

Critics suspected that GPALS was a new cloak for SDI; an assault on the symptoms of a problem, which might exacerbate the deeper causes; the high-tech equivalent of swallowing a horse to catch a fly. One congressman, a critic of SDI, complained of people trying to 'piggyback their own pet projects on the back of the success story known as Patriot'.[62] The problem addressed by GPALS might be better tackled through a global regime to monitor and control military exports. Efforts in this area have always been paltry compared with efforts to build new weapons. The USA, the USSR, Germany and Italy all sold arms to Saddam Hussein. US military equipment was diverted to Iraq, despite the United Nations embargo, right up to January 1991. Only a week after the end of the Gulf War, the US was proposing to sell arms worth $18 billion to the Middle East.[63] Moscow's willingness to co-operate creates new opportunities for 'prevention before cure': a mutually agreed and internationally enforced code of restraint. If GPALS were unilaterally imposed, states would regard it, in the same light as the Non-Proliferation Treaty, as a token of superpower condominium, asking to be broken. But if a wider pact were devised by consent, between the superpowers and Third World countries, GPALS might then be a welcome, supplementary measure.

What of the future? Much will depend on whether the USA 'sells' GPALS as effectively as Saddam Hussein inadvertently managed in early 1991. In efforts to promote GPALS, the SDI Office had by April 1991 'visited almost every member of the House Armed Services Committee', their lobbying 'the most aggressive since Abrahamson left'.[64] The SDIO is a powerful institutional voice for GPALS. The navy apparently has little to gain from it.[65] The attitude of

189

the other Services, particularly in a harsh budgetary climate, awaits clarification.

The Soviet Union (or its successor), perhaps more exposed to Third World attack than the USA, might agree to GPALS, if it were confident that relations with the USA would remain friendly. SDI might be converted into a mutually agreed GPALS, or even superseded by an epoch of space co-operation. Existing plans to launch a Soviet cosmonaut on the US shuttle and to launch a US astronaut to the Soviet's Mir space station might be the seed of further co-operation. If, on the other hand, détente crumbled, the SDI budget might be revived as part of a wider arms build-up, reverting to its anti-Soviet rationale. Abrogation of the ABM Treaty by either side would remove the great constraint, and full-scale development could ensue.

The future of strategic defence is linked to the broadest and least predictable trends: North/South relations; moves towards inter-dependence and integration; the extent of technological diffusion; the pace of integration in Western Europe and disintegration in the East. Sensitive to seemingly remote events, SDI might be eclipsed by recession, ecological crisis, nuclear accident, the unforeseen or adven-titious. The symbolic dimension, innate in SDI, makes it especially hard to predict the exact course it will take. Because SDI makes headlines, it is vulnerable to the politics of gesture. In 1988 the House cut $600 million from SDI and gave the money to drug interdiction.[66] Other unlikely causes may impact on SDI in the future. There is no saying where the political football will be kicked next. SDI could be bargained away as a gesture of goodwill, part of a 'peace dividend' or to show that the President was 'getting tough' with the deficit. Or SDI might be increased to placate the far Right, perhaps whilst far-reaching arms control agreements are pushed through Congress.

In an uncertain world, some things seem sure. SDI/GPALS will be valued for its position on the 'cutting edge' of military technology. Noam Chomsky predicted in 1986 that the US will welcome a reduction in nuclear arms providing that 'an intimidating posture permitting the free exercise of subversion and intervention must remain in place and the "Pentagon system" of forced investment for the benefit of high-tech industry must not be challenged. Star Wars combined with build-down is thus a natural US stance. Appropriate strategic doctrines can be designed as needed.'[67]

Continued research, compliant with the ABM Treaty, would require little intervention from above and would go some way towards satisfy-ing the interests of SDI contractors and the armed forces. 'The generals and admirals will take most of the money and the technology, and they'll put it toward things they want to do.'[68] Though the name and rationale may change, the network of laboratories and military agencies engaged on BMD projects looks set to endure, aided by institutional inertia and continuing strategic uncertainty.

Research into strategic defence will encourage advances in other weapons, especially ASATs. In congressional hearings for FY 1991 the Pentagon noted that the 'SDIO is developing technologies in both Kinetic Energy and Directed Energy areas that have ASAT potential or applicability'. 'The Department would be remiss in the current budget environment if we did not fully utilize those research efforts wherever they might be applicable (whether for ASAT or other defense programs), leveraging the substantial investment made by SDIO to date.'[69] The dangers posed by space weapons, especially ASATs, which are likely to be more prominent over the next decade, might be lessened by further Confidence Building Measures (CBM) or an ASAT Treaty.

SDI, or GPALS, retains cultural currency, as well as a formidable industrial constituency and institutional momentum. Following military triumph in the Gulf, US patriotism flourishes; myths of the High Frontier and the superweapon live unchallenged; space-age military hardware retains its exciting gloss; the images of 'Star Wars' continue to be linked with power, fun and entertainment. Strategic defence offers both excitement and security, a blend of the exotic and the familiar, a marriage of prized military technology and political popularism. It will be funded for many years to come.

191

# 15  THE CAUSES OF SDI

Herman Kahn established the Hoover Institute to 'think the unthinkable'. SDI may seem more a case of explaining the inexplicable. By placing the search for explanation within the myriad theories about the dynamics of the arms race, we may have overlooked the most obvious of causes. Situated in a different context, such as the demise of the Soviet Union, SDI could be seen as quite simply a good idea, a coercive tool or bargaining chip which proved devastating – an idea propounded by Mrs Thatcher:

> I firmly believe that it was the determination to embark upon the SDI program and to continue it that eventually convinced the Soviet Union that they could never, never, never achieve their aim by military might because they would never succeed.[1]

This suggestion supplies a satisfyingly simple explanation for the swirling currents of Soviet policy; and suggests an equally simple explanation for SDI. It sails over any deeper consideration of the origins of 'new thinking' prior to 1983; the arms control record of Brezhnev in the 1970s; and the rise of liberal think tanks which promoted *globalistika* (global studies) and 'mutualist' approaches to the arms race, no longer seen as external imposition or symptom of class struggle, but as a 'panhuman' issue requiring interactive solutions.[2]

An extension, or reduction, of Mrs Thatcher's belief holds that Star Wars actually *caused* the collapse of the Soviet Union: Edward Teller and his crew won their 'end-run' on Marxism-Leninism. The idea may yet be corroborated or negated by the memoirs of the Soviet leadership, should they appear. Until then, devoid of proof, we can only assess the theory's plausibility. Though SDI might be judged 'the straw that broke the Communists' back', it pales in significance besides the chronic dislocations already fracturing the body politic. Compared with the traumatic birthpangs of Soviet socialism, invasion from without and insurrection within, armies marching to 'strangle communism in its crib', the famines of the twenties, the internal and external terrors of the thirties, the 'Great Purges' and the 'Great Patriotic War', social and sexual repression, mass militarisation, the One Party electorally unaccountable, the spread of bureaucracy and nepotism, the plague of stagnation and sycophancy, the cancer of conformism and careerism, the smothering of innovation, enterprise finding its sole outlet in corruption, the systematic blocking of dissent at the national level, its flourishing at the level of the republics, the complacency of the geron-tocracy – besides these massive, structural problems, SDI scarcely warrants mention. The fire of revolution had long since consumed itself. The disintegration of the USSR has seemed so sudden partly because its causes were shrouded so obsessively. Once the collective belief in socialism was eroded below a critical level, no motivation to work remained. Demoralisation and recrimination set in. To state that Star Wars knocked the will out of the Soviet leadership may be a chunk of infinite truth, but it commonly functions more as a slogan or thought-stopper than a useful hypothesis.[3]

SDI can therefore be accounted for by magnifying it into a knock-out blow to the Kremlin. Conversely it could be discounted by minimising its significance, treating it as a secondary appearance covering the key (military) realities of its time:

> When we are confronted with any manifestation which someone has permitted us to see, we may ask, what is it meant to conceal? What is it meant to draw our attention from? What prejudice does it seek to raise? and how far does the subtlety of the dissimulation go?[4]

Nietzsche's *Hinterfrage* may apply to SDI. Just as the 'ABM debate' distracted attention from the development of MIRVs in the 1960s, so, it may be argued, SDI is a mere sideshow next to the modernisation of US offensive nuclear forces: the growth of Space Command, the Midget-man land-based missile, the navy's Ohio-class submarine, the Trident II D-5 warhead, sea-based cruise missiles, air-launched cruise missiles, the B-1 and the Stealth bomber. 'Without question', Nolan argues, 'these modernisation programs will determine the future of American defense capabilities far more than anything envisioned or pursued as part of the SDI. Ironically, the SDI has served to paralyze its critics in exaggerated polemics of what *might* happen, while the real future of nuclear forces was being determined elsewhere.'[5]

Before returning to SDI's ultimate historical 'place', significance and relation to other phenomena, we must summarise the explanations, strategic and otherwise, for its development. The baseline rationale for BMD, that it is a prudent hedge against Soviet research, has great longevity:

> The Soviets give every appearance of preparing for [BMD] deploy-
> ment whenever they believe they will derive significant strategic
> advantage from doing so. Their activities include some that are
> questionable under the ABM Treaty ... Active US R&D programs on
> advanced defensive systems can assist in deterring a Soviet deploy-
> ment designed to exploit an asymmetry in their favor.[6]

The above sentence, which could have come from almost any
justification for BMD in the last twenty years, epitomises the strategic
mindset which has driven BMD inexorably onwards. Our programmes
deter theirs. Theirs necessitate improvements in ours. When both sides
research as a hedge against the other, the result is likely to be an
upward spiral of weapons development. Since there is already
'vigorous research', 'resources must continue':

> Since the United States is conducting vigorous BMD Research and
> Development, resources must continue to insure program vitality.
> Fortunately, the technological edge still favours the United States. The
> potential to improve the edge, avoid surprise and promote stability –
> even including substantive arms control – rests with continued fund-
> ing which protects the current level of effort. Selective increases would
> enhance those areas of BMD R&D which promise high pay-off.[7]

In justifications for BMD, military strength is often confused with
national security: a far from synonymous concept. In an age of mass
destruction, mutual vulnerability and interdependence, security is
better conceived in terms of mutual confidence and common security.
It would be hard to demonstrate that the vast funds poured into BMD
since 1945 have left either superpower with a jot more security. SDI
may well produce an increase in US military power, but further
degradation of common security.[8]

The specific strategic rationales for SDI have not been prime
historical movers. At most they have been important subsidiary factors;
at worst, post hoc justifications, or specious apologetics. That said, a
post hoc justification, however casuistic, can, if widely accepted,
become an important rationale, contributing its own momentum to the
programme. Although the specific strategic rationales for SDI have
often been inconsistent and blind to the historical lessons of BMD, they
wielded considerable authority. Strategic defence is indeed intertwined
in strategic theory, but strategic theory alone is insufficiently reflexive,
resourceful and wide-ranging to show precisely how the demand for
SDI was constructed; or how both SDI and strategic logic are structured
by the political and ideological dimensions in which they are suffused.

The relation between strategic demand and economic supply-side interests can be illustrated by analogy. The medieval crusaders prayed before battle that with the aid of God they would extend His Kingdom and win much booty. When the House Majority leader urged his colleagues to 'muzzle the mad dog missile threat of the Soviet Union, loose the Zeus [BMD] through America's magnificent production line'[9] – or a Pentagon official invites a professor of computer science 'to "save the world from nuclear conflagration" and be paid $1000 per day'[10]– a double motivation similar to that of the crusaders is operating. Neither the strategic nor religious rationale should be dismissed as mere piety or pretence. Both are a cover for self-interest, but the cover is crucial. The official rationale serves to legitimise and mystify: to metamorphose worldly drives into moral duties. It provides an explanation which is publicly available and socially endorsed. Its atavistic simplicity (Us/Them, Good/Bad) opens endless prospects for exculpation and victimisation.

Could one ever *prove* that the specific strategic arguments for BMD have never been more than important, subsidiary rationales? Could the 'supply' side survive the demise of 'demand': the collapse of the 'strategic threat' and the disappearance of the enemy? This was a prospect dreamed by some in spring 1990, before the crisis in Kuwait. Would SDI sink with the Soviet threat? Would the interest groups galvanise themselves to perpetuate the programme? Would a new threat be manufactured? To what extent could the power of the 'supply side' compensate for the decline of the 'demand side'? The questions stand unanswerable because a new 'threat' soon emerged. Self-interest and strategy remain riveted to each other. They can be analysed apart, but for the purposes of experience and experiment they are practically inseparable.

A few of the theories discussed in Chapter 1 are of limited value. The theory of the 'baroque arsenal' is probably correct to suggest that strategic defences would be overly sophisticated and unreliable. SDI, however, is not an example of 'gold plating': superfluous increments being endlessly tacked on to existing systems, until they become super-saturated. SDI research explores *new* areas. The danger is not that the applications will be ineffectual, but that they are likely to be devastating. The 'Marxist' (or Trotskyist) theories of Mandel and Kidron that capitalism needs high arms expenditures in order to maintain demand and stave off a 'realisation crisis' do little to illuminate strategic defence.

Most of the other theories, however, can contribute to a rounded explanation of BMD and SDI. Most apply to every stage in the programme's history. Technological progress, the climate of superpower hostility, ideological antagonism, action/reaction, 'hedging' against the enemy, institutional incrementalism, bureaucratic inertia, the profit motive and coincidence of interest are endemic to the development of BMD since the 1950s.

BMD has long been an oblique way of securing federal funding of value to the commercial development of space, and some 'space enthusiasts' expect it to spur economic growth. Of its very nature, research into BMD goes hand in hand with development of more accurate nuclear weapons, space control and ASAT. Spin-offs range from ATBMs to futuristic beam weapons. The main SDI contractors are also busy manufacturing counter-force nuclear weapons: the Pershing missile (Martin Marietta), the Trident missile (Lockheed), the cruise missile (Boeing, Litton), the B-1 bomber (Boeing, LTV, AVCO, Rockwell) and the MX 'Peacekeeper' missile (AVCO, Rockwell, TRW, Martin Marietta). SDI could be as profitable for these firms in the 1990s as the production of highly accurate missiles was in the 1980s. SAIC, a small firm highly dependent on SDI contracts, has also won a $24 million contract to analyse *offensive* techniques by which US missiles could penetrate a Soviet BMD.[11] On the balance sheet, 'offence' and 'defence' are a profitable dialectic.

The policy process for BMD has often been highly complex. Responsibility is dispersed across institutions with different perceptions, preoccupations and priorities. It is made and unmade in the midst of uncertainty about information, environment and outcomes, with single decisions bearing on multiple objectives, with unpredictable trade-offs between the different values affected. BMD 'policy-making' passes through several stages: the formulation of the decision (context and options), the decision itself and the implementation of that decision. The complexities of the policy process are as nothing compared to the complexities of the relationship between it and other factors.

The policy process has been consistently dominated by members of the BMD infrastructure. In the late 1970s, the federal weapons laboratories were essential in maintaining BMD R&D, away from publicity. They provided 'experts' who argued the case for BMD before congressional committees. The official history of the Army Strategic Defense Command correctly noted that SDI was 'made possible by the technology kept alive in the Army's BMD activities of the past'.[12] Members of the BMD interest groups skilfully promoted the prospects for BMD in the early 1980s. The pro-BMD group based at the Heritage Foundation, which had several meetings with President Reagan, comprised leading industrialists (Joseph Coors, William Wilson and Karl Bendetsen), a weapons scientist (Edward Teller) and an 'ideological' supporter of BMD (Lt-Gen. Graham). Their efforts were aided by the wider political climate, the rise of the 'New Right' and the wave of anti-Soviet feeling which swept the USA in the early 1980s.

BMD could be seen as a triumph of narrow self-interest and the short-term view, the result of appalling weakness and almost paranoid insecurity; the senator who gives way to lobbying; the blinkered representatives of self- and corporate interest; the reporter who resorts to stereotypes of the Enemy; the executive preoccupied by his sales; the politician who exploits fear and anxiety; the statesman who seeks contracts for his nation; the military who want to guard against all eventualities except the arms race itself.

Apart from the wider contexts which continually shape BMD, some factors predominate at a particular moment. In the late 1960s, public protest was critically important in the cancellation of Sentinel. The arms control community held sway in the early 1970s, during the successful negotiation of the ABM Treaty. Thereafter, bureaucratic politics and strategic 'hedging' were vital in sustaining BMD. In the early 1980s it seemed that improved satellite, laser and $C^3I$ technologies might enable directed energy weapons to destroy enemy missiles in their boost phase.[13] These technological advances, coupled with the fear that the Soviets might exploit them, were an underlying cause of SDI.

The form which the new BMD programme took and the promise of 'eliminating nuclear weapons' were shaped by the character of the President. To the sober quiescence of strategic defence, Reagan added an intoxicating dash of Hollywood and Disneyland. He transmogrified BMD into SDI: a populist initiative which appealed to a latent desire for protection against the nuclear threat. Reagan and his Administration marketed SDI as the 'peace shield', a symbol of American commitment to peace through strength, along with the promise of space exploration and the elimination of nuclear weapons. SDI became a 'sexy' concept, appealing to motifs from popular culture: the 'super-weapon', the final frontier, the technical fix and the ultimate defence. Whereas BMD had survived largely beyond the realm of publicity, the arrival of SDI signalled a renewed role for domestic politics. As one adherent noted, it offered the chance to 'disarm BMD opponents, either by stealing their language and cause (arms control), or by putting them into a tough political corner through their explicit or de facto advocacy of classical anti-population war crimes'.[14]

In the establishment of the SDI programme between 1983 and 1985, decisions were taken with scant regard for the history of BMD. The large, significant questions were fragmented into small issues by the advisory panels. The Fletcher panel focussed on technical feasibility;

197

the Hoffman panel on strategy. Neither considered adequately the crucial issues, which concern the overlap and interaction of technology and strategy. The panels neglected the broad historical record, which would have led to more consideration of Soviet counter-measures and more caution about the prospects of BMD. They were dominated by those who stood to gain from the advice given. Over half the members of the Fletcher panel came from firms which have since profited from SDI. Fifty-three out of 65 had a direct financial interest in SDI-related research.[15] Seventeen of the 24 members of the Hoffman panel were drawn from SDI contractors. The Miller panel was also composed of 'defense insiders'. The few qualifications made by the panels were apparently edited out in the summary of their reports prepared for the President by the National Security Council.

The armed forces might have resented and resisted the coming of a rival, whose rhetoric of 'eliminating nuclear weapons' subverted the rationale for the offensive nuclear arsenal. The SDI Office could have disrupted the established roles and traditions of established BMD units in the army, air force, navy, Department of Energy, Defense Advanced Research Projects Agency and Defense Nuclear Agency. Friction was minimised by the director of the SDI Office, Lt-Gen. Abrahamson.[16] Because SDI funds were nearly all contracted to these established agencies, the programme was a new channel of funding to existing empires, rather than a new empire itself. The air force and the army both stood to gain in terms of budget and prestige. SDI was peripheral to the navy, which, under Lehman and Watkins, was already doing well financially, thanks to the increased total military budget. The armed forces and established BMD agencies had ample opportunity to shape SDI according to their wishes. The Defensive Technologies Executive Committee, which implemented Reagan's decision, was dominated by Pentagon officials. So too was the SDI Office Executive Committee, to which the SDI Office was answerable.[17]

In the mid 1980s the role of interest groups and institutional momentum was central to the expansion of the SDI infrastructure. SDI contracts were widely distributed, creating a powerful constituency of interest, spread among congressional districts and composed of corporations, federal laboratories and universities.[18] The sums already won by these groups would be dwarfed by the enormous contracts available if SDI moves to full-scale procurement. This engenders a degree of self-perpetuating institutional momentum. Once funds have been invested, it is hard to disband a weapons programme. Constituencies would be offended, facilities closed and jobs lost. Paul Warnke, senior arms control negotiator under President Carter, spoke of 'the rapid conversion of the President's Star Wars proposal from star-dust and moonbeams to that great pork barrel in the sky'.[19]

The beneficiaries of SDI wielded significant influence on the making of policy. Half of the members of the SDI Advisory Committee, which had overall responsibility for supervising the SDI programme, were employees of SDI contractors. Others had a distinguished record of BMD advocacy. One member was a director of 1 firm doing SDI work, a stock-holder in 7 and a paid consultant to 7. Despite this he failed to file any disqualification statement and by 1988 the SDI Office had still not reviewed his financial disclosure form.[20] By 1988, 2 of the 12 members had still not filed financial disclosure forms. Of the other 10, 5 reported that they were paid consultants to SDI contractors, 6 were trustees or directors and 8 held stock in such firms. Senator Levin remarked that 'you cannot have a much riper situation for a conflict of interest'.

The SDI Advisory Committee, the Defense Science Board and the Eastport Group point to a pattern of non-compliance with the regulations of the Federal Advisory Committee Act, which are designed to prevent conflict of interest. Committees were not chartered; members failed to file financial disclosure forms; written records were not kept; and consultants were paid four times the statutory amount.

In the 1980s prominent individuals from the laboratories were eager to promote SDI on the public agenda. Edward Teller advised Reagan's chief arms negotiator, Paul Nitze, not to compromise at Geneva, because of the promise of the X-ray laser project at Lawrence Livermore. The head of that project, Roy Woodruff, said that Teller and Lowell Wood gave 'overly optimistic, technically incorrect statements' on the subject.[21] In late 1986, Teller, Wood and pro-SDI congressmen combined to urge early deployment of partial strategic defences 'while the political will to do so undeniably exists'.[22] Deployment of an early Initial Operating Capability (IOC) was also advocated by Lockheed, the Heritage Foundation, High Frontier and the Marshall Institute.

The changes in BMD have not been solely influenced by the activities of interest groups, any more than by deliberate choice, personal or presidential desire. The correlation of forces was never predetermined. BMD has been an arena of struggle, in which, at each stage, the interest groups have contended for influence. The state of SDI in the 1990s, the advent of GPALS, is very probably distinct from what any BMD policy-maker intended ten, six or even four years ago. It is the result of large organisations, with conflicting preferences and unequal power, pulling in different directions, in an environment itself subject to change.

The successful establishment of the SDI programme between 1983 and 1986 may therefore be ascribed to bureaucratic momentum, the politics of influence, 'cultural' motifs and popularist marketing. The interest groups had little need to shape the programme at this stage since there were funds aplenty. They could concentrate on establishing the programme, an objective they all shared. In the years after 1986, as the SDI budget levelled off, the interest groups had to some extent to struggle among themselves to shape the SDI programme and win contracts. This led to some fragmentation, although the internecine struggles were limited and the BMD constituency retained a collective desire to preserve SDI. It is doubtful whether SDI could have survived as it has without the solid support of its institutional base and the individuals it succoured. However, the interests of SDI contractors were thwarted in important ways. The ABM Treaty was not openly renounced; there was no early IOC deployment and no large SDI Institute.[23]

From 1983, BMD became an Alliance issue. The SDI Office wanted some participation by Allied firms and the endorsement represented by governmental agreements on SDI. The Europeans wanted to stay abreast of technological developments.[24] In late 1985 and 1986, the SDI Office negotiated Memoranda of Understanding (MoUs) with Allied countries, using exaggerated promises of SDI funding. It awarded 'architecture studies' to Allied firms which were of such nominal value that they would not offend US contractors. They might help to identify and mobilise potential SDI and ATBM contractors in Europe. By the end of the 1980s, Allied expectations about lucrative SDI contracts had been dashed and SDI had slipped off the Alliance agenda. If SDI or GPALS is to be deployed, the question of alliance management is sure to re-emerge.

From about 1986, the changing international climate is central to understanding the troubled fortunes of SDI. The end of the Reagan era, the end of Soviet-style Marxism-Leninism and the end of the Cold War all undermined the ideology of anti-Communism on which SDI had initially rested. The revival of détente and arms control discouraged premature deployment of SDI. The reincarnation of SDI as GPALS illustrates the inseparability of supply and demand. The attractiveness of the GPALS concept grew as the Soviet threat receded. The Gulf War offered an ideal opportunity for a much-needed reorientation of SDI. The chance was swiftly seized by SDI supporters.

All the factors outlined in this book are necessary but not sufficient in explaining the genesis and development of SDI. The arms race is not monocausal. To identify a single 'main cause' would be as fraught as naming a single main reason for the Second World War or a uniquely 'correct' interpretation of *King Lear*.

The role of interest groups has been emphasised, partly because this aspect is neglected in other accounts. Theories about 'coincidence of interest', 'bureaucratic politics' and the 'industrial imperative', which emerged in the late 1950s or even before, were developed in the following two decades. Considering their usefulness, it is disappointing that they were not further refined in the 1980s. The time is ripe for them to be extended and applied in creative, transdisciplinary ways.

The thesis is not that the 'supply side' and the 'military industrial complex' are all-embracing; but that they are of key importance in the development of SDI. A combination of demand and supply perspectives is needed for rounded analysis. The co-existence of different factors and the conjunction of technological, corporate, bureaucratic and strategic dynamics, backed up by cultural and economic conditions, give BMD an awesome momentum, regardless of its advisability. SDI confirms the validity, wisdom and insight of most of the literature about the dynamics of the arms race.

The momentum for SDI comes from the perpetual complementarity and unceasing interaction of supply and demand factors.[25] The two thrive off each other. The supply side ensures that powerful individuals and institutions have a vested interest in SDI. The demand side provides the altruistic rationale (national security, defending the population) to mobilise strategic and political constituencies. It is a devastatingly productive alliance. The challenge is to comprehend precise connections and configurations, to specify the 'joint force and full result of all'.

Causes could be categorised in other ways: for instance, into underlying, precipitating and trigger causes. Underlying causes tend to be structural or systemic, whereas trigger causes involve agency, the 'personal' or 'accidental'. Precipitating causes may be concerned with the institutional or that which mediates structure and agency. The trigger in the case of SDI, the origin of the promise of eliminating nuclear weapons by building space weapons, was President Reagan. The trigger may have been primed or pulled by a secretive coalition of BMD supporters, associated with the Heritage Foundation and including Edward Teller.[26] The precipitating and underlying causes have been examined in some detail in Chapters 2, 11 and 12.

Clearly, this study could often have gone much further. It could have tested the theories of the arms race much more thoroughly against the early history of BMD and ASAT, and then extended the comparison between the different causes of ASAT, BMD and SDI. It has paid scant attention to technological detail. Above all, if further research were pursued, it would be compelling to record the unfolding of GPALS in the new strategic conditions of the 1990s.

The causes assigned to SDI depend on how we place it in context – its role in and influence on everything else. Since explanation involves evaluation, how is SDI finally to be evaluated? Some hail it as the critical factor which forced the USSR into serious arms control; and produced a defensive insurance against the threat of proliferating weapons; and broke the power of the Kremlin; and offered an era of defence-dominated deterrence. Others see cynicism, waste and deceit. Posterity may pronounce Reagan's idea a folly, blind to the lessons of history, consequences and the consequences of consequences; an eccentricity which stumbled on a function; or a sound idea courageously pursued. SDI may be seen as a radical innovation, an inspiration, or a tale of repeated response, a failure to imagine alternatives.

The next millennium may concur with Caspar Weinberger that 'the best characteristics of democratic politics are inherent in our SDI program, the hope of transcending a policy of deterrence based upon retaliation; open and honest debate in our own country and with our allies; and an ongoing effort to discuss with the Soviet Union the possibility of a transition to a deterrence based upon strategic defense'.[27] Or it may condemn the building of space weapons as an evil past imagination. Which of the available perspectives has most validity and what new prospects will unfold, history will tell.

# NOTES

## INTRODUCTION

1 United States Congress, Senate, Committee on Appropriations, *DoD Appropriations for Fiscal Year 1991. Hearings on H.R. 5803/S. 3189. Part 2* (Washington, D.C.: United States Government Printing Office, 1990) (S. Hrg. 101-936, part 2), p. 390.
2 In fact they do: the official SDI library, whose unclassified section is open to academics, is based at the Institute for Defense Analysis in Virginia.
3 SDI bibliographies include: Congressional Research Service, *SDI: Selected References* (periodically updated); Oryx Science Bibliographies, Space Weapons series; SDIO/IDA SDI Library Bibliography; Library of Congress on-line catalogues.
4 See Chapter 7 below.
5 Union of Concerned Scientists, *Empty Promise: The Growing Case Against Star Wars* (Boston: Beacon Press, 1986).
6 R. Curnow *et al.*, 'General and Complete Disarmament: A Systems Analysis Approach', *Futures* (October 1976).


## 1 THEORY

1 Matthew Evangelista, *Innovation and the Arms Race: How the United States and the Soviet Union Develop New Military Technologies* (Ithaca: Cornell University Press, 1988), p. 52.
2 See Scilla McLean (ed.), *How Nuclear Weapons Decisions are Made* (London: Macmillan, 1986). H. Miall, *Nuclear Weapons: Who's in Charge?* (London: Macmillan, 1987).
3 John Steinbruner, *The Cybernetic Theory of Decision* (New Jersey: Princeton University Press, 1974).
4 Harvey M. Sapolsky, *The Polaris System Development: Bureaucratic and Programmatic Success in Government* (Cambridge, Mass.: Harvard University Press, 1972); R. F. Coulam, *Illusions of Choice: The F-111 and the Problem of Weapon Acquisition Reform* (Guildford, N.J., 1977); Lauren H. Holland and Robert A. Hoover, *The MX Decision: A New Direction in US Weapons Procurement?* (Boulder, Colo.: Westview Press, 1985); Edmund Beard, *Developing the ICBM: A Study in Bureaucratic Politics* (Guildford, N.Y.: Columbia University Press, 1976).

5 Henry D. Levine, 'Some Things to All Men: The Politics of Cruise Missile Development', *Public Policy*, vol. 25, no. 1 (Winter 1977).
6 See Chapter 5 below.
7 'The Air Force buys more than 100,000 items from sole sources simply because the data on which a second supplier could work is either locked up legally by the original producer, incomplete or non-existent.' *Financial Times* (14 July 1987). General Dynamics has a virtual monopoly on the Trident submarine and Lockheed on Submarine Launched Missiles.
8 Gordon Adams, *The Iron Triangle: The Politics of Contracting* (New Brunswick, N.J.: Transaction Books, 1981). For profiles of main DoD contractors, including company–government relationship and personnel interchange, see Investor Responsibility Research Centre, *The Nuclear Weapons Industry* (Washington, D.C.: Investor Responsibility Research Center, 1984).
9 J. E. Kurth, 'Why We Buy the Weapons We Do', *Foreign Policy*, no. 11 (1973), pp. 38, 40.
10 John Pike, quoted in the *Washington Post* (20 October 1985).
11 President Dwight D. Eisenhower, 'Farewell Address to the American Nation', US Department of State, *Bulletin*, vol. 44 (6 February 1961).
12 Lord Solly Zuckerman, 'The Deterrent Illusion', *The Times* (21 January 1980). His 'hypothesis' is assessed in M. Blunden and O. Greene (eds.), *Science and Mythology in the Making of Defence Policy* (London, Brassey's Defence Publishers, 1989).
13 Retired Admiral William J. Crowe (chair of JCS from 1985 to 1989). Interviewed in *Washington Post* (18 February 1990), p. 18.
14 See Chapter 3 below.
15 'Coincidence of interest' is a less emotive term than 'Military Industrial Complex' (MIC). The MIC has generated more heat than light, as the weapons of criticism become confused with the criticism of weapons. Defence Industry Management Science (see, e.g., Jacques Gansler, *The Defense Industry* (Cambridge, Mass.: MIT Press, 1980)) has similar subject matter, but seeks efficiency in the MIC rather than its reduction. Examples of the MIC genre include Sidney Lens, *The Military-Industrial Complex* (Philadelphia: Pilgrim Press, 1970); S. Rosen (ed.), *Testing the Theory of the Military Industrial Complex* (Lexington, Mass.: Lexington Books, 1973); Georgi Tsagolov, *War is their Business* (Moscow: Progress Publishers, 1985).
16 Marek Thee, *Military Technology, Military Strategy and the Arms Race* (London: Croom Helm, 1986).
17 A. R. Sunseri, 'The Military Industrial Complex in Iowa', in B. F. Cooling (ed.), *War, Business and American Society* (New York: Kennikat Press, 1977).
18 Adam Yarmolinsky, 'The Problem of Momentum', in Abram Chayes and Jerome B. Wiesner, *ABM: An Evaluation of the Decision to Deploy an Anti Ballistic Missile System* (New York: Harper & Row, 1969).
19 'Servants or Masters: The B-1 Bomber', *Los Angeles Times*, part VI (10 July 1983), pp. 9, 10.
20 Eisenhower, 'Farewell Address to the Nation'.
21 Senator William Proxmire, 'Retired High-ranking Military Officers', chapter

17 of Carroll W. Pursell (ed.), *The Military-Industrial Complex* (New York: Harper & Row, 1972).
22 United States, General Accounting Office, 'Extent of Compliance with DoD's Requirement to Report Defense-related Employment' (10 June 1985).
23 United States, General Accounting Office, 'DoD Revolving Door: Processes have Improved but Post-DoD Employment Reporting Still Low' (13 September 1989).
24 United States, General Accounting Office, 'DoD Revolving Door: Few Are Restricted from Post-DoD Employment and Reporting has Some Gaps' (February 1990), GAO/NSIAD–90–103.
25 United States, Congress, House of Representatives, *DoD Appropriations for 1987, Part 6*, pp. 442–3.
26 *Ibid.*, p. 443.
27 *Aviation Week and Space Technology* (27 June 1988), 'Federal Investigators Pursue Dozens of Defense Contractors'. Also (4 July 1988), 'US Fraud Probe Rekindles Military Waste Controversy', and (12 September 1988), 'Carlucci Prohibits Appointment of Consultants for Rest of Term'. The *Financial Times* (14 July 1987), 'US Competition Takes on a Dizzying Aspect'.
28 *Aviation Week and Space Technology* (20 June 1988), 'Nationwide FBI Bribery Probe Centers on Defense Consultants', p. 19.
29 United States Congress, Senate, Committee on Governmental Affairs, *DoD/ SDIO Compliance with the Federal Advisory Committee Act* (19 April 1988), pp. 2, 4, 104–31. See Chapter 8 below.
30 Not intended to be sexist – most 'congressmen' are men.
31 Rep. George Brown (D. – Calif.), quoted in *IEEE Spectrum* (September 1985), p. 56.
32 Edward Roedner, *PACs Americana: A Directory of Political Action Committees (PACs) and their Interests* (Washington, D.C.: Sunshine Services Corp., 1982). Details of PACs are kept by the Federal Election Commission. The Defense Budget Project monitored PAC contributions from SDI contractors. See also Marvin Weinberger and David U. Greevy, *The PAC Directory: A Complete Guide to Political Action Committees* (Ballinger: PAC Researchers Ltd, 1982).
33 Senator Proxmire, quoted in Tristram Coffin, *The Passion of the Hawks* (New York: Macmillan, 1964), p. 166.
34 Noam Chomsky, 'The Evil Empire', *New Socialist* (January 1986).
35 Paul A. Baran and Paul M. Sweezy, *Monopoly Capital* (London: Penguin), chapter 7.
36 Noam Chomsky, 'The Cold War is a Device by which the Superpowers Control their Own Domains. That is Why it Will Continue', *The Guardian* (15 June 1981), p. 7. This could be categorised as an 'alliance management' theory.
37 See Helen Caldicott, *Missile Envy: The Arms Race and Nuclear War* (New York: William Morrow, 1984); Diana H. Russell (ed.), *Exposing Nuclear Phallacies* (Oxford: Pergamon Press, 1989); Brian Easlea, *Fathering the Unthinkable: Masculinity, Scientists and the Nuclear Arms Race* (London: Pluto Press, 1983).
38 See Crispin Aubrey (ed.), *Nukespeak: The Media and the Bomb* (London: Comedia, 1982).

39 See Lynn Barnett and Ian Lee (eds.), *The Nuclear Mentality: A Psychosocial Analysis of the Arms Race* (London: Pluto Press, 1989).

40 President Ronald Reagan, 'Transcript of Televised Address to the American Nation on 23 March 1983', p. 17.

41 For a list of early strategic texts on SDI, see United States Congress, Office of Technology Assessment, *Ballistic Missile Defense Technologies* (1985), Appendix L, 'References on Strategic Nuclear Policy' and Appendix M, 'References on Soviet Strategic Policy'.

42 Walter Zegveld and Christien Enzing, *SDI and Industrial Technology Policy* (London: Frances Pinter, 1987); E. P. Thompson (ed.), *Star Wars* (London: Penguin, 1985). See Chapter 10 below.

43 Colin S. Gray, *American Military Space Policy* (Cambridge, Mass.: Abt. Books, 1982), p. 19.

44 In practice, few writers explain weapons in terms of technology alone. Yanarella speaks of 'the paramount role played by the American technological planning process in fueling the strategic arms race'. Ernest J. Yanarella, *The Missile Defense Controversy: Strategy, Technology and Politics, 1955–1972* (Lexington, Ky.: University Press of Kentucky, 1977).

45 See Gwyn Prins (ed.), *Defended to Death* (Harmondsworth: Penguin, 1983), p. 135.

46 United States Global Strategy Council, 'Space Support of US National Security'.

47 For the case of cruise missiles, see R. K. Betts, *Cruise Missiles: Technology, Strategy, Politics* (Washington, D.C.: Brookings Institution).

48 James Fallows, *National Defense* (New York: Vintage Books, 1981).

49 See Mary Kaldor, *The Baroque Arsenal* (London: André Deutsch, 1982).

50 Thee, *Military Technology*, pp. 123–4.

## 2 THE HISTORY OF STRATEGIC DEFENCE IN THE USA

1 Arthur J. Downey, *The Emerging Role of the US Army in Space*, National Security Affairs Monograph (Washington, D.C.: National Defense University Press, November 1985). See also Tom Bower, *The Paperclip Conspiracy: The Battle for the Spoils and Secrets of Nazi Germany* (London: Michael Joseph, 1987).

2 CONUS excludes Hawaii and Alaska. It refers to the other forty-eight states.

3 Allison and Morris, 'Armaments and Arms Control', p. 114.

4 Gerald M. Steinberg (ed.), *Lost in Space: The Domestic Politics of the Strategic Defense Initiative* (Lexington, Mass.: Lexington Books, 1988).

5 Quoted in Coffin, *Passion of the Hawks*, p. 168.

6 Eugene Rabinowitch and Ruth Adams (eds.), *Debate the Antiballistic Missile*, Bulletin of the Atomic Scientists 1967 Review – Science and Public Affairs (Chicago, 1967), p. 8.

7 United States, Department of Defense, Army Strategic Defense Command, *The U.S. Army Strategic Defense Command*, Official History.

8 McNamara, 'Defense Posture Statement for 1967', presented on 23 January 1967. Reprinted in Rabinowitch and Adams, *Debate*, p. 145. The budget

status of BMD programmes from fiscal year 1962 to fiscal year 1987 is given in the *Congressional Record* (4 April 1985), E1444.

9  Halperin, 'The Decision to Deploy the ABM', pp. 71–2.
10  *Ibid.*, pp. 69–70.
11  *Ibid.*, p. 71.
12  Quoted in Seymour M. Hersh, 'The Great ABM Pork Barrel', *War Peace Report* (January 1968).
13  *Ibid.*, p. 4.
14  *Business Week* (23 September 1967), p. 37.
15  Hersh, 'The Great ABM Pork Barrel', p. 4.
16  Allison and Morris, 'Armaments and Arms Control', p. 114.
17  Roger P. Main, 'Beam Weaponry', unpublished manuscript (1985).
18  Halperin, 'The Decision to Deploy the ABM', p. 83.
19  *Ibid.*, p. 92.
20  R. S. McNamara, 'Text of McNamara's Speech on Anti-China Missile Defense and US Nuclear Strategy'. Text of address to editors of United Press International in San Francisco, 18 September 1967, as issued by the Pentagon and reprinted in the *New York Times* (19 September 1967) (hereafter, McNamara, 'Anti-China Missile Defense').
21  *Ibid.*
22  United States Congress, House of Representatives, Armed Services Committee, *Hearings on Military Posture*, 90th Congress, 1st session, 1967, p. 874.
23  United States Congress, House of Representatives, *House Defense Appropriations*, 1964, part 1, pp. 438–9. Quoted in Adams, 'McNamara's ABM Policy', p. 206.
24  McNamara, 'Anti-China Missile Defense'.
25  McNamara, 'Defense Posture Statement for 1967'.
26  Kaplan, *The Wizards of Armageddon*, p. 347.
27  *Business Week* (23 September 1967), p. 36.
28  Halperin, 'The Decision to Deploy the ABM', pp. 89–90.
29  United States, Department of Defense, Army Strategic Defense Command, Official History, p. 7.
30  'Major Lobby Effort Surrounds Sentinel ABM System', *Congressional Quarterly* (21 March 1969), p. 409.
31  *Ibid.*
32  Quoted in United States Congress, Office of Technology Assessment, *Ballistic Missile Defense Technologies*, p. 48.
33  'Battle over ABM Switches to Nation's Grassroots', *Congressional Quarterly* (30 May 1969), pp. 845–50.
34  *Ibid.*
35  Dr Harold Brown to House Armed Services Committee hearings, 1965. Quoted in Adams, 'McNamara's ABM Policy 1961–1967', *Orbis*, vol. 12, no. 1 (spring 1968) (Foreign Policy Research Institute, University of Pennsylvania).
36  United States, Department of Defense, Army Strategic Defense Command, Official History, p. 15.

37 Zuckerman, 'The Deterrent Illusion'.
38 Anne Hessing Cahn, 'Eggheads and Warheads: Scientists and the ABM', Science and Public Policy Program, Department of Political Sciences and Center for International Studies, Massachusetts Institute of Technology, 1971, p. 215.
39 Herbert York, *Race to Oblivion: A Participant's View of the Arms Race* (New York: Simon & Schuster, 1970), p. 180. Italics in the original. See also Sanford Lakoff and Herbert F. York, *A Shield in Space? Technology, Politics and the Strategic Defense Initiative* (University of California Press, 1989). The argument of this later work by Herbert York is summarised in the subtitle: *How the Reagan Administration Set Out to Make Nuclear Weapons 'Impotent and Obsolete' and Succumbed to the Fallacy of the Last Move.*
40 McNamara, 'Anti-China Missile Defense'.
41 McNamara, *Annual Posture Statement*, p. 27. Quoted in Adams, 'McNamara's ABM Policy', p. 213.
42 Hon. Malcolm R. Currie, United States Congress, House of Representatives, Armed Services Committee, *DoD Authorization of Appropriations, FY 1975. RDT&E. Title II*, p. 3526.

### 3 THE 'SDI' SPEECH

1 Reagan, 'Transcript of Televised Address to the American Nation on 23 March 1983', p. 17.
2 *Ibid.*, p. 20.
3 *Ibid.*, pp. 19, 20.
4 *Ibid.*, pp. 17–18.
5 See Chapter 13 below.
6 General Alexander Haig, speech at Lawrence Livermore, August 1984. Quoted in William J. Broad, 'Long Stream of People and Ideas Led to "Star Wars" Speech', *New York Times* (4 March 1985).
7 Martin Anderson, *Revolution* (New York: Harcourt Brace Jovanovich, 1988), p. 98.
8 Frank Greve, 'Star Wars', *San José Mercury News* (17 November 1985), p. 1A.
9 George Ball, 'The War for Star Wars', *New York Review of Books* (11 April 1985).
10 Janne E. Nolan, *Guardians of the Arsenal: The Politics of Nuclear Strategy* (New York: Harper & Row, 1989), p. 8.
11 Anderson, *Revolution*, p. 98; Nolan, *Guardians of the Arsenal*, p. 7.
12 Greve, 'Star Wars'.
13 Steinberg, *Lost in Space*, p. 26; Greve, 'Star Wars', p. 21A.
14 Edward Frieman, quoted in Steinberg, *Lost in Space*, p. 26.
15 United States, Department of Defense, Army Strategic Defense Command, Official History, p. 17.
16 For background on the US 'New Right' see Robert W. Whitaker, *The New Right Papers* (New York: St Martin's Press, 1982); and Ronald Brownstein and Nina Easton, *Reagan's Ruling Class: Portraits of the President's Top 100 Officials* (Washington, D.C.: Presidential Accountability Group, 1982).

17  Colin S. Gray and Keith Payne, 'Victory is Possible', *Foreign Policy*, 39 (1980), p. 21.

18  John Quirt, 'Washington's New Push for Anti-Missiles', *Fortune* (19 October 1981), p. 144.

19  *Ibid.*

20  Office of the White House Press Secretary, 1982.

21  *Department of Defense Authorizations for Appropriations for Fiscal Year 1980. Research Development Test and Evaluation. Title II* (Washington, D.C.: United States Government Printing Office, 1979), p. 801. Also, United States Senate, Armed Services Committee, *Authorization for Appropriations for Fiscal Year 1981. Part 5. Research and Development* (Washington, D.C.: United States Government Printing Office), p. 2900.

22  United States Congress, House of Representatives, Armed Services Committee, *Hearings on Military Posture and H.R. 6495*, p. 920.

23  United States, Department of Defense, Army Strategic Defense Command, Official History, p. 17.

24  Garry Wills, *Reagan's America: Innocents at Home* (New York: Doubleday, 1987), chapter 3.

25  Edward Teller, 'SDI: The Last, Best Hope', *Insight* (*Washington Times* magazine) (28 October 1985), p. 75.

26  Robert Scheer, *With Enough Shovels: Reagan, Bush and Nuclear War* (London: Secker and Warburg, 1983), pp. 232–3.

27  Anderson, *Revolution*, p. 85.

28  *Ibid.*, p. 86. General Graham, who advised Reagan in the 1976 and 1980 campaigns, made the same point. Lt-Gen. Daniel O. Graham, USA (Ret.), *High Frontier: A New National Strategy* (Washington, D.C.: High Frontier Inc., 1982), foreword, p. ix.

29  Graham, *High Frontier*, p. 4.

30  Gregg Herken, 'The Earthly Origins of Star Wars', *Bulletin of the Atomic Scientists* (October 1987), p. 21.

31  Anderson, *Revolution*, p. 94.

32  Broad, 'Long Stream'.

33  Anderson, *Revolution*, pp. 94–5.

34  Broad, 'Long Stream'.

35  Nolan, *Guardians of the Arsenal*, p. 161. Both Graham and his deputy at High Frontier, General Robert Richardson, served on the advisory board of the Moonie-sponsored organisation, Causa. *Nuclear Times* (June 1985), p. 12.

36  Correspondence between Bendetsen and Herken. Herken, 'Earthly Origins', p. 22.

37  Greve, 'Star Wars', p. 21A. Greve says that this account by his source was independently confirmed by another participant.

38  Anderson, *Revolution*, p. 97.

39  Quoted in Greve, 'Star Wars', p. 21A.

40  Anderson, *Revolution*, p. 98.

41  Greve, 'Star Wars', p. 21A. Nolan, *Guardians of the Arsenal*, p. 13.

42  Greve, 'Star Wars', p. 21A.

43 Anderson, *Revolution*, p. 99.
44 *Ibid.*, p. 97; Greve, 'Star Wars', p. 21A.
45 Herken, 'Earthly Origins', p. 24.
46 Graham, *High Frontier*, pp. 1, 12, 13, 14.
47 *Ibid.*, foreword, p. x and summary, p. 10.
48 *Ibid.*, p. 4.
49 Teller, 'SDI: The Last, Best Hope'.
50 G. Harry Stine, *Confrontation in Space* (Englewood Cliffs, N.J.: Prentice-Hall, 1981), pp. 183–4. Italics in original. Quoted in Gray, *American Military Space Policy*, p. 19.
51 See also David Carlton, 'Rendering Nuclear Weapons Impotent and Obsolete: The Origins of a Pipedream', in M. Blunden and O. Greene (eds.), *Science and Mythology in the Making of Defence Policy* (London: Brasseys Defence Publishers, 1989).
52 Herken, 'Earthly Origins', p. 25.
53 Herbert F. York, 'Nuclear Deterrence and the Military Uses of Space', *Daedalus*, vol. 114, no. 2 (spring 1985), p. 31.
54 Anderson, *Revolution*, p. 93.
55 Greve, 'Star Wars', p. 21A.
56 Herken, 'Earthly Origins', p. 22.
57 *Ibid.*
58 Teller, 'SDI: The Last, Best Hope'.
59 *New York Times* (13 February 1990), p. C1.
60 Anderson, *Revolution*, p. 93; Broad, 'Long Stream'.
61 Ball, 'The War for Star Wars', p. 3.
62 Graham, *High Frontier*, foreword.

### 4 CONTEXTS

1 The PEs were Surveillance Acquisition Tracking Kill Assessment (SATKA), Directed Energy Weapons (DEW), Kinetic Energy Weapons (KEW), Systems Analysis/Battle Management (SA/BM) and Survivability Lethality Key Technologies (SLKT).
2 United States Congress, Congressional Budget Office, 'Analysis of the Costs of the Administration's Strategic Defense Initiative', p. 12 and appendix A. The study shows the associated 1984 budget structure for each of the SDI PEs.
3 Fred Hoffman, 'Ballistic Missile Defenses and US National Security', Summary Report, prepared for the Future Security Study (October 1983), p. 2. The Hoffman Report, also called the Future Security Strategies Study (FS³), was published as only a dozen pages; and the classified version was apparently not much longer. Donald L. Hafner, 'Assessing the President's Vision: The Fletcher, Miller and Hoffman Panels', *Daedalus*, vol. 114, no. 2 (spring 1985), pp. 91–107.
4 'Ballistic Missile Defenses and US National Security', p. 2.
5 *Ibid.*, p. 8.
6 *Ibid.*, p. 7.

7  *Ibid.*, p. 2.

8  *Ibid.*, p. 3.

9  *Ibid.*, p. 3.

10  *Ibid.*, p. 6.

11  The contradictions are captured in the booklet from which many of the quotes below are taken: 'Star Wars: An Anthology of Quotes by the Administration, Congress and Outside Experts' (Washington, D.C.: Arms Control Association, June 1985).

12  President Reagan, Address to National Space Club, Washington, D.C., 29 March 1985.

13  NBC, 'Meet the Press' (27 March 1983).

14  Keyworth, 1 May 1985. Quoted in Steinberg, *Lost in Space*, p. 28.

15  Address to aerospace contractors, 21 May 1985.

16  President Reagan, interviewed by *Wall Street Journal* (8 February 1985). Once again the President ignores submarine-based nuclear missiles, which could ensure a devastating retaliation, regardless of SDI.

17  Lt-Gen. Abrahamson, *Science* (10 August 1984).

18  Lt-Gen. Abrahamson, *Christian Science Monitor* (21 September 1984).

19  The popular idea of 'deterrence' misrepresents actual strategies of flexible response and counter-force targeting, as described in the Pentagon's Single Integrated Operational Plan (SIOP). Robert C. Aldridge, *First Strike! The Pentagon's Strategy for Nuclear War* (London: Pluto Press, 1983). Peter Pringle and William Arkin, *SIOP: Nuclear War from the Inside* (London: Sphere, 1983).

20  Reagan, interviewed in *Wall Street Journal* (3 February 1984).

21  Reagan, Press conference, Washington, D.C., 14 June 1984. See also his interview with the *New York Times* (12 February 1985). Weinberger said that the Soviets were 'far ahead of the United States', *New York Times* (3 December 1983).

22  *Science* (10 August 1984).

23  After a long public debate about the best way of siting new land-based missiles, so as to minimise their vulnerability to a first strike, the Scowcroft Commission had been appointed to try to settle the matter.

24  Ashton Carter, *Directed Energy Missile Defense in Space* (Office of Technology Assessment, April 1984). Also, United States Congress, Office of Technology Assessment, *Ballistic Missile Defense Technologies*.

25  Union of Concerned Scientists, *The Fallacy of Star Wars* (New York: Random House, 1984).

26  The shooting down of the civilian Iran Air flight 665 by the US Cruiser Vincennes was, according to a senior officer, due to 'compression of time'. The danger of error would be even greater with the vastly more complex decisions required by SDI.

27  WJLA-TV reports, 23 June 1988, 6.00 p.m., transcript. *Current News* (24 April 1988), p. 2.

28  'State Department: Security Issues Related to Selected Employees', GAO/NSIAD-89-86. 'Embassy Security: Background Investigations of Foreign Employees', GAO/NSIAD-89-76.

29 High Frontier cited numerous instances where scientists derided as impossible feats which were shortly after achieved. They said that SDI too would disprove the technological doubting Thomases.

30 Words of the US Acting Permanent Representative to the UN Security Council.

31 Abrahamson, 29 October 1984, quoted in Arms Control Association, 'Star Wars'.

## 5 INTEREST GROUPS

1 $69 billion was the market forecast prepared by the Electronic Industries Association in 1984.

2 Senator Larry Pressler to Senate Foreign Relations Committee, 25 April 1984.

3 James R. Schlesinger, *International Security*, vol. 10, no. 1 (summer 1985), 'Rhetoric and Realities in the Star Wars Debate', p. 4.

4 United States Congress, House of Representatives, Armed Services Committee. [HASC 98-21], p. 17, 10 November 1983. DeLauer estimate in Garwin testimony.

5 *Washington Post* (20 October 1985).

6 By April 1988, the air force had won 2,831 contracts, or $1,646.167 million in outlays. The army had won 2,618 SDI contracts, and $2,511.698 million in outlays. For the role of the air force in the SDIP, see 'Charter of the Strategic Defense Initiative Program (SDIP)'.

7 United States, Department of Defense, Air Force, Space Division.

8 *Air Force Magazine* (July 1985).

9 Air Force Space Technology Center, publicity material (1989).

10 Air Force Weapons Laboratory, fact sheet (September 1987).

11 *Ibid*.

12 *Newsreview*, Air Force Systems Command internal magazine, vol. 29, no. 21 (22 November 1985).

13 Air Force Space Technology Center, publicity material.

14 John T. Bosma and Richard C. Whelan, *Guide to the Strategic Defense Initiative* (Pasha Publications, June 1985), p. 44.

15 *Air Force Magazine* (May 1984).

16 See Bosma and Whelan, *Guide*; SDIO Contract Management Information System; also United States, Department of Defense, Navy Research Laboratory, *Directive Systems Checklists, Fact Books* and *Organization Manuals*.

17 See LLNL Institutional Plan FY 1984–1989. Also *Energy and Technology Review* (monthly), LLNL.

18 United States, Department of Defense, SDIO, 'A Technical Progress Report Submitted to the Secretary of Defense' (June 1985), p. 16.

19 For the Construction Project Data Sheet, see the FY 1986 Budget Justifications in United States Congress, House of Representatives, *Energy and Water Hearings*, FY 1986, part 4, pp. 139–42. For other information, see Sandia National Laboratory Institutional Plan FY 1985–90.

20 SDIO Contract Management Information System (April 1988).
21 For a list of forty-five contractees for SDI work to DNA, with the initial amount awarded to each (totalling $29,089,809), see United States, Department of Defense, Defense Nuclear Agency, 'SDI by performer 1985'. This is a print-out, dated 3 May 1985, of SDI contractees to DNA. The acronyms for the performers can be read using the unclassified 'Performer Code Directory by Acronym'.
22 Retired Admiral William J. Crowe, chair of the JCS from 1985 to 1989. Interviewed in *Washington Post* (18 February 1990), p. 18.
23 Special Projects Offices had been successfully used to expedite other programmes, including the Cruise Missile and Midgetman. See Sapolsky, *The Polaris System Development*.
24 Magraw, 'SDI', p. 11.
25 Steinberg, *Lost in Space*, p. 49.
26 *Ibid.*, pp. 43, 46.
27 Organisational charts of the SDIO are given in the SDIO's annual *Report to Congress*.
28 In FY 1986, 83 per cent of the SDI budget was managed for the SDIO by the armed services and defence agencies. Quoted in Steinberg, *Lost in Space*, p. 50.
29 SDIO, *Report to Congress* (1985), p. 5.
30 Congressman Dickinson (Alabama). United States Congress, House of Representatives, Armed Services Committee, Hearings, no. 99-30, *SDI Program* (6 June 1985), p. 21.
31 United States, Senate, Committee on Governmental Affairs, *DoD/SDIO Compliance with the Federal Advisory Committee Act* (19 April 1988). Nolan paints a picture of Abrahamson's ineptitude in *Guardians of the Arsenal*, pp. 191–7.
32 *Guardians of the Arsenal*, p. 89.
33 United States, Department of Defense, Army Strategic Defense Command, Official History, p. 27.
34 *Ibid.*, p. 38.
35 Magraw, 'SDI', p. 25.
36 United States, Department of Defense, Army Strategic Defense Command, Official History, p. 39.
37 *Ibid.*
38 *Army Research Development and Acquisition Magazine* (March/April 1985).
39 *Los Angeles Times* (8 November 1987).
40 See SDIO Contract Management Information System; Council on Economic Priorities, *The Strategic Defense Initiative*, part 3, and appendices 2, 3 and 4. Also, Frost and Sullivan Inc., *The Space Defense Market in the US* (New York, May 1983), section 13. Defense Marketing Services, *Space Based Defense Systems: Market Study and Forecast* (June 1984), appendix 11, arranges data by company, city/state and programme.
41 *Washington Post* (21 October 1985), p. A10.
42 *Ibid.*
43 SDIO Contract Management Information System (April 1988).

44 Alan Benasuli, financial analyst, quoted in *Washington Post* (20 October 1985), 'Defense Inc.', part 1.

45 *Ibid.*

46 Quoted in Council on Economic Priorities, *Star Wars*, p. 66. Telephone interview with Marshall Gehring of 5 December 1984.

47 *Washington Post*, Washington Business (14 September 1987), 'Martin Marietta Sets Sights on SDI Work'. The facility was opened in November 1985.

48 '$3,000,000,000.00 has been approved by the Senate to fund the SDI in FY 1986 . . . Opportunities for your organization abound in the SDI Program . . . **Guide to the Strategic Defense Initiative** will give you a running start. Don't miss it. Don't even delay . . . call Allen Powers toll-free . . . and use your credit card.' Bosma and Whelan, *Guide*, publicity brochure.

49 *Defense Week* (13 August 1984), 'Star Wars Manager offers Bright Prospects for Aggressive Firms'.

50 *Christian Science Monitor* (22 April 1985), p. 3.

51 *Fortune* (15 April 1985), p. 121.

52 Interview with senior Lockheed executive.

53 United States, Army Strategic Defense Command, News Release no. 85–08–13.

54 *Aviation Week and Space Technology* (2 September 1985).

### 6 THE POLITICS OF INFLUENCE

1 National Security Decision Directive 85, para. 2.

2 *Ibid.*

3 Also known as the Defensive Technologies Study Team (DTST), the Fletcher panel was named after its chairman, James Fletcher. Its final report ran to eight volumes.

4 Senate, Armed Services Committee, *DoD Authorization of Appropriations*, FY 1985, part 6, p. 2996.

5 Quoted in Hafner, 'Assessing the President's Vision', p. 95.

6 Transcript of Pentagon news conference, 27 March 1984, 11.40 a.m. My italics.

7 *Aviation Week and Space Technology* (17 October 1983).

8 Memorandum from Secretary of Defense. Subject: Organization of Defensive Technologies Executive Committee – Action Memorandum. United States, Department of Defense, Washington, D.C. (28 March 1983).

9 Interim Charter of the SDIO. Memorandum from the Secretary of Defense. Subject: Management of the Strategic Defense Initiative (24 April 1984).

10 The six institutions are Physical Dynamics Inc.; Braddock Dunn and McDonald; John Allen Associates Inc.; John Jamieson Inc.; the Scripps Institute of Oceanography; and (a Lieutenant-Colonel from) the Office of Science and Technology Policy. The Scripps Institute is part of the University of California, which is an SDI contractor.

11 United States, Department of Defense, Army Strategic Defense Command, Official History, p. 29.

12 United States Congress, Senate, Committee on Governmental Affairs, *DoD/ SDIO Compliance with the Federal Advisory Committee Act* (19 April 1988).

13 *Ibid.*, p. 166, Extracts from Personal Log. D. W. Ream, 1983. Office of General Counsel, Office of the Secretary of Defense. Record for 1 June 1983.

14 See *ibid.* and Scheer, 'The Man who Blew the Whistle on Star Wars'.

15 Roy Woodruff, quoted in Scheer, 'The Man who Blew the Whistle on Star Wars'.

16 Wood visited the SDIO eleven times in 1985. Blum, 'Weird Science'.

17 Roy Woodruff, quoted in Scheer, 'The Man who Blew the Whistle on star Wars'.

18 It is reasonable to suppose that others in a similar dilemma to Woodruff are still unknown.

19 1986 letter from DoE Assistant Secretary for nuclear weapons research to the director of Livermore. Quoted in Union of Concerned Scientists, *Empty Promise*, p. 20.

20 Major-General Eugene Fox, April 1989. Quoted in 'Pseudo-Science and SDI', *Arms Control Today* (October 1989), p. 15.

21 'Near-Fatal Blow Dealt to the Star of "Star Wars"', *New York Times* (21 October 1990); 'X-ray Laser Research Slashed as Congress Cuts SDI Funding', *Aviation Week and Space Technology* (12 November 1990). See also *Washington Post* (18 October 1990), p. 31.

22 Quoted in Sweedler, 'Congress and the Strategic Defense Initiative', in Steinberg, *Lost in Space*.

23 Senator Larry Pressler, *Star Wars: The Strategic Defense Initiative Debates in Congress* (New York: Praeger, 1986), p. 67 and chapter 7.

24 23 Congressional hearings were held on SDI between February and June 1985. Steinberg, *Lost in Space*, p. 63.

25 Carl T. Bayer, quoted in the *Washington Post* (20 October 1985), 'Defense Inc.', part 1.

26 *Ibid.*

27 8–9 May 1985.

28 *Christian Science Monitor* (22 April 1985), p. 3.

29 *Science*, vol. 222 (21 October 1983).

30 Company prospectus, quoted in the *Washington Post* (21 October 1985).

### 7 CONTEXTS AND CONSTITUENCIES

1 President Reagan, remarks at a briefing on SDI, Washington, D.C., 6 August 1986.

2 State of the Union address to a joint session of Congress, *Financial Times* (29 January 1987). See also Reagan's address to the nation of 26 February 1986.

3 See, for instance, the joint Department of State and DoD report, 'Soviet Strategic Defense Programs' (October 1985). The 'Report to the Congress' of 1988 by the Secretary of Defense paid the merest lip service to population defence. It justified the programme as a response to Soviet actions and as an aid to offensive arms negotiations. The statement on 'Military Posture' for

215

FY 1989 presented SDI as a 'necessary, prudent response' to the Soviet BMD effort, which would reduce Soviet confidence in a successful first strike.

4 Quoted in Union of Concerned Scientists, *Empty Promise*, p. 18.
5 Douglas James Bruce and Douglas Cook, 'SDI: Progress and Challenges', staff report submitted to Senators Proxmire, Johnston and Chiles (17 March 1986).
6 'Star Wars in transition', *IEEE Spectrum* (March 1989), p. 37. See also Peter Stein, 'The SDI Battle Management System' Technical Report 14, Program in Science and Technology for International Security (Massachusetts Institute of Technology: December 1985).
7 United States, Senate, Committee on Governmental Affairs, *Need for and Operation of a Strategic Defense Initiative Institute*, p. 125.
8 Quoted in survey by the Cornell Institute for Social and Economic Research, October 1986.
9 'Eye on Wall Street', *Defense News* (27 April 1987).
10 In nominal terms, the DoD budget was $144 billion in 1980, and $293 billion by 1987.
11 The National Security Council had been instrumental in drafting Reagan's SDI speech and then implementing it. See Chapters 3 and 6 above.
12 In the crash of 1987, the computer-programmed trading system reacted to a strong bout of selling with a self-sustaining trend of further sales. This might give pause for thought about the wisdom of relying in a crisis on computer-controlled missile launching and strategic defence systems.
13 For example, Donald Regan, former chief of staff at the White House, claimed that Nancy Reagan had influenced the President through astrology.
14 Jack Mendelsohn, 'Gorbachev's Preemptive Concession', *Arms Control Today* (March 1989), p. 10.
15 The debate is more fully explored in K. Luongo and W. T. Wander (eds.), *The Search for Security in Space* (Ithaca: Cornell University Press, 1989), chapters 13 and 14 (by the State Department's legal adviser and Sam Nunn, respectively); and M. Bunn, *Foundation for the Future: The ABM Treaty and National Security* (Washington, D.C.: Arms Control Association, 1990). Also reports for the Federation of American Scientists, Washington, D.C.: John E. Pike, 'ABM Negotiations', September 1987 and John E. Pike, 'SDI Report Card: Technical Progress and Compliance with the ABM Treaty', March 1988.
16 I.e. principles other than ABM interceptors, ABM launchers and ABM radars.
17 The Administration's somewhat clumsy, autocratic approach needlessly incensed those, such as Sam Nunn, who upheld the Senate's constitutional prerogative to interpret treaties. Nolan, *Guardians of the Arsenal*, pp. 223–7.
18 Reagan's decision to abide by the treaty was another sign of the decline of hard-liners from the New Right.
19 United States, Congress, House of Representatives, Armed Services Committee, *Hearings on National Defense Authorization Act for Fiscal Years 1988/1989: H.R. 1748. RDT&E Title II*, p. 42.

20 United States Congress, Senate, Committee on Governmental Affairs, *DoD/ Senate Compliance with the Federal Advisory Committee Act* (19 April 1988), p. 90.
21 Steinberg, *Lost in Space*, p. 50.
22 'Auditors Troubled by SDI Contracts', *Defense Week* (30 October 1989), p. 1.
23 See SDI Program Descriptive Summaries, 1988: 'RDT&E Facilities Project Data'; 'Military Construction Project Data'; 'Major Improvements to and Construction of Government-Owned Facilities Funded by RDT&E'.
24 See Chapter 11 below.
25 *National Security Record*, no. 110 (Heritage Foundation, February 1988).
26 Quoted in Morrison, 'Shooting Down Star Wars', p. 2545.
27 George Ball, 11 April 1985. Quoted in Council on Economic Priorities, *Star Wars*, p. 93.
28 Wolfgang Demisch, quoted in Charles E. Bennett (R. – Fla.), 'The Rush to Deploy SDI', *The Atlantic* (April 1988).
29 SDIO Contract Data Base, 5 August 1988. Fortune 500, 24 April 1989.
30 Magraw, 'SDI', p. 17.
31 Rockwell brochure, 'Strategic Defense Center: A Synthesis of Resources'.
32 'Ford Operating Command Center Lab to Strengthen SDI Contract Position', *Aviation Week and Space Technology* (2 May 1988).
33 *Ibid.* (April 1987).
34 Aerospace specialist at Shearson Lehman Brothers, quoted in 'SDI and the Business Outlook', *MILTECH* (April 1987), p. 76. I have found no evidence that SDI contracts as a whole gave lower profitability than comparable programmes.
35 Quoted in Pike, 'SDI and Corporate Contractors'.
36 *Los Angeles Times* (29 January 1988), pp. IV-5. $10.4 million had already been expended and ninety people worked on the job.
37 See Chapter 6 above.
38 Quoted in *The New Republic* (20 April 1987). Wallop's aide called SDI a 'welfare program for scientists'. Angelo Codevilla, *While Others Build: A Commonsense Approach to the Strategic Defense Initiative* (New York: Free Press, 1989).
39 See Chapter 13 below.

**8 INTEREST AND INFLUENCE**

1 The article is published in the winter 1989 edition of *Strategic Review*.
2 Dr Kane also argued for a partial strategic defence system to provide early warning of an initial Soviet nuclear attack, thereby ensuring the US a (pre-emptive) counter-attack capability. Duke Kane, 'Protracted Peace: The Role of Strategic Defenses in Preventing War', *Rockwell News, Rocketdyne Division* (16 December 1988), p. 2.
3 United States, Department of Defense, Army Strategic Defense Command, Official History, p. 17.
4 'Report of the Technical Panel on Missile Defense in the 1990s' (Washington, D.C.: Marshall Institute, 1987).

5 The fourth director, Karl Bendetsen, was an industrialist and member of the group meeting at the Heritage Foundation in the early 1980s, which proposed BMD increases to Reagan.

6 United States Congress, House of Representatives, Armed Services Committee, *Hearings* [HASC. no. 100–31] (15 September 1987), Prepared Statement of Edward Gerry, p. 253.

7 SDI Contract Data Base, run date 5 August 1988.

8 United States, Senate, Committee on Armed Services, *DoD Authorization for Appropriations for FY 1985. Hearings*, Part 6 (8 and 22 March 1984) (Washington, D.C.: United States Government Printing Office, 1984), p. 3016.

9 Steinberg, *Lost in Space*, p. 133. McDonnell Douglas had $288.963 million of SDI contracts by mid 1988. SDI Contract Data Base, run date 5 August 1988.

10 At one stage Dukakis spoke of limiting SDI funding to $1 billion a year. This was probably an attempt to exploit the issue of budget deficits and to outflank Jesse Jackson, by appealing to the liberal and 'peace' vote, when Jackson was making his strongest running, just after winning the Michigan primary.

11 Magraw, 'SDI', p. 22.

12 Jack Coakley, a former aerospace official and High Frontier staff member. Quoted *ibid.*, p. 19.

13 United States Global Strategy Council, 'Space Support of US National Security'.

14 The SDIAC was a Pentagon committee, dealing specifically with oversight of the SDI.

15 United States Congress, Senate, Committee on Governmental Affairs, *DoD/ SDIO Compliance with the Federal Advisory Committee Act* (19 April 1988), p. 23.

16 *Ibid.*

17 *Ibid.*, p. 22.

18 *Ibid.*, p. 6.

19 Council on Economic Priorities, *Star Wars*, p. 48.

20 'Contracts in Descending Funds Order', SDIO, run date 5 August 1988.

21 *Washington Post* (9 July 1987).

22 *Ibid.*

23 S. Hrg. 100–37, p. 75.

24 United States Office of Government Ethics, 'Inquiry into the Eastport Group Advisors', p. 4.

25 S. Hrg. 100–681, p. 94.

26 *Ibid.*, p. 98.

27 *Ibid.*, pp. 4, 28.

28 *Ibid.*, p. 94.

29 'Statement of Senator Carl Levin before the Senate Subcommittee on Federal Services, Post Office and Civil Service, Concerning Defense Consultants' (8 July 1988), p. 4.

30 S. Hrg. 100–681, p. 17.

31 The interim rule is published in 48 Federal Register 19234. The General Counsel's defence of SDIO is found in S. Hrg. 100–681, pp. 61–86.

32 Quoted in Steinberg, *Lost in Space*, p. 79.
33 *Ibid.*
34 Rep. Charles E. Bennett of the House Armed Services Committee. Quoted in *MILTECH* (April 1987), p. 82.
35 Council on Economic Priorities, *Star Wars*, p. 94.
36 *Ibid.*, p. 106.
37 Scheer, 'The Man who Blew the Whistle on Star Wars'.
38 Quoted *ibid.*
39 George Miller, December 1987, quoted *ibid.*
40 The question of early IOC is considered in the next chapter.
41 *SDIO Report to the Congress* (1987), appendix E, 'Need for a Federally Funded Research and Development Center (FFRDC)'. Also United States, General Accounting Office, 'SDIP: Experts' Views on DoD's Organizational Options and Plans for SDI Technical Support', GAO/NSIAD–87–43.
42 The proposed salary was more than President Reagan's. S. Hrg. 100–37, p. 4.
43 S. Hrg. 100–37, pp. 44 and 134.
44 Council on Economic Priorities, *Star Wars*, p. 50.
45 S. Hrg. 100–37, p. 131.
46 *Ibid.*, p. 22.
47 *Ibid.*, p. 5.
48 *Ibid.*, p. 29.
49 The SDIO used instead three public affairs officers from the Office of the Secretary of Defense. *Spacewatch Fortnightly* (16 November 1987), p. 3.
50 S. Hrg. 100–681, p. 165.
51 'Anti-SDI Sentiments Snag Chief's Promotion', *Washington Times* (29 June 1987), p. 4.
52 United States, Senate, Committee on Armed Services, *National Defense Authorization Act for Fiscal Year 1989*, Report (4 May 1988) (Washington, D.C.: United States Government Printing Office), pp. 61, 62. My italics.

#### 9 EARLY DEPLOYMENT?

1 Angelo M. Codevilla, 'How SDI is Being Undone From Within', *Commentary* (May 1986), pp. 26–7.
2 Quoted in Douglas Waller, James Bruce and Douglas Cook, 'SDI: Progress and Challenges. Part Two', staff report submitted to Senators Proxmire, Johnston and Chiles (19 March 1987).
3 United States, Congress, House of Representatives, Armed Services Committee, *Hearings on National Defense Authorization Act for Fiscal Years 1988/1989 – H.R. 1748*, pp. 474–7.
4 *Aviation Week and Space Technology* (13 October 1986), p. 17.
5 Marshall Institute, 'Report of the Technical Panel on Missile Defense in the 1990s', p. 8. For the authorship of the report, see Chapter 8, p. 101 above.
6 *Ibid.*, p. 5.
7 *Ibid.*, p. 6.
8 *Ibid.*, p. 11.

9 Quoted in Waller *et al.*, 'SDI: Part Two', p. 6.
10 *Ibid.*
11 *Ibid.*
12 *Ibid.*, p. 9.
13 'General Accounting Office Challenges SDI Phase I Weapons Cost Estimate', *Aviation Week and Space Technology* (3 April 1989).
14 William Loomis, in United States, Congress, House of Representatives, Armed Services Committee. *Hearings on National Defense Authorization Act for Fiscal Years 1988/1989 – H.R. 1748*, p. 476.
15 *Ibid.*
16 *Ibid.* It is not clear whether Mr Loomis intended to mean Soviet or US break-out.
17 See Chapter 11 below.
18 Quoted in Waller *et al.*, 'SDI: Part Two', p. 4.
19 Allan Mense, quoted in 'SDI Supporters Work to Nudge Reagan towards R&D', Radio Free Europe, 18 January 1987, 9.09 p.m., transcript (FF108), R. Jeffrey Smith, *Washington Post*.
20 Tony Battista, staff member of the House Armed Services Committee, HASC no. 100-7, p. 478 (18 March 1987).
21 In 1988 the House passed an amendment to restrict funds for early deployment, but difficulties in defining early IOC work prevented the measure from being enacted.
22 See Waller *et al.*, 'SDI: Part Two'.
23 'Program Descriptive Summaries for SDI, FY 1988', pp. 722, 748.
24 'Star Wars in Transition', *IEEE Spectrum* (March 1989), p. 38.
25 HASC no. 100-7, p. 477.
26 S. Hrg. 101–936, part 2, p. 456.
27 United States, Department of Defense, 'Global Protection Against Limited Strikes (GPALS): Briefing on the Refocussed Strategic Defense Initiative' (12 February 1991), 'BMD Budget Evolution' (no pagination).

## 10 EUROPE

1 *Science*, vol. 229 (20 September 1985), p. 1243, 'A European Defense Initiative: The Idea that European Nations Band Together for a Strictly European Version of SDI is Gaining Support'. For a detailed account of EDI and related proposals, see Hans Gunter Brauch (ed.), *Star Wars and European Defence* (Macmillan, 1987), especially chapter 14, 'From SDI to EDI: Elements of a European Defense Architecture'.
2 Weinberger later dropped his initial demand that the Allies respond within sixty days.
3 *Aviation Week and Space Technology* (29 April 1985), 'SDIO Moves to Promote Non-US Share of Research Work'.
4 For the role of pulsed power at Aldermaston, see *Financial Times* (21 August 1985), 'British Finger on the Star Wars Pulse'.
5 For a full analysis, see: UK Ministry of Defence, 'UK Participation in SDI: Company Capabilities' (no date), 135 pages. Also, 'SDI Research: British

Capabilities and Interests' (Armament Disarmament Information Unit (ADIU), University of Sussex, May 1986).

6 *Wehrtechnik*, vol. 7 (July 1986), 'Das SDI Forschungs-programm', quoted in Michael Lucas, 'SDI and Europe', *World Policy* (Spring 1986).

7 See John Fenske, 'France and the Strategic Defense Initiative: Speeding up or Putting on the Brakes?', *International Affairs* (1986).

8 For example, Konrad Seitz, 'SDI: The Technological Challenge for Europe', *The World Today* (August/September 1985). See also Klaus Gottstein, 'The Debate on SDI in the Federal Republic of Germany', paper presented to the 47th Pugwash Symposium, London, 5–8 December 1985.

9 The case is summarised in Sir Peter Emery, MP, 'SDI – An Offer Europe Shouldn't Refuse', *Armed Forces Journal International* (March 1986), p. 75.

10 See John E. Pike, 'Barriers to European Participation in the Strategic Defense Initiative', statement to the Subcommittee on Economic Stabilisation, Committee on Banking, Finance and Urban Affairs, House of Representatives, 10 December 1985.

11 ABM Treaty, article IX and agreed statement G.

12 DoD Federal Acquisitions Regulations, supplement (25.7007), 'Restrictions on R&D Contracting with Foreign Sources'. See United States Congress, House of Representatives, Committee on Foreign Affairs, *Technology Transfer and the Strategic Defense Initiative Research Agreements*, Hearing (10 December 1985), p. 39. Competition need not be provided if the foreign government shoulders some of the costs. This is only the case in a few SDI contracts with the Allies: the Israelis contributed $31.6 million to their total of $173.719 million in SDI contracts. The Netherlands contributed $7 million to their total of $12.043 million (SDIO data, October 1989).

13 United States Congress, House of Representatives, Committee on Foreign Affairs, *Technology Transfer and the SDI Research Agreements* (10 December 1985), p. 171.

14 EDI was sometimes known as EVI: the Europäische Verteidigungs-Initiative.

15 *Aviation Week and Space Technology* (9 December 1985), 'German Minister Proposes Initiative to Improve European Defences'. Also, *The Guardian* (3 December 1985), p. 7, 'West Germany Seeks Support for European SDI'.

16 *Jane's Defence Weekly* (5 April 1986), p. 603, 'SDI Talks Cast Doubt on Need for Separate European Ballistic Defence'.

17 Stewart Menaul, 'A European Defence Initiative', *Journal of Defense and Diplomacy*, vol. 4, no. 2 (February 1986). Also Stewart Menaul, 'The European Defense Initiative: Some Implications and Consequences' (Rotterdam: High Frontier Europa, no date), 50 pages.

18 The chairman of the far Right CSU, Franz Josef Strauss, called for a European 'complement to the SDI' in the spring of 1985, months before Manfred Worner proposed EDI.

19 See Lucas, 'SDI and Europe'.

20 The Foundation is closely linked to the ruling German CDU party. *Aviation Week and Space Technology* (7 July 1986), 'German Study Encourages

Development of Antitactical Ballistic Missiles'. Also *Aviation Week and Space Technology* (14 July 1986), p. 30, 'NATO Planners Drafting Guidelines for Europe-Based ATBM Development'.

21 International Institute for Strategic Studies, *Strategic Survey* (1985–6), p. 45, 'Soviet ATBM Programmes'.

22 *Aviation Week and Space Technology* (29 September 1986), p. 22, 'Army Missile Intercept Success Spurs SDI Theater Defense Study'.

23 *Aviation Week and Space Technology* (9 April 1984), p. 46, 'US Develops Anti-tactical Weapon for European Role'.

24 A NATO-sponsored group, AGARD, wrote a classified report on ATBMs in 1980, which was regularly updated. *Aviation Week and Space Technology* (7 July 1986), p. 84. AGARD is the Advisory Group for Aerospace Research and Development.

25 Hoffman, 'Ballistic Missile Defenses and US National Security: Summary Report', p. 3.

26 United States Congress, House of Representatives, Committee on Foreign Affairs, *Technology Transfer and the SDI Research Agreements* (10 December 1985), p. 165. See also Hans Gunter Brauch, 'Antitactical Missile Defense: Will the European Version of SDI Undermine the ABM Treaty?', AFES Press Report, no. 1 (Mosbach, West Germany, 1988).

27 John Bosma, 'Anti-Tactical Missile Defense: The Eyes have it', *NBC Defense and Technology International* (April 1986), p. 24. The joint army and air force Anti-Tactical Missile (ATM) programme, started in 1982, was intended to supplement older air defence efforts such as Patriot and Hawk. By FY 1986 this ATM programme was funded at $62.7 million, independently of SDI. The work of the US Army Strategic Defense Command at Huntsville, which specialises in terminal and midcourse interception, would also be prioritised in an ATBM programme.

28 FY 1986. Defense Authorization Bill.

29 Quoted in Steinberg, *Lost in Space*, p. 8.

30 Brauch, *Star Wars and European Defence*, p. 477.

31 The British signed a $10 million contract for an ATBM 'architecture study' in June 1986. Of 14 contracts for the UK in the SDIO 'Contracts System' (run date 16 October 1989), 12 are for the 'Allied Architecture Study' and 2 for Extended Air Defence.

32 *Aviation Week and Space Technology* (21 April 1986), 'Aerospatiale Studies Missile System to Counter Tactical Soviet Threat'.

33 *Financial Times* (11 July 1986), 'Anglo-French Tie Proposed for Anti-Missile System'. The SDIO 'Contract System' (run date 16 October 1989) includes a $300,000 contract with British Aerospace for 'Vertical Launch Seawolf'.

34 'EAD' was sometimes used for '*European* Air Defense'.

35 'NATO Study Ties SDI to European Air Defense', *Jane's Defence Weekly* (31 May 1986), p. 970.

36 This was the Air Command and Control System (ACCS). A multinational ACCS team produced 'baseline' descriptions in 1985. See *NATO's Sixteen Nations*, Special Issue no. 2, vol. 30 (6 October 1985), p. 76, 'The Development of an Air Command and Control System for NATO's Forces in Europe'.

37 The NATO Airborne Early Warning (NAEW) Command, based in Maisières, Belgium. See M. J. Jackson, 'Trends in Air Warfare: Airborne Early Warning', in RUSI and Brassey's *Defence Yearbook* (1985).

38 The German Air Defence Ground Environment (GEADGE); the Système de traitement et de représentation des informations de défense aerienne (STRIDA); and the Combat grande.

39 Sheena Phillips, 'Britain, France and the Future of ATBM', paper presented to the ATBM seminar, Amsterdam Free University, 27–8 November 1986.

40 Derek Wood, 'UK rebuilds its Air Defences', *Jane's Defence Weekly* (17 March 1984), p. 412. Also Graham Warwick, 'Building the Big Picture', *Flight International* (27 April 1985).

41 Phillips, 'Britain, France and the Future of ATBM'.

42 *Ibid.*

43 One candidate for upgrading the Hawk was a French team of Thomson-CSF (radar) and Aerospatiale (the Aster-30 missile). A West German team comprised Siemens and AEG Telefunken (radar) and Messerschmitt-Bolkow-Blohm (missile).

44 'Army Plans $9.3 Billion for Air Defense Package', *Defense News* (17 March 1986), p. 4.

45 'Cloudy Skies for the ADI?', *Defense Electronics* (January 1987), p. 59.

46 63716F, Atmospheric Surveillance Technology. 63424F, Cruise Missile Surveillance Technology.

47 63368F, Air Defense Battle Management, $C^2$ technology. 63369F, Cruise Missile Engagement Systems Technology.

48 'SDI Talks Cast Doubt on Need for Separate European Ballistic Defence', *Jane's Defence Weekly* (5 April 1986).

49 Brauch, *Star Wars and European Defence*, p. 454.

50 For example, JSTARS and JTACM.

51 *The Independent* (15 June 1987), p. 15, 'Phoney War is Over as Airbus Takes on the Two American Giants'.

52 This included the space shuttle (Hermes), the launch vehicle (Ariane) and the space station (Columbus).

53 European Strategic Program of R&D in Information Technology (the largest EEC scientific programme); Basic Research in Industrial Technologies for Europe; R&D in Advanced Communication technologies for Europe; Strategic Programme for Innovation and Technology transfer; and Basic Research in Adaptive Intelligence and Neurocomputing.

54 Brauch, *Star Wars and European Defence*, chapter 9.

55 Jacques Isnard (Defence Editor of *Le Monde*), 'The Eureka Project and the SDI', *International Defense Review* (June 1985), p. 858.

56 *The Engineer* (3 July 1986), p. 10, 'Europe Agrees on £1.4 Billion for High-Tech Projects'.

57 France, Canada, Norway, Netherlands, Greece, Denmark.

58 This sum is uncannily close to the estimate by the Federation of American Scientists that the Allies would win $300 million over the first five years of SDI. Pike, 'Barriers to European Participation in the Strategic Defense Initiative', p. 2.

NOTES TO PAGES 135–41

59 Lockheed Missile and Space Company are to 'assist the IAI [Israel Aircraft Industries] in US and international marketing efforts', *Janes's Defence Weekly* (21 January 1989), p. 74. Eighty per cent of funding for the Israeli Arrow comes from the SDI Program.

60 Bill Davies, 'The SDI Participation Office: The Interface with Industry', paper presented to the British Defence Exports Conference, 24-5 April 1986, Advanced Technology International Ltd.

61 Letter from Michael Bentley, seminars manager, Crown Eagle Communications Ltd (29 September 1987).

62 See also United States, General Accounting Office, 'Strategic Defense Initiative Program: Extent of Foreign Participation' (February 1990) (GAO/NSIAD 90-2), table 2.1. Another source gives the total of SDIO allied contracts as $479.2 million: *Armed Forces Journal International* (January 1991), p. 23.

63 Off-the-record interviews with officials in Paris and Bonn. Correspondence with Stuart Croft, International Institute for Strategic Studies.

## 11 MILITARY ECONOMY

1 United States, Department of Defense, 'Program Descriptive Summaries, RDT&E. FY 1987'. No pagination.

2 United States, Department of Defense, Strategic Defense Initiative Organization, Office of Technology Applications, 1987.

3 Donald Latham, Assistant Secretary of Defense for C³I. United States Congress, House of Representatives, Committee on Appropriations, Subcommittee on Defense, *Hearings* (29 April 1985) [Microfiche H181–88.5, p. 543].

4 John E. Pike, 'The Strategic Defense Initiative: Areas of Concern', Federation of American Scientists Staff Paper (10 June 1985), p. 43. United States Congress, Senate, Armed Services Committee, *DoD Authorization of Appropriations for Fiscal Year 1985. Hearings on S. 24145. part 6*, p. 3034, lists 22 PEs 'which provide collateral benefit to SDI' and 58 PEs which benefit 'a broad range of military applications', including the SDI.

5 See Thomas Karas, *Star Wars: The New High Ground* (Sevenoaks: Hodder & Stoughton, 1988), chapter 8, 'Space Lasers: The Ultimate Weapon?'. Also 'Laser-Guided Systems: An Overview', *Marine Corps Gazette* (August 1990).

6 United States Congress, House of Representatives, Armed Services Committee. *Hearings on H.R. 4428. DoD Authorization of Appropriations for Fiscal Year 1987. RDT&E. Title II.* (HASC 99-38), p. 763.

7 Mr Naef, quoted in Magraw, 'SDI', p. 23.

8 *Ibid.*

9 *FY 1987 Defense Authorization Act*, section 215. *FY 1988 Defense Authorization Act*, section 233.

10 The panel is chaired by the director of defense research and engineering (DDR&E).

11 Lt-Gen. Abrahamson, keynote address to the National Defense University Space Symposium dinner. Reprinted in United States, Department of

224

Defense, National Defense University, *America Plans for Space*, p. 10. See also *Air Force Magazine* (August 1990).

12 Air Force Space Command fact sheet (May 1988).

13 United States Congress, House of Representatives, Committee on Appropriations, Subcommittee on Defense, *Hearings*, 1987, part 1, p. 817.

14 Co-ordination between SDI and Space Command is being increased. *Aviation Week and Space Technology* (7 April 1989), p. 19.

15 Quoted in Brauch, *Military Technology*, p. 429.

16 Yevgeny Velikhov, Roald Sagdeyev and Andrei Kokoshin (eds.), *Weaponry in Space: The Dilemma of Security* (Moscow: Mir Publishers, 1986), chapter 4, 'Potential Uses of Space-Based Weapons against Air and Ground Targets'.

17 United States, Department of Defense, Air Force, *Air Force Space Systems Architecture* (SSA 2000), interim version (29 January 1985). The document, obtained under the Freedom of Information Act, has three pages on strategic defence (appendix D, 50–3), and these are mainly blanked out.

18 *Ibid.*, vol. I, p. 3. Also vol. II, C-19.

19 *Ibid.*, vol. I, p. 9.

20 *Ibid.*, vol. II, C-11 and C-19.

21 See, for example, *ibid.*, vol. III, appendix F, 2–74.

22 *Space News* (7–20 January 1991), p. 22.

23 Bhupendra Jasani and Christopher Lee, *Countdown to Space War* (London: Taylor and Francis, 1984), pp. 1, 83.

24 Over 70 per cent of all US military communications are transmitted via satellite: see 'Space Weapons and Intelligence Satellites', *Armed Forces Magazine* (August 1985), p. 224. For a list of US and Soviet military satellites, see Union of Concerned Scientists, *The Fallacy of Star Wars*, chapter 10, tables 3 and 4.

25 See Karas, *Star Wars*, chapter 5, 'Force Multipliers: Navigation and Weather Satellites'.

26 Paul B. Stares, *The Militarization of Space: US Policy, 1945-1984* (Ithaca: Cornell University Press, 1985), p. 126.

27 John Foster, DDR&E, FY 1970 NASA budget hearings. Quoted in Stares, *The Militarization of Space*, p. 120.

28 Such at least was the view of Allan Mense, acting chief scientist at the SDIO until April 1988. Quoted in 'Star Wars in Transition', *IEEE Spectrum* (March 1989), p. 36.

29 Aspen Strategy Group, ed. Joseph S. Nye Jr and James A. Schear, *Seeking Stability in Space* (Lanham, Md.: Aspen Strategy Group and University Press of America, 1987).

30 United States Congress, Office of Technology Assessment, *Anti-Satellite Weapons* (OTA-ISC 281), p. 9.

31 See the works of Seymour Melman, Robert Reich and the Council on Economic Priorities.

32 *Wall Street Journal* (11 March 1981). Every ten years, the US Department of Commerce, Bureau of Economic Analysis, publishes an exhaustive data base on US investment overseas (under authority of the International Investment Survey Act 1976). See *US Direct Investment Abroad* (Washington,

D.C.: United States Government Printing Office, 1981). See also Seymour Melman, *Profits Without Production* (New York: Knopf, 1983), appendix 1. For a fuller picture, which includes foreign direct investment *within* the USA, see *Transnational Corporations in World Development: Trends and Prospects* (New York: United Nations, Centre on Transnational Corporations, 1988).

33 The Philippines, South Korea, Haiti, Peru, etc.

34 United States, Senate, Armed Services Committee (11 March 1986), p. 68.

35 Barry M. Blechman and Stephen S. Kaplan, *Force without War: United States Armed Forces as a Political Instrument* (Washington, D.C.: Brookings Institution, 1978), p. 517.

36 *Ibid.*, p. 517.

37 See the report of that title by the US General Accounting Office. GAO/PEMD–90–13.

38 See Paul L. Ferrari, Jeffrey W. Knopf and Raul L. Madrid, *U.S. Arms Exports: Policies and Contractors* (Washington, D.C.: Investor Responsibility Research Center, 1987). Apart from FMS, other security assistance programmes include the Military Assistance Program (MAP), International Military Education and Training (IMET) and Economic Support Fund (ESF).

39 The argument may be refined: increased US arms expenditures, of which SDI is a part, encourage rises in the interest rate, as the US government needs to fund the deficit. The interest rate rises increase the burden on debtor nations to repay or service their debts – which amounts to a subtle form of 'low intensity conflict'.

40 Paul Kennedy, *The Rise and Fall of the Great Powers* (London: Fontana, 1989).

41 Zegveld and Enzing, *SDI and Industrial Technology Policy*.

42 United States, Department of Defense, Air Force, *Air Force Space Systems Architecture*, (SSA 2000), p. 11. Italics in the original.

43 Nozette, Stewart (ed.), *Commercializing SDI Technologies* (New York: Praeger, 1987). Also SDIO, 'The SDI Technology Applications Program' (1987). The American Defense Preparedness Association sponsored a conference on 'SDI Technology Transfer Opportunities'.

44 Institute for Defense Analysis, 'Benefit to Industry and Tactical Forces from SDI Innovative Science and Technology Programs' (1985).

45 See Chapter 9 above.

46 Council on Economic Priorities, *The Strategic Defense Initiative*, chapters 3 and 5. Council on Economic Priorities, *Star Wars*, chapter 8. Also *Aviation Week and Space Technology* (5 December 1988), 'US Faces Potential Shortage of Engineers'. For the alternatives forgone in terms of welfare programmes, see Council on Economic Priorities, 'Research Report' (October/November 1988).

47 Nozette (ed.), *Commercializing SDI Technologies*, pp. 3, 39.

48 Kaldor, *The Baroque Arsenal*, p. 4.

49 *Ibid.*, p. 5.

50 *Ibid.*, pp. 3, 219–30. Also Melman, *Profits without Production*, chapter 11.

51 V/STOL aircraft were too effective to be denigrated as 'baroque'. FRS-1 Harriers and GR-3 Ground Attack Harriers flew over 1,000 sorties, achieving an availability rate of 80–90 per cent.

52 Later reports suggested that only 7 per cent of US explosives dropped in the war were smart bombs; and that 'seventy per cent of the 88,500 tons of bombs dropped on Iraq and Kuwait missed their targets completely'. *New Statesman and Society* (12 April 1991), pp. 6–7.

53 One baroque failure was the Apache AH-64 attack helicopter, which had a low availability rate and had jammed guns. *Financial Times* (20 February 1991). US General Accounting Office, *Apache Helicopter: Serious Logistical Support Problems Must Be Solved to Realize Combat Potential* GAO/NSIAD–90–294 (September 1990).

54 Kaldor, *The Baroque Arsenal*, pp. 173–4, 226, did allow that precision-guided munitions might be a 'process' improvement perhaps challenging the stultification of the baroque.

55 *Ibid.*, p. 3.

56 N. D. Kondratiev, 'The Long Waves in Economic Life', *Review of Economic Statistics* (17 November 1935), pp. 105–15. C. Perez, 'Structural Change and the Assimilation of New Technologies in the Economic and Social Systems', *Futures* (October 1983), pp. 357–75.

57 Roger Hutton, 'The SDI: Technology and Politics', M.Sc. thesis, University of Lancaster, 1984.

58 Ernest Mandel, *Late Capitalism* (London: New Left Books, 1975), p. 277.

59 *Ibid.*, p. 306.

60 Michael Kidron, *Capitalism and Theory* (London: Pluto Press, 1974), p. 20.

### 12 THE CULTURE OF 'STAR WARS'

1 Reagan's idea was 'metaphysical' in that it was an 'attempt to set right the nature of things', which rested on 'unexamined assumptions about reality', 'supposed to be non-negotiable and embedded in nature'. Jeff Smith, 'Reagan, Star Wars and American Culture', *Bulletin of the Atomic Scientists* (January/February 1987).

2 Henry T. Nash, 'The Bureaucratization of Homicide', in E. P. Thompson and D. Smith (eds.), *Protest and Survive* (Harmondsworth: Penguin, 1980). Aubrey, *Nukespeak*; Cohn, 'Sex and Death in the Rational World of Defense Intellectuals', in Diana E. H. Russell (ed.), *Exposing Nuclear Phallacies* (New York: Pergamon Press, 1989).

3 Dennis Hayes, 'The Cloistered Work-Place', in Les Levidow and Kevin Robins (eds.), *Cyborg Worlds: The Military Information Society* (London: Free Association Books, 1989), p. 82.

4 Robert Jay Lifton and Richard Falk, *Indefensible Weapons: The Political and Psychological Case against Nuclearism* (New York: Basic Books, 1982), chapter 10, 'On Numbing and Feeling'.

5 United States Congress, House of Representatives, Armed Services Committee, *Strategic Defense Initiative Program* (6 June 1985) [HASC 99–30], p. 37, Mrs Lloyd.

6 United States Congress, House of Representatives, Armed Services Committee, *Hearings on HR. 4428. DoD Authorization of Appropriations for Fiscal Year 1987. RDT&E. Title II.* (HASC 99–38), p. 684.

7 Mr Battista, United States Congress, House of Representatives, Armed Services Committee, *Hearings on National Defense Authorization Act for Fiscal Years 1988/1989 – H.R. 1748* (13 October 1986), p. 478.

8 United States Congress, House of Representatives, Armed Services Committee, *Strategic Defense Initiative Program* (6 June 1985) [HASC 99–30], p. 24.

9 SDI Office, 'Brilliant Pebbles' fact sheet (18 April 1989).

10 Dennis Hayes, 'The Cloistered Work-Place: Military Electronics Workers Obey and Ignore', in Levidow and Robins, *Cyborg Worlds*.

11 George Kennan, 'Idea Whose Time is Up', *The Guardian* (25 April 1988).

12 York, *Race to Oblivion*, pp. 234-5.

13 United States, Department of Defense, National Defense University, *America Plans for Space*, p. 11.

14 Lt-Gen. Abrahamson. Quoted in *The Guardian* (19 February 1986). Reagan borrowed the same line in a speech at the National Space Club. Herken, 'Earthly Origins', p. 26.

15 Rod Hyde, quoted in William J. Broad, *Star Warriors: The Weaponry of Space: Reagan's Young Scientists* (London: Faber & Faber, 1986), p. 134.

16 Franklin, *War Stars*, parts I and II.

17 Quoted in Rogin, *Ronald Reagan*, p. 1. See also Wills, *Reagan's America*, p. 361.

18 Congressman George Brown (California). Speech to Congress, 'GAO Report on the X-ray Laser Program', 14 July 1988.

19 Congressman Floyd Spence. United States, Congress, House of Representatives, Armed Services Committee, *Hearings before The Defense Policy Panel and R&D Subcommittee* (26 March, 8 July and 15 September 1987), p. 22 (Washington, D.C.: United States Government Printing Office, 1988).

20 Teller, 'SDI: The Last, Best Hope'.

21 Schlesinger, 'Rhetoric and Realities'.

22 *Washington Times* (3 September 1990), p. 4.

23 Broad, *Star Warriors*, p. 207.

24 Blum, 'Weird Science', p. 11. See also 'Science Fiction: "The Root of Star Wars"', *USA Today* (Society for the Advancement of Education) (9 May 1990), p. 52.

25 'Star Warriors: Starfighter Combat in the Star Wars Universe'. West End Games. Back cover.

26 Franklin, *War Stars*, p. 203.

27 'Crow's Account of the Battle', in Ted Hughes, *Crow* (London: Faber & Faber, 1972), p. 27.

28 Lt-Gen. Abrahamson, United States Congress, House of Representatives, Armed Services Committee, *Hearings on H.R. 4428. Authorization of Appropriations for Fiscal Year 1987. RDT&E. Title II* (Washington, D.C.: US Government Printing Office, 1986) [HASC. 99–38], p. 763.

29 *Ibid.*, p. 679.

30 'Brilliant Pebbles' fact sheet.
31 See also Herbert C. Kelman and V. Lee Hamilton, *Crimes of Obedience* (New Haven: Yale University Press, 1989).
32 'Star Warriors', back cover.
33 Quoted in Rogin, *Ronald Reagan*, p. 23.
34 *The Guardian* (5 January 1986).
35 David Cortwright and Richard Pollock, 'Summary Findings of the Peace Media Exploratory Project' (25 July 1985), p. 14.

### 13 THE SELLING OF SDI

1 Reagan, 'Transcript of Televised Address to the American Nation on 23 March 1983', p. 1.
2 'Now this is not to say that the Soviet Union is planning to make war on us', *ibid.*, p. 4.
3 *Ibid.*, pp. 8–10.
4 *Ibid.*, p. 8.
5 Seven months later, Grenada was invaded by the US in Operation Urgent Fury.
6 *Ibid.*, p. 4.
7 *Ibid.*, pp. 6–7.
8 *Ibid.*, pp. 6–7.
9 *Ibid.*, pp. 2, 11.
10 Twice in the speech (pp. 4, 15), Reagan used the 1930s as an analogy, implying that Communists are equivalent to Nazis and liberals to appeasers. The analogy, which has a strong resonance in lived experience, ignores the right-wing motivations of most appeasers. For a different basis of comparison, see Robert Jay Lifton, *The Genocide Mentality: Nazi Holocaust and Nuclear Threat* (London: Macmillan, 1991).
11 In the lingo of the insurance salesman, 'pull up the hearse and let them smell the flowers'. A whiff of gulags was the political equivalent.
12 Nixon, 'Announcement of the Safeguard Decision, March 14, 1989', reprinted in William R. Kintner (ed.), *Safeguard: Why the ABM Makes Sense* (New York: Hawthorn Books, 1969), pp. 3, 6.
13 Wills, chapter 31.
14 Retired Admiral William J. Crowe, interviewed in *Washington Post* (18 February 1990), p. 18.
15 USAF official biography of Lt-Gen. James A. Abrahamson, in Defense Marketing Services, *Space Based Defense Systems*, appendix II.
16 Program Descriptive Summaries, RDT&E, FY 1987. No pagination. My italics.
17 Interim charter of the SDIO.
18 Teller, 'SDI: The Last, Best Hope'.
19 Representative Henry Hyde (R. – Ill.), quoted in Steinberg, *Lost in Space*, p. 69.
20 Daniel J. Boorstin, *The Americans: The National Experience* (London; Weidenfeld & Nicolson, 1966), chapters 34 and 35.

21 'The Selling of Star Wars: A Childishly Simple Task', *International Herald Tribune* (7 November 1985).
22 Reagan, March 1988, quoted in Ronald L. Tammen, James T. Bruce and Bruce W. MacDonald, 'Star Wars after Five Years: The Decisive Point', *Arms Control Today* (July/August 1988).
23 *Ibid.*, p. 7.
24 'CIA: Soviet Strategic Defense Funding 15 Times U.S.', *Defense Daily* (1 December 1986), p. 138.
25 *Ibid.*
26 See 'The Soviet Propaganda Campaign against the US Strategic Defense Initiative', United States, Department of State, Arms Control and Disarmament Agency (August 1986). In the 1960s the Liberty Lobby warned that 'the Communist Party is orchestrating a massive drive against the Safeguard system'. *Congressional Quarterly* (30 May 1969), p. 850.
27 See Chapters 6 and 8 above.
28 Maxwell Glen, 'Star Wars Future Remains Uncertain Despite its Early Successes in Congress', *National Journal* (10 August 1985), p. 1836.
29 USAF official biography of Lt-Gen. James A. Abrahamson.
30 Glen, 'Star Wars Future Remains Uncertain Despite its Early Successes in Congress', p. 1833.
31 These officials included Secretary of Defense Weinberger, Under-Secretary of Defense Fred Ikle, and Assistant Secretary of Defense for International Security Policy Richard Perle. See *Aviation Week and Space Technology* (11 March 1985), 'US Launches Program to Bring NATO into SDI Research Role'.
32 'German–American Conference on SDI', Cologne–Bonn air base, 28–9 June 1985. Report obtained from the American Defense Preparedness Association.
33 BDM had $55,410,000 in SDI contracts by August 1988. SDIO Contract Management Information System.
34 *Defense News* (10 November 1986), p. 21.
35 *The Times* (19 February 1986).
36 Michael Marshall (Conservative – Arundel). Notes for the House of Commons Defence Committee on a meeting at the Pentagon with Frank Gaffney, Deputy Assistant Secretary of Defense, Nuclear Forces and Arms Control Policy, 21 October 1985.
37 Chairman LaFalce, United States Congress, House of Representatives, Committee on Banking, Finance and Urban Affairs, *Impact of Strategic Defense Initiative [SDI] on the U.S. Industrial Base*, Hearing (10 December 1985), p. 69.
38 See Chapter 10 above.
39 *The Sun* (14 October 1986), p. 6.
40 Paul Quiles (French Defence Minister), interview with *Le Monde* (13 November 1985), p. 12. Reproduced in *The Guardian* (5 January 1986).
41 After long preparation, the letter, titled 'The Challenge of Peace: God's Promise and Our Response' was issued in May 1983.
42 Franklin, *War Stars*, p. 197.
43 *Milwaukee Sentinel* (3 December 1986), p. 10. The claim is made by R. James

Woolsey. Others who saw SDI as specifically a counter to the Freeze included Les Aspin, chairman of the House Armed Services Committee, and Father Brian Hehir, staff director for the pastoral letter.

44 Edward Tabor Linenthal, *Symbolic Defense: The Cultural Significance of the Strategic Defense Initiative* (Champaign, Ill.: University of Illinois Press, 1989).

45 John T. Bosma, 'A Proposed Plan for Project on BMD and Arms Control (Final)'. High Frontier/Heritage Foundation document (no date). The eleven-page plan was leaked to Richard Garwin in the summer of 1984. Bosma denied authorship, then claimed it with pride. Correspondence with Richard Garwin.

46 Bosma said that he returned his $1,000 consultancy fee when he learnt of High Frontier's links with the 'Moonie' Unification Church. *Nuclear Times* (May 1985), p. 12.

47 Edward Teller, quoted in Scheer, 'The Man who Blew the Whistle on Star Wars', p. 9.

48 Reagan, 'Televised Address', p. 12.

49 Hoffman, 'Ballistic Missile Defenses and US National Security', p. 5.

50 *Aviation Week and Space Technology* (31 October 1988), p. 23, 'Bush Links Domestic, Defense Themes to Keep Dukakis Campaign off Stride'. Dukakis had one 'sound bite' on SDI: 'we need Star Schools, not Star Wars'.

51 It had supported paedophiles.

52 'Crown Jewel of "Star Wars" has Lost its Luster', *New York Times* (13 February 1990), p. C1.

### 14 INTO THE 1990S

1 Meeting of the Soviet Foreign Minister and US Secretary of State at Jackson Hole, Wyoming. The Soviets reserved the right to cancel a START Treaty should the USA violate the traditional reading of the ABM Treaty.

2 *Washington Times* (9 July 1990).

3 'SDIO Continues String of Successes', *Defense Daily* (11 May 1990), p. 242. Also United States Congress, House of Representatives, Committee on Appropriations, Subcommittee on Defense, *DoD Appropriations for 1991. Hearings*, part 7, p. 610.

4 'Technical Failures Bedevil Star Wars', *New York Times* (18 September 1990), p. C1.

5 'SDI Budget Cutbacks to Delay Near Term Weapons Deployments', *Aviation Week and Space Technology* (22 May 1989). ' "Star Wars" Plan Facing a Delay, its Director Says', *New York Times* (12 May 1989). Also 'Strategic Defense System Criteria for Deployment Will Not be Met by 1993: Critical Issues Must be Resolved', United States Congress, House of Representatives, Committee on Government Operations (30 November 1990). DoD criticised this report. 'Pentagon calls SDI Report a "rewrite"', *Washington Times* (18 December 1990), p. 6.

6 'Hackers Steal SDI Information in Internet System', *Washington Times* (24 December 1990), p. 3.

7 Frank Carlucci, quoted *ibid*.
8 *Congressional Quarterly* (1 April 1989), p. 705.
9 *The Guardian* (29 March 1989).
10 ' "Star Wars" Goal Cut, Quayle Says', *Los Angeles Times* (7 September 1989), p. 1.
11 Unclassified paragraph from National Security Decision Directive 14 on 'ICBM Modernization and Strategic Defense Initiative'. Quoted in Bruce W. MacDonald, 'Lost in Space: SDI Struggles through its Sixth Year', *Arms Control Today* (September 1989), p. 22.
12 General Robert Herres, quoted *ibid*.
13 *Aviation Week and Space Technology* (22 May 1989), p. 23.
14 'SDI: "Brilliant Pebbles" detailed', *Jane's Defence Weekly* (27 May 1989). See also a description by Lowell Wood: 'From "Smart Rocks" Come "Brilliant Pebbles" ', *Aerospace America* (April 1990).
15 Other cost estimates are four times this figure. 'Sharp Rise in Brilliant Pebbles Interceptor Funding Accompanied by New Doubts about Technical Feasibility', *Aviation Week and Space Technology* (22 May 1989).
16 Nine days after retiring as director of the SDIO, Abrahamson backed the Pebbles, saying they could be deployed by 1995 at a total cost of $25 billion. *Congressional Quarterly* (1 April 1989), p. 703, 'Phase One Scenarios'.
17 'Technical, Economic Challenge to "Brilliant Pebbles" Concept', *San Francisco Chronicle* (12 September 1990), p. B1.
18 *Aviation Week and Space Technology* (22 May 1989).
19 Richard Garwin, 'Are Brilliant Pebbles all that Brilliant?', *Aerospace America* (December 1990), p. 6.
20 'Pentagon Science Advisers Criticize SDIO's Rush to Adopt Brilliant Pebbles', *Aviation Week and Space Technology* (9 April 1990).
21 Sen. Jeff Bingamann (D. – N.Mex.), quoted in *Aviation Week and Space Technology* (14 August 1989), p. 23.
22 Rep. Edward Markey (D. – Mass.), quoted in *San José Mercury News* (5 May 1990), p. 1.
23 'Pentagon Develops New SDI Rocket', *Financial Times* (4 April 1991). 'Particle beam Reactor Central to SDI Nuclear Rocket Project', *Aviation Week and Space Technology* (8 April 1991), p. 18.
24 *Washington Post* (18 February 1990), p. 18.
25 'Pentagon Seeks to Protect Funding for Critical Technology Development', *Aviation Week and Space Technology* (16 April 1990).
26 *Inside the Pentagon* (6 September 1990), p. 1. As the first SDI project due to enter full-scale development, BSTS faced constraints because of the ABM Treaty. The relabelling was also a way of negotiating this problem.
27 S. Hrg. 101–936, part 2, p. 390. Testimony of SDIO director.
28 'Carter Calls "Star Wars" a Wasteful Scheme to "Legally Bribe" Lawmakers', *Atlanta Journal & Constitution* (30 January 1990), p. A12.
29 'Will Tight Budgets Finally Shoot Down SDI?', *Investor's Daily* (9 January 1990), p. 1. See also 'SDI Troops Rallied for Hill Battle', *SDI Monitor* (30 March 1990), p. 82.
30 S. Hrg. 101–49, part 6, pp. 913–15.

31 Reagan, news conference, September 1985. Quoted in Herken, 'Earthly Origins'.
32 See *Arms Control Today* (March 1988).
33 Admiral William Crowe, March 1989, quoted in MacDonald, 'Lost in Space'.
34 United States Senate, Committee on Appropriations, *Hearings on DoD Appropriations for FY 1986 and H.R. 3629. Part 4*, p. 311.
35 'New SDI Film is on Target', *Dayton Daily News* (23 September 1989), p. 11.
36 'Prodded by Quayle and Cheney, Bush Becomes Fervent Supporter of Strategic Defense Initiative', *Wall Street Journal* (23 February 1990), p. 12.
37 *Ibid.*, p. 12.
38 *Defense Industry Report* (19 October 1989).
39 *Wall Street Journal* (23 February 1990), p. 12.
40 'Strategic Defense for the 1990s', *Nature* (19 April 1990).
41 'Pentagon should Change Emphasis from Soviet to Third World', Washington – United Press International (10 May 1990).
42 'SDI Backers See Third World Missile Threat', *Air Force Times* (9 April 1990), p. 25.
43 Henry F. Cooper, 'SDI and Arms Control', in Kim R. Holmes and Spring Baker (eds.), *SDI at the Turning Point: Readying Strategic Defenses for the 1990s and Beyond* (Washington, D.C.: Heritage Foundation, 1990).
44 'Iraqi Threat Boosts Interest in SDI Spin-Off', *Washington Times* (17 September 1990), p. 4. 'SDI Gets a Boost through Saddam', *Insight* (29 October 1990), p. 25.
45 'Senate Makes Major Changes to "Star Wars" Program', Washington – United Press International (4 August 1990).
46 'Defenseless Against Missile Terror', *Reader's Digest* (October 1990), p. 112.
47 'The New Case for Star Wars', *Fortune* (3 December 1990), p. 121.
48 'SDIO Retools for Limited Threats', *SDI Monitor* (21 December 1990).
49 Rep. John Kyl (R. –Ariz.), *Defense News* (8 October 1990), p. 3.
50 'SDI Won't Die', *Washington Times* (20 December 1990). 'Several conservative leaders declined to sign the letter because they considered it "too polite".'
51 *The Guardian* (24 January 1991).
52 Some, including Senator Malcolm Wallop and Angelo Codevilla, asserted that the SDI programme hindered the development of Patriot. ('The whole [SDI] program was designed to study forever and build never. It hurt more than it helped.') See William J. Broad, 'The Patriot's Success: Because of "Star Wars" or in Spite of it?' (10 February 1991).
53 'Lesser "Star Wars" May See the Light', *Washington Times* (31 January 1991), p. 1.
54 *Financial Times* (6 February 1991), p. 1.
55 'Sky Wars Delivers the Victory', *Financial Times* (1 March 1991).
56 *The Guardian* (22 January 1991). See also 'US Defence Sector Unlikely to Gain from War Dividend', *Financial Times* (31 January 1991).
57 'State of the Union Address', 29 January 1991 (Washington, D.C.: United States Government Printing Office, 1991), p. 7.

58 *SDI Monitor* (4 February 1991).
59 'In Test, "Star Wars" Picks Off a Warhead in Space', *New York Times* (30 January 1991), p. 1.
60 *Congressional Quarterly Weekly Report* (9 February 1991), p. 376. Also 'SDI Downsized to Protect Against Limited Strikes', *Defense Daily* (5 February 1991).
61 'Army Leadership Faulted for Losing ATBM Work to SDIO', *Defense Daily* (26 November 1990).
62 Rep. Charles Bennett (D. – Fl.), 'Patriot and SDI', *Washington Post* (5 February 1991).
63 See *Financial Times* (17 and 18 April 1991 and 3 May 1991), 'Arms to Iraq: Under the Nose of the White House Kickbacks and Illegal Deals Funded Saddam'. Also, 9 March 1991.
64 Joe Cirincione, professional staff member of the House Armed Services Committee and, later, the Government Operations Committee. Telephone interview, 17 April 1991.
65 'Navy SDI Facing Extinction as Funds Dwindle', *Navy News and Undersea Technology* (12 November 1990), p. 1.
66 *Defense Daily* (6 May 1988), p. 37.
67 Chomsky, 'The Evil Empire'. SDI's contribution to US power projection is discussed in Chapter 11 above.
68 Joseph Campbell, defence industry analyst at Paine Webber, quoted in the *Boston Globe* (14 September 1987).
69 United States Congress, House of Representatives, Committee on Appropriations, Subcommittee on Defense, *DoD Appropriations for 1991, Part 7*, p. 678. The US Army Strategic Defense Command, the main SDI agency, is also responsible for the Kinetic Energy ASAT. USASDC fact sheets (February 1991).

## 15 THE CAUSES OF SDI

1 Mrs Thatcher, speaking at the National Test Facility in Colorado Springs. Quoted by the director of the SDI Office, Henry Cooper, 'Trying to Get SDI Off the Ground', *Washington Times* (14 September 1990), p. F3.
2 J. P. Litherland, 'Soviet Views of the Arms Race and Disarmament', Ph.D. thesis, University of Bradford, 1987, chapter 6.
3 The counter-argument would be that, by strengthening the hand of the Soviet military, a mainly conservative force, SDI and other US threats delayed the liberalisation of the USSR.
4 Nietzsche, *The Dawn of Day*, section 523.
5 Nolan, *Guardians of the Arsenal*, p. 24. Also conclusion.
6 Hoffman, 'Ballistic Missile Defenses', p. 6.
7 United States, Department of Defense, Department of the Army (1980?). Army issue papers prepared in response to the Special Assistant's 11 November 1980 memorandum on presidential transition.
8 National security may even be inverse to military strength. Although by the mid 1980s the USA had over 25,000 nuclear weapons, never before had the

country been less secure. Never before had it faced the prospect of such total annihilation.

9 Coffin, *Passion of the Hawks*, p. 168. See Chapter 2 above.

10 United States Congress, Senate, Committee on Governmental Affairs, *DoD/ SDIO Compliance with the Federal Advisory Committee Act* (19 April 1988), p. 94.

11 *Space News* (22 January 1990), p. 18.

12 United States, Army Strategic Defense Command, Official History, p. 63.

13 See Chapter 3 above.

14 Bosma, 'A Proposed Plan'. See Chapter 13 above.

15 See Chapter 6 above.

16 See Chapter 5 above.

17 See Chapter 6 above.

18 See Chapters 5, 6, 7 and 8 above.

19 Council on Economic Priorities, *The Strategic Defense Initiative*, preface.

20 See Chapter 8 above.

21 See Chapter 8 above.

22 See Chapter 9 above.

23 See Chapters 8 and 9 above.

24 See Chapter 10 above.

25 A study of Fleet Ballistic Missile Guidance Systems concludes that 'technology' and 'politics' interact, only '"interact" is too weak a word for their labyrinthine interconnections and intermingling'. Donald MacKenzie and Graham Spinardi, 'The Shaping of Nuclear Weapon System Technology: US Fleet Ballistic Missile Guidance and Navigation', *Social Studies of Science*, 18 (1988), p. 612.

26 See Chapter 4 above.

27 Caspar Weinberger, 'SDI, Ethics and Soviet Hypocrisy', *Insight* (13 January 1986).

# SELECT BIBLIOGRAPHY

Adams, Benson, D. 'McNamara's ABM Policy, 1961–1967', *Orbis*, vol. 12, no. 1 (spring 1968), Foreign Policy Research Institute, University of Pennsylvania.

Allison, Graham T. and Frederic A. Morris. 'Armaments and Arms Control: Exploring the Determinants of Military Weapons', *Daedalus*, 105 (summer 1975).

Anderson, Martin. *Revolution*, New York, Harcourt Brace Jovanovich, 1988.

Anderton, Charles Harold. 'Arms Race Modelling: Systematic Analysis and Synthesis', Ph.D. thesis, Cornell University, 1986.

Arkin, William M. and Richard W. Fieldhouse. *Nuclear Battlefields: Global Links in the Arms Race*, Cambridge, Mass., Ballinger, 1985.

Arms Control Association. 'Star Wars: An Anthology of Quotes by the Administration, Congress and Outside Experts', Arms Control Association, Washington, D.C., June 1985.

Baran, Paul A. and Paul M. Sweezy. *Monopoly Capital: An Essay on the American Economic and Social Order*, London, Penguin, 1968.

Blum, Deborah. 'Weird Science: Livermore's X-ray Laser Flap', *Bulletin of the Atomic Scientists* (July/August 1988).

Bosma, John T. 'A Proposed Plan for Project on BMD and Arms Control (Final)', High Frontier/Heritage Foundation Document (no date).

Bosma, John T. and Richard C. Whelan. *Guide to the Strategic Defense Initiative*, Pasha Publications, June 1985.

Bowman, Robert. *Star Wars: a Defense Expert's Case Against the Strategic Defense Initiative*, Los Angeles, Jeremy P. Tarcher, 1986.

Brauch, Hans Gunter (ed.), *Star Wars and European Defence*, Macmillan, 1987.
  *Military Technology, Armaments Dynamics and Disarmament*, Macmillan, 1989.

Broad, William J. 'Long Stream of People and Ideas Led to "Star Wars" Speech, *New York Times* (4 March 1985).
  *Star Warriors: The Weaponry of Space: Reagan's Young Scientists*, London, Faber & Faber, 1986.

Bulkeley, Rip and Graham Spinardi. *Space Weapons: Deterrence or Delusion?* Cambridge, Polity Press, 1986.

Bunn, Matthew. *Foundation for the Future: The ABM Treaty and National Security*, Washington, D.C., Arms Control Association, 1990.

Chayes, Antonia Handler and Paul Dity (eds.). *Defending Deterrence: Managing the ABM Treaty into the 21st Century*, Pergamon-Brasseys, 1989.

236

Chomsky, Noam. 'The Evil Empire', *New Socialist* (January 1986).

Coalition for the Strategic Defense Initiative, launch booklet (1985).

Coffin, Tristram. *The Passion of the Hawks: Militarism in Modern America*, New York, Macmillan, 1964.

Cohn, Carol. 'Sex and Death in the Rational World of Defense Intellectuals', in Russell (1989).

Council on Economic Priorities. *The Strategic Defense Initiative: Costs, Contractors and Consequences*, New York, 1985.

*Star Wars: The Economic Fallout*, Cambridge, Mass., Ballinger, 1988.

Defense Budget Project. 'Military Spending Data Base: MX and SDI Contractors', PAC Contributions to Congressional Candidates', printout (July 1985).

Defense Marketing Services. *Space Based Defense System: Market Study and Forecast* (June 1984).

Eisenhower, President Dwight D. 'Farewell Address to the Nation' of 17 January 1961. US Department of State, *Bulletin*, vol. 44 (6 February 1961). Reprinted in Carroll W. Pursell (ed.), *The Military-Industrial Complex*, New York, Harper & Row (1972), chapter 13.

Electronics Industries Association. 'Proceedings of the Military Electronics Market: Exploring the Opportunities: SDI Program', 9–11 October 1984, Century Plaza Hotel, Los Angeles, EIA Market Planning Reference Publications.

Evangelista, Matthew. *Innovation and the Arms Race: How the United States and the Soviet Union Develop New Military Technologies*, Cornell University Press, 1988.

Franklin, H. Bruce. *War Stars: The Superweapon and the American Imagination*, Oxford University Press, 1988.

Frost and Sullivan Inc. *The Space Defense Market in the US*, New York, May 1983.

Graham, Lt-Gen. Daniel O., USA (Ret.). *High Frontier: A New National Strategy*, Washington, D.C.: High Frontier Inc., 1982.

Gray, Colin S. *American Military Space Policy: Information Systems, Weapon Systems and Arms Control*, Cambridge, Mass., Abt. Books, 1982.

Greve, Frank. 'Star Wars', *San José Mercury News* (17 November 1985).

Hafner, Donald L. 'Assessing the President's Vision: The Fletcher, Miller and Hoffman Panels', *Daedalus*, vol. 114, no. 2 (spring 1985), pp. 91-107.

Halperin, Morton H. 'The Decision to Deploy the ABM: Bureaucratic and Domestic Politics in the Johnson Administration', *World Politics*, Princeton University Press.

Herken, Gregg. 'The Earthly Origins of Star Wars', *Bulletin of the Atomic Scientists* (October 1987).

Hoffman, Fred S., study director, 'Ballistic Missile Defenses and US National Security', Summary Report ('The Hoffman Report'), prepared for the Future Security Strategy Study (October 1983).

Jastrow, Robert. *How to Make Nuclear Weapons Obsolete*, Boston, Little, Brown, 1985 (1st edition, 1983).

Kaldor, Mary. *The Baroque Arsenal*, London, André Deutsch, 1982.

Kaplan, F. *The Wizards of Armageddon*, New York, Simon & Schuster, 1983.

Karas, Thomas. *Star Wars: The New High Ground*, Sevenoaks, Hodder & Stoughton, 1988.

Kidron, Michael. *Capitalism and Theory*, London, Pluto Press, 1974.

Kintner, William R. (ed.). *Safeguard: Why the ABM Makes Sense*, New York, Hawthorn Books, 1969.

Kiser, John W. 'How the Arms Race Really Helps Moscow', *Foreign Policy*, no. 60 (fall 1985).

Lakoff, Sanford and Herbert F. York. *A Shield in Space? Technology, Politics and the Strategic Defense Initiative*, University of California Press, 1989.

Lawrence, Robert M. *SDI: Bibliography and Research Guide*, Boulder, Colo., Westview Press, 1987.

Lawrence Livermore National Laboratory. 'Institutional Plan', FY 1984–1989.

Levin, Senator Carl. 'Statement before the Senate Subcommittee on Federal Services, Post Office and Civil Service, Concerning Defense Consultants', 8 July 1988.

Longstreth, Thomas K., John E. Pike and John B. Rhinelander. 'The Impact of the US and Soviet Ballistic Missile Defense Programs on the ABM Treaty'. A Report for the National Campaign to Save the ABM Treaty (March 1985).

Luongo, K. and W. T. Wander (eds.). *The Search for Security in Space*, Ithaca, Cornell University Press, 1989.

McNamara, Robert S. 'Text of McNamara's Speech on Anti-China Missile Defense and US Nuclear Strategy'. Text of address to editors of United Press International in San Francisco, 18 September 1967, as issued by the Pentagon and reprinted in the *New York Times* (19 September 1967).

Magraw, Katherine. 'SDI: Fading Fantasy or Fait Accompli?', Washington, D.C.: Spacewatch, 1988.

Marshall Institute. Report of the Technical Panel on 'Missile Defense in the 1990s', Washington, D.C., Marshall Institute, 1987.

Morrison, David C. 'Shooting Down Star Wars', *National Journal* (25 October 1986), p. 2544.

Natural Resources Defense Council. *Nuclear Weapons Databook* series, Ballinger, 1984.

Nolan, Janne E. *Guardians of the Arsenal: The Politics of Nuclear Strategy*, A New Republic Book, Harper & Row, 1989.

Phillips, Sheena. 'Britain, France and the Future of ATBM', paper presented to the ATBM seminar, Amsterdam Free University, 27–8 November 1986.

Pianta, Mario. *New Technologies Across the Atlantic: US Leadership or European Autonomy?*, Hertfordshire, Harvester, Wheatsheaf Press, and Tokyo, The United Nations University, 1988.

Pike, John E. 'The Strategic Defense Initiative: Areas of Concern', Federation of American Scientists Staff Paper (10 June 1985).

'Barriers to European Participation in the Strategic Defense Initiative', Statement to the Subcommittee on Economic Stabilisation, Committee on Banking, Finance and Urban Affairs, House of Representatives (10 December 1985).

'The Emperor's Newest Clothing: Changes to the SDI as a result of Phase 1 Architecture Studies', Federation of American Scientists (16 February 1986).

'SDI and Corporate Contractors: Momentum, Ambivalence and a Push for Early Deployment', Federation of American Scientists, Public Interest Report, vol. 40, no. 4 (April 1987).

'SDI Contracts after 5 Years', Federation of American Scientists (15 March 1988).

Reagan, President Ronald. 'Transcript of Televised Address to the American Nation on 23 March 1983', Weekly Compilation of Presidential Documents, 28 March 1983. Reprinted in Defense Marketing Services, *Space Based Defense Systems*, appendix 1.

Rhea, John. *SDI: What Could Happen: 8 Possible Star Wars Scenarios*, Harrisburg, Pa., Stackpole Books, 1988.

Rockwell International. 'Space: America's Frontier for Growth, Leadership and Freedom' (no date; *c*. 1981).

Rogin, Michael Paul. *Ronald Reagan, the Movie and Other Episodes in Political Demonology*, University of California Press, 1987.

Russell, Diana E. H. (ed.). *Exposing Nuclear Phallacies*, New York, Pergamon, 1989.

Scheer, Robert. *With Enough Shovels: Reagan, Bush and Nuclear War*, London, Secker and Warburg, 1983.

'Teller's Obsession Became Reality in Star Wars Plan', *Los Angeles Times*, part VI (10 July 1983).

'The Man who Blew the Whistle on Star Wars', *Los Angeles Times Magazine* (17 July 1988).

Schlesinger, James R. 'Rhetoric and Realities in the Star Wars Debate', *International Security*, vol. 10, no. 1 (summer 1985).

Schneider, William (ed.). *Why ABM? Policy Issues in the Missile Defense Controversy*, New York, Hudson Institute, 1969.

Stares, Paul B. *The Militarization of Space: US Policy, 1945-1984*, Ithaca, New York, Cornell University Press, 1985.

*Space Weapons and US Strategy*, London, Croom Helm, 1985.

Steinberg, Gerald M. (ed.). *Lost in Space: The Domestic Politics of the Strategic Defense Initiative*, Lexington Books, 1988.

Tammen, Ronald L., James T. Bruce and Bruce W. MacDonald, 'Star Wars after Five Years: The Decisive Point', *Arms Control Today* (July/August 1988).

Teller, Edward. 'SDI: The Last, Best Hope', *Insight* (*Washington Times* magazine) (28 October 1985), p. 75.

Thee, Marek. *Military Technology, Military Strategy and the Arms Race*, London, Croom Helm, 1986.

Thompson, E. P. (ed.). *Star Wars*, London, Penguin, 1985.

Union of Concerned Scientists. *The Fallacy of Star Wars*, New York, Vintage Books, Random House, 1984.

*Empty Promise: The Growing Case Against Star Wars*, Boston, Beacon Press, 1986.

United States Congress, Congressional Budget Office
'Analysis of the President's Strategic Defense Initiative 1985–1989' (May 1984).
United States Congress, *Congressional Quarterly*
'Major Lobby Effort Surrounds Sentinel ABM System' (21 March 1969), p. 409.
'Battle over ABM Switches to Nation's Grassroots' (30 May 1969), p. 845.
United States Congress, House of Representatives, Armed Services Committee
*Hearing on Military Posture and H.R. 12564. DoD Authorization for Appropriations for FY 1975. RDT&E Title II*, Washington, D.C., United States Government Printing Office, 1976.
*Hearing on Military Posture and H.R. 1872 (H.R. 4040). DoD Authorization for Appropriations for Fiscal Year 1980. RDT&E Title II*, Washington, D.C., United States Government Printing Office, 1979.
*Hearing on Military Posture and H.R. 6495 (H.R. 6974). DoD Authorization for Appropriations for Fiscal Year 1981. R&D Title II*, Washington, D.C., United States Government Printing Office, 1980.
*DoD Authorization Act 1986. Hearings*, 10 May 1985, Washington, D.C., United States Government Printing Office.
*Hearings on H.R. 4428. DoD Authorization of Appropriations for Fiscal Year 1987. RDT&E. Title II*, Washington, D.C., United States Government Printing Office, 1986.
*Hearings on National Defense Authorization Act for Fiscal Years 1988/1989. H.R. 1748. RDT&E. Title II* (Y4 Ar5/2a: 987-8/7), Washington, D.C., United States Government Printing Office, 1987.
United States Congress, House of Representatives, Armed Services Committee, Subcommittee on Defense
*DoD Appropriations* for Fiscal Years 1985–91
United States Congress, House of Representatives, Committee on Appropriations, Subcommittee on Energy and Water Development
FY 1986. *Hearings*, parts 4 and 7.
United States Congress, House of Representatives, Committee on Banking, Finance and Urban Affairs, Subcommittee on Economic Stabilization
*Impact of Strategic Defense Initiative [SDI] on the U.S. Industrial Base*, 10 December 1985, Washington, D.C., United States Government Printing Office, 1986 (Y4.B 22/1: 99-59).
United States Congress, House of Representatives, Committee on Foreign Affairs, Subcommittees on Arms Control, International Security and Science, on Europe and the Middle East, and on International Economic Policy and Trade
Joint Hearing. *Technology Transfer and the Strategic Defense Initiative Research Agreements*, 10 December 1985, Washington, D.C., United States Government Printing Office, 1986 (Y4.F 76/1: T22/5).
United States Congress, House of Representatives, Committee on Government Operations
*The SDI Organisation: Management Deficiencies in Key Areas*, 53rd Report by Committee on Government Operations, House Report, 100-728, 23 June

1988, Washington, D.C., United States Government Printing Office, 1988 (H403-24).

United States Congress, House of Representatives, Committee on Government Operations, Subcommittee on Legislation and National Security

*Management of the Strategic Defense Initiative*, Hearing, 29 March 1988 (H401-49).

*National Defense Authorization Act for Fiscal Years 1988 and 1989*, Conference Report to accompany H.R. 1748.

United States Congress, Office of Technology Assessment

*Ballistic Missile Defense Technologies*, OTA–ISC–254, Washington, D.C., United States Government Printing Office (September 1985).

*Anti-Satellite Weapons. Counter-Measures and Arms Control*, OTA–ISC–281, Washington, D.C., United States Government Printing Office (September 1985).

United States Congress, Senate, Armed Services Committee

*Authorization of Appropriations*. FY 1981 to FY 1991.

United States Congress, Senate, Committee on Appropriations

*Hearings on H.R. 3629. Part 4*, Washington, D.C., United States Government Printing Office, 1986.

*Hearings on H.R. 3072. Part 6*, Washington, D.C., United States Government Printing Office, 1990 (S. Hrg. 101–49).

*Hearings on H.R. 5803/S. 3189. Part 2*, Washington, D.C., United States Government Printing Office, 1990 (S. Hrg. 101–936, part 2).

United States Congress, Senate, Committee on Governmental Affairs

*DoD/SDIO Compliance with the Federal Advisory Committee Act*, Hearing, 19 April 1988, Washington, D.C., United States Government Printing Office, 1988 (Y4.G74/9: S. Hrg. 100–681) (S401–71).

United States Congress, Senate, Committee on Governmental Affairs, Subcommittee on Oversight of Government Management, and Committee on Armed Services, Subcommittee on Strategic Forces and Nuclear Deterrence

*Need for and Operation of a Strategic Defense Initiative Institute*, S. Hrg. 100–37, 6 May 1987, Washington, D.C., United States Government Printing Office, 1987.

United States, Department of Defense

*The Strategic Defense Initiative: Defensive Technologies Study* (summary of the 'Fletcher Panel' study) (April 1984).

*RDT&E Program Descriptive Summaries/Justification of the Estimates*, fiscal years 1985–8.

*Military Posture FY 1989*, prepared by the Joint Staff.

*Report of the Secretary of Defense Frank C. Carlucci to the Congress on the Amended FY 1988/FY 1989 Biennial Budget*, 18 February 1988.

United States, Department of Defense, Air Force

'Current News': SDI special editions.

*Air Force Space Systems Architecture* (SSA 2000), interim version, vols. 1–3 (29 January 1985).

241

United States, Department of Defense, Space Division
'Organization and Functions Chart Book'.

United States, Department of Defense, Defense Nuclear Agency
'SDI by Performer 1985'. Computer print-out, run date 3 May 1985. To be read using the unclassified 'Performer Code by Acronym'.

United States, Department of Defense, Department of the Army
Issue Papers on Presidential Transition, 'BMD: A Key to Improving Strategic Deterrence' (no date: 1980?).
Annual Historical Summaries, 'Ballistic Missile Defense' (FY 1981 and FY 1982).

United States, Department of Defense, Department of the Army, Strategic Defense Command
The U.S. Army Strategic Defense Command: Its History and Role in the Strategic Defense Initiative, Official History by Ruth Currie-McDaniel and Claus R. Martel, 3rd edn, 1989.

United States, Department of Defense, Institute for Defense Analysis/SDIO Official Library
'Bibliography of the Unclassified Section' (July 1985).
'Benefit to Industry and Tactical Forces from SDI Innovative Science and Technology Programs', quoted in Congressional Record (12 June 1985), E2709.

United States, Department of Defense, National Defense University
America Plans for Space, Washington, D.C., National Defense University Press, 1984.

United States, Department of Defense, Strategic Defense Initiative Organization
Reports to the Congress on the Strategic Defense Initiative, 1985–90.
'A Technical Progress Report Submitted to the Secretary of Defense' (June 1985).
'The Eastport Report' (December 1985).
'Contract Management Information System', run dates 26 January 1988, 13 April 1988.
Contract Data Base, various dates.
'Charter of the SDIP' (draft form, no marking).
'Global Protection Against Limited Strikes (GPALS): Briefing on the Refocussed Strategic Defense Initiative' (12 February 1991), Ambassador Henry Cooper, director SDIO and Honorable Stephen J. Hadley, Assistant Secretary of Defense, International Security Policy.

United States, Department of State, Arms Control and Disarmament Agency
'The Soviet Propaganda Campaign against the US Strategic Defense Initiative' (August 1986).

United States, General Accounting Office
'Extent of Compliance With DoD's Requirement to Report Defense-related Employment'. GAO/NSIAD–85–98 (10 June 1985).
'Status of the US Antisatellite Program', GAO/NSIAD–85–104 (14 June 1985).
'SDIP: Information on Contracting and Other Activities', GAO/NSIAD–86–151FS (July 1986).

'SDIP: Controls Needed Over Construction and Operational Support Funds', GAO/NSIAD–86–145 (July 1986).

'SDIP: Better Management Direction and Controls Needed', GAO/NSIAD–88–26 (November 1987).

'SDIP: Status of Space Surveillance and Tracking System', GAO/NSIAD–88–61 (November 1987).

'SDIP: Information on Reprogramming and Department of Energy Efforts', GAO/NSIAD–88–162FS (May 1988).

'DoD Revolving Door: Processes have Improved but Post-DoD Employment Reporting Still Low', GAO/NSIAD–89–221 (13 September 1989).

'Strategic Defense Initiative: Funding Needs Through Completion of Phase 1 System', GAO/NSIAD–90–79FS (29 January 1990).

'Strategic Defense Initiative Program: Basis for Reductions in Estimated Cost of Phase 1', GAO/NSIAD–90–173 (May 1990).

'Strategic Defense System: Stable Design and Adequate Testing Must Precede Decision to Deploy', GAO/IMTEC–90–61 (July 1990).

United States, Office of Government Ethics
'Inquiry into the Eastport Group Advisors to the Strategic Defense Initiative Organization'.

United States, White House
'National Security Decision Directive 116' (2 December 1983).
'National Security Decision Directive 119' (6 January 1984).

United States, White House, Office of the Press Secretary
'National Space Policy', fact sheet (4 July 1982).

United States Global Strategy Council
'Space Support of US National Security', report of a conference in Washington, D.C., 24 November 1987.

Waller, Douglas, James Bruce and Douglas Cook. 'SDI: Progress and Challenges', staff report submitted to Senators Proxmire, Johnston and Chiles (17 March 1986).

'SDI: Progress and Challenges. Part Two', staff report submitted to Senators Proxmire, Johnston and Chiles (19 March 1987).

Who Owns Whom, North American edition, 1987, London, Dun and Bradstreet International, 1987.

York, Herbert. Race to Oblivion: A Participant's View of the Arms Race, New York, Simon & Schuster, 1970.

'Nuclear Deterrence and the Military Uses of Space', Daedalus, vol. 114, no. 2 (spring 1985).

Zegveld, Walter and Christien Enzing. SDI and Industrial Technology Policy: Threat or Opportunity?, London, Frances Pinter, 1987.

Zuckerman, Lord Solly. 'The Deterrent Illusion', The Times (21 January 1980).

# INDEX

ABM, definition, 3
  history, 21–36
ABM Treaty, 32, 34, 40, 56, 72, 90, 91, 111, 119, 127, 129, 179, 197
Abrahamson, Lt-Gen. James A., 51, 54–5, 58, 64–5, 70–1, 79, 82, 87, 91–2, 110–11, 117, 119–20, 140–1, 157, 167–70, 180–1, 198
'Absolute Bomb', 16, 156, 159
Accidental launch, 116, 183–5, 186
Acronyms, 153, 160
Action/reaction, 16, 34, 195
Adams, Gordon, 102
Adelmann, Kenneth, 40
Adenauer Foundation, 128
'Ad hocracy', 65, 107
Aerojet Electro Systems, 70; see also Gencorp
Aerospace Industries Association, 30, 110
Aggression, 162
Airborne Early Warning, 133
Air defense, see Extended Air Defense
Air Defense Initiative, 131, 137–8
Air Force, US, 21–4, 33, 76, 93, 95–7, 138, 141, 143, 198
  agencies working on SDI, 61–2
  Electronic Systems Division, 8, 62
Air–Land Battle, 133
Aldrin, Buzz, 81
Allen, Richard, 43
Alliance management, 17, 128, 133-4, 200
'Alpha' laser, 96
ALPS, 184; see also accidental launch
American Defense Preparedness Association, 81, 101–2
American Institute of Aeronautics and Astronautics, 81, 183
American Security Council, 30
American Space Frontiers Committee, 81
Anderson, Martin, 42–3
Anti-Communism, 156–7, 195, 197, 200, 229 n. 10
Anti-Satellite Weapons, see ASATs
Anti-Tactical Ballistic Missiles, see ATBM

AOA, 66, 70
AOS, 118
Apathy, 161
Arms control, 32–3, 40, 58, 73, 89–91, 119, 132–3, 179, 189; see also ABM Treaty
'Arms economy', 14–15, 151–2
Arms race, definition, 3
  individuals' motivation, 157
  theories of, 7–20
Army, US, 21–5, 29, 62, 76, 95–6, 138, 141, 143–4, 188, 212 n. 6
Army Strategic Defense Command, 8, 33, 65–8, 78, 97, 186, 196
ARPA, 22, 144
Arrow ATBM, 121, 135, 188
ASATs, 40, 117, 137, 139, 143–5, 191, 201
AT&T, 24, 129
ATBMs, 125–36, 170, 186
Avoidance, 153–6

B-1 bomber, 12
'Bail-out imperative', 9, 131
BAMBI, 22
Baran, Paul A., 15
Baroque arsenal, 19, 148–50, 195
BASICO, 167
Battle Management/C³, 180
BDM Corp., 130, 169
Belgium, 135
Bell (Telephone) Laboratories, 24–5, 31, 75
Bendetsen, Karl, 42–4, 46, 218 n. 5
Benson, Lucy, 82
Bethe, Hans, 68
BMD, definition, 3
BMD Infrastructure, definition, 3
  extent of, 60, 182, 191
BMD Organization, 32, 39, 61–2, 65–8
Boeing, 30–1, 40, 47, 69–70, 77, 97, 118, 184
Bosma, John, 70, 173, 197, 222 n. 27
Braudel, Fernand, 16
Brilliant Pebbles, 155, 161, 180–2, 185
Britain, 126, 130–1, 135–6, 149, 170–1, 188
Brookhaven Lab., 63
BSTS, 64, 118, 140, 180, 182

244

Lawrence Livermore Laboratory, 30, 39,
  62–3, 69, 74, 77–9, 97, 105, 108, 181,
  184–5; *see also* 'O' Group
Leboyer, Frederic, 162
Levin, Senator Carl, 78, 104, 106, 110, 199
Levine, H. D., 8
LoADS, 41
Lockheed, 30–1, 56, 67, 69, 97, 102, 114,
  116, 118, 120, 140, 144, 184–6,
  224 n. 59
Los Alamos Laboratory, 30, 39, 63, 69, 74,
  78, 97, 140, 184
LTV, 18, 25, 69, 97, 118, 185–6
Lukens, Rep. "Buz' (Ohio), 103

M-16 rifle, 19
McDonnell Douglas, 24–5, 28, 30–1, 40, 67,
  69–70, 74, 95, 97, 101, 118, 184–6
McElroy (US Secretary of Defense), 22
McFarlane, Robert, 44, 46, 79
McNamara, Robert, 23, 26, 166, 183
MAD, 18
Mandel, Ernest, 14, 151–2, 195
Marketing, *see* selling
Marquet, Dr L., 76, 169
Marshall Institute, 120
Marshall Report, 101, 114
Martin Co., 24–5, 28, 30
Martin Marietta, 31, 40, 69–70, 77, 97, 102,
  185
Masculinity, 15, 161–2
Meese, Edwin, 43, 115
Mense, Allan, 220 n. 19, 225 n. 28
Metaphors, 162
Meyer, General Stewart C., 76, 100
Military economy, 139–52
Military Industrial Complex, 204 n. 15; *see
  also* interest groups, industrial
  imperative, bureaucratic politics,
  politics of influence
Miller panel, 51, 198
MIRACL, 87, 144
MIRVs, 32
MIT, 69, 74, 77–8, 97, 184
Mitre Corp., 75, 104–5
Monahan, Major-Gen. George, 154, 161,
  176, 180–1
Mondale, Walter, 174
Moral Majority, 81
Motorola, 25, 30–1
MOUs, 126–7, 133, 171, 200
'Mudflap', 23, 144
MX missile, 41, 140

NASA, 22, 66, 96, 167
National Academy of Scientists (US), 2,
  89
Nationalism, 15

National Security Council, 44, 47, 72, 89,
  185, 198
National Security Decision Directive
  (6–83), 72
National Security Decision Directive
  (119), 51, 73
National Space Policy (1982), 40
National Test Bed, 57
NATO, 125, 135
Navy (US), 24, 62, 95–6, 141, 189
Netherlands, 135, 221 n. 12
New Right, 39, 45, 71, 98, 147, 197
Nichols Research, 95, 184
Nierenberg, Professor William A., 103,
  105
Nike-Ajax, 21
Nike-Hercules, 21
Nike Project, 21
Nike-X, 23, 25
Nike-Zeus, 22, 144
Nitze, Paul, 26, 40, 78–9, 199
'Nitze criteria', 88, 179, 183
Nixon, President Richard, 29, 166, 183
Nolan, Janne E., 193
NORAD, 42, 131, 137
Northrop, 77
Nukespeak, 153–6
Nunn, Senator Sam, 184

'O' Group (at Lawrence Livermore), 79,
  157, 160
Office of Naval Research, 96, 106
Office of Technology Assessment, 57, 59,
  82
Opinion polls, 163, 172
'Overdeveloped technology', 18

'Paperclip', Operation, 21
Parnas, David, 106
Partial Test Ban Treaty, 31
Particle beam weapons, 26, 63, 88, 96, 139,
  144
Patriot missile, 121, 127, 129, 131, 149,
  187–9
Peace Dividend, 179
Pentagon, *see* Defense Department (US)
'Pentagon system", 14, 134, 147, 190
People Protection Act, 80
Perez, Carlota, 150
Perle, Richard, 170, 230 n. 31
Physical Dynamics, 77
Policy process, 7–8, 196; *see also* politics of
  influence
Political Action Committees (PACs), 13,
  81, 108
Politics of influence, 11–14, 29–30, 39,
  73–83, 100–12, 129–30, 179–91,
  196–200; *see also* interest groups,

247